NUCLEAR WEAPONS AND SCIENTIFIC RESPONSIBILITY

C.G. Weeramantry
Professor of Law, Monash University

Longwood Academic
Wolfeboro, NH

Published by
LONGWOOD ACADEMIC
A Division of Longwood Publishing Group, Inc.
27 South Main Street
Wolfeboro, NH 03894-2069
USA

Library of Congress Cataloguing in Publication Data:

Weeramantry, C.G.
  Nuclear weapons and scientific responsibility.

  Includes index.
  1. Nuclear weapons (International law) 2. Scientists—
Professional ethics. I. Title.
JX5133.A7W44 1987   341.7'34   87-2804

ISBN 0-89341-542-1

For
my children
Ravi, Shalini, Nilmini, Romesh and Roshini

That their generation and its successors
may know a world
free
from the spectre of instant destruction

FOREWORD

by His Excellency Judge Nagendra Singh,
President of the International Court of Justice

The subject of this learned treatise attracted attention for the first time immediately following the events of World War II. It also captured my imagination then, and in a work published by Stevens & Sons, London, in 1958 I addressed the problem of Nuclear Weapons and International Law. However, during the decades that followed, the subject attracted less attention, only to come back to prominence in recent years. With the Chernobyl incident this year and the expansion of nuclear weaponry, this topic has again become one of worldwide importance. Professor Weeramantry has used his legal talents, which are of an exceptionally high order, to produce a work of worldwide interest. It will serve the best interests of the community by enlightening both the common man as well as the specialist. He addresses the problem from the legal angle in a manner relevant to all who are interested in the rule of law and its use to evolve international peace.

The learned author is a distinguished scholar of that branch of the law which the International Court of Justice administers. I have an abiding interest in this particular branch of legal scholarship, and when the author approached me to write the Foreword, I acceded to his request for many reasons. First, I know the author well, and his sincerity as a scholar is indeed compelling. Secondly, the subject is now a prime concern of the law and of foremost interest to all who strive for the promotion of peace. Thirdly, the author enjoys a position of great advantage in writing on this vital subject. He comes from the Third World, being by birth and origin a Sri Lankan, but he also belongs to the great legal tradition of the English-speaking people and the Commonwealth. His cross-cultural perspectives give him much versatility in the legal field.

In regard to the book itself, I must say that what interests me most is the appeal to the scientist to adopt a human approach to a problem which could destroy the entire race and with it all life on this planet. This appeal concerns not merely the peripheries of the scientist's activities, but goes to the core of the matter and is made at a critical hour in human history. The politicians often take no heed and ignore popular sentiments frequently expressed through persistent protests and mammoth meetings not merely in one country, but in several. To whom therefore could one appeal, except to the scientist who, having been responsible in the past for these discoveries, is even now actively engaged in finding still more devastating means to destroy all Creation? The author is right when he says the scientist must now give up his efforts in that direction and concentrate all his efforts towards promoting peaceful uses of nuclear energy to help and serve humanity but not to annihilate it and the great civilization that human effort has produced.

The book covers a wide spectrum, viewing the problem from several angles including, in particular, the deterrence aspect. May I, in this connection, quote my submission made on the 40th Anniversary Celebrations of the UN when the Court greeted Her Majesty, the Queen of the Netherlands, the Head of the host country of the World Court. I said:

> The old adage had it that if you desire peace you must prepare war. The paradox has, however, turned sour, and though the Charter of the United Nations makes copious provision for a system of collective security, it is certain that the articles devoted to the social and economic development of mankind are more attuned to the candid logic of our younger generations, who say: if you desire peace, prepare peace.

This treatise, devoted to preparing peace through law, is therefore at once useful to students, instructive to politicians, and a warning to the scientists who must now take thought before so acting as to facilitate the destruction of their innocent brothers and sisters and of future generations by perfecting inventions which are purely destructive. The ancient saying of my country is "always endeavor to create so as to help and never even think to destroy, for beware one day that destructive habit may destroy you also."

NAGENDRA SINGH

Preface

The year 1985 marked the forty-second anniversary of the bombs dropped on Hiroshima and Nagasaki. For 42 years now, all mankind has lived under the shadow of the bomb. All human beings on the planet have become hostages; their fundamental right to live has been appropriated by those who have the least right to control it—the controllers of nuclear weapons. Every day we live is a day of grace granted to us by these lords of life and death, and we have grown resigned to our fate. There are those who point with satisfaction to the fact that we have not had a World War for 42 years and thank the bomb for this indulgence. The bomb has warped our thinking so grievously that we tend to accept such arguments.

Rationality has long since departed from the scene, and viewers from outer space would no doubt conclude that some grievous epidemic of lunacy has swept over the entire planet. While millions starve, we channel our choicest material and intellectual resources into this quest for death. The possessors of the skills to change this situation—the scientists—only drift along with the current, seemingly helpless to struggle against its force.

The world has spent over three trillion dollars on nuclear weapons and has increased its stockpile from three bombs in 1945 to more than 50,000 in 1985. Some 50% of the skilled scientific manpower in the world is now engaged in military research and development. Less than 1% devotes its skill to solving global problems of underdevelopment which cost millions of lives every year. Though it is not generally understood as such, this is one of the great public issues of our time.

Recent research on the consequences of using nuclear weapons establishes beyond doubt the enormity of the damage which they can cause. They not only threaten humanity, but all life forms on the planet. The unprecedented scale of this capacity for destruction attracts special legal consequences in international law.

The nuclear weapons that have been built since 1945 have a combined firepower of more than a million Hiroshima-type bombs. It is the politicians who have ordered the production of these weapons and the military who are prepared to use them. But they were not made by politicians or generals; they were made by scientists.

iv

Those who play a part in nuclear weapons manufacture cannot shut their eyes to the probable consequences of their activities. Nor can international law fail to hold them responsible for their work. In this work we shall not consider the case of those scientists who are unaware of the part their work plays in nuclear weapons manufacture, or whose primary work lies apart from subsequent weapons applications. Instead we shall deal with the clear-cut case of those who knowingly and deliberately participate in the manufacture or improvement of nuclear weaponry.

Needless to say, in speaking of the illegality of nuclear weapons we do not mean to imply that all other weapons are, or should be, legal. The illegality of biological weapons and chemical weapons deserves a full-scale treatment which lies outside the compass of this book. Also, in speaking of the illegality of nuclear war we do not mean to imply that all other wars are legal.

The legal issues involved in nuclear weaponry have to be understood in their political/military context, both that of the past and that of the present. The first two chapters of this book provide some of the historical background to the present arms race. The next two chapters speak of the present situation, discussing the distinctiveness of nuclear weapons and the status of current arsenals. Chapter 5 provides an introduction to the legal dimension of the problem by discussing the historical background of the international law of war. Chapters 6 through 9 develop, respectively, four propositions that logically proceed from each other. The first proposition, dealt with in Chapter 6, is that nuclear weaponry is illegal under prevailing principles of international law and constitutes a crime against humanity as well as an international delict or tort (i.e., a civil wrong). This proposition has already been the subject of much writing in the field of international law. This book briefly examines the principles from which this proposition comes and attempts to point out the deficiencies of various objections that have been raised to it. Having thus established in Chapter 6 the illegality of *use,* Chapter 7 goes on to show how this illegality also attaches to the *production* of nuclear weapons. Chapter 8 examines the question of responsibility, discussing both the responsibility of private individuals and that of such public figures as statesmen and generals. In Chapter 9, which discusses the specific responsibility of scientists, there is a summing up and focusing of all the issues previously discussed. In that chapter and in the conclusion, which follows, there is an outline of some of the principles of personal responsibility which follow from the legal principles currently applicable in international law.

Although there is a fairly universal sentiment that the use of nuclear weaponry is clearly contrary to morality and that its production is probably so, this position does not go far enough. It is not just a question of morality but a question of law. It is hoped that by showing how the legal issues dovetail with the moral issues, we may find a way to stop this madness before it is too late.

In 1956 President Eisenhower said: "One day both sides must meet at the conference table with the understanding that the era of armaments has ended and the human race must conform its actions to that truth or die." President Carter warned in his farewell address that "The survivors, if any, would live in despair amid the poisoned ruins of a civilization that had committed suicide." On its side, the Soviet Union has officially pronounced that it views nuclear war as a universal disaster which would most probably mean the end of civilization and may lead to the destruction of all mankind. These views are confirmed by the latest scientific research on the effects of nuclear weapons.

Many of the legal principles in this book are adduced on the basis of these same scientific facts. It is hoped that in citing them there will be some counterbalance to those planners who are still proposing strategies based on scenarios of "limited" nuclear war and equations of nuclear weaponry with conventional weaponry. Such plans succeed in being, at one time, both unrealistic and illegal.

Since President Reagan's "Star Wars" announcement in 1983, there has been a major increase in awareness of the problem of nuclear weaponry. Yet neither scientists nor lawyers—two very influential groups—have given it sufficient consideration. Hopefully this can still be remedied. This book will have been worth writing if it manages to persuade even a few scientists. When even a few begin to ask some of the fundamental questions which have been buried beneath the folklore of the nuclear age, there is no telling where it will end.

An old proverb tells us that a journey of a thousand miles begins with the first step. Our journey towards disarmament has not even begun. The scientific community could well enjoy the privilege of taking that vital first step on behalf of all mankind.

TABLE OF CONTENTS

CHAPTER 1 The Beginnings...................................1

CHAPTER 2 The Cold War....................................15

CHAPTER 3 The Distinctiveness of Nuclear Weapons.................29

The Nuclear Winter   29
a) Atmospheric Effects   34
b) Agricultural Effects   37
c) Medical Effects   40
d) Social Effects   42

CHAPTER 4 The Arsenals....................................50

Analysis of U.S. Firepower   53
Analysis of Soviet Firepower   53
A Comparative Survey   54
a) Intercontinental Ballistic Missiles (ICBMs)   55
b) Submarine-launched Ballistic Missiles (SLBMs)   55
c) Bombers   56
d) Launch-on-Warning Systems   56
e) Weapons Sites   57
The Other Weapons States   60
Proliferation   61

CHAPTER 5 The Origins and Current Status of the
International Law of War.............................64

Does International Law Exist?   64
The Sources of International Law   66
The Characteristics of a Legal Prescription   67
a) Policy Content   67
b) Authority Signal   68
c) Control Intention   69
Swings toward International Law   70
The Framework of the Law relating to War   71
The Jus ad Bellum   72
The Jus in Bello   77
The Human Rights Dimension   79

CHAPTER 6   Is the Use of Nuclear Weapons Illegal?....................83

What Principles of International Law Render
the Use of Nuclear Weapons Illegal?   83
    1. Causation of indiscriminate harm to
        combatants and non-combatants   84
    2. Aggravation of pain and suffering   84
    3. Violation of the laws of humanity   89
    4. Contradiction of the principle of proportionality   90
    5. Nullification of a return to peace   91
    6. Destruction of the eco-system   92
    7. The extermination of populations and
        the decimation of mankind   93
    8. The possibility of extinction of the human race   94
    9. Intergenerational damage   95
   10. The express prohibition of asphyxiating
        gases and analogous materials   95
   11. Destruction and damage to neutral states   96
The Delictual Dimension   97
Alleged Justifications and their Inadequacy   98
    1. Abrogation of international law by contrary practice 98
    2. The necessities of war   99
    3. Practical military strategy   101
    4. The concept of a just war   102
    5. Self-defence   102
    6. The preservation of one's way of life   106
    7. Preventing destabilization of areas of influence   106
A More Humanistic Approach to International Law   107

CHAPTER 7   Is the Manufacture of Nuclear Weapons Illegal?............111

Deterrence   111
a) The impracticality of deterrence   113
b) The illegality of deterrence   115
A Contained Nuclear War   116
a) Theatre nuclear war   118
b) Limited nuclear war   119
c) Star Wars: the objections   121
Other considerations   124
a) The unpredictability of the outbreak of war   124
b) The unpredictability of the course of war   125
c) The uncontrollability of war   125
d) Launch-on-warning capability (LOWC)   126
e) The electro-magnetic pulse (EMP)   129
f) The absence of a limited war concept
   in Soviet nuclear strategy   129
g) Incentives towards a first strike strategy   130
h) Scientific research as an impediment to de-escalation   131
i) The increase in the likelihood of war   132
The Violation of Human Rights   134

CHAPTER 8   The Concept of Personal Responsibility
             in International Law................................ 138

CHAPTER 9   The Responsibility of the Scientist..................... 148

             Conscious Involvement   149
             The Principle of Causation   153
             The Principle of Foreseeability   154
             Changes in Public Attitudes   155
             Levels of Scientific Involvement   155
             Scientific Involvement through Information Technology   156
             Alleged Justifications for Scientific Involvement   157
                 1. The principle of freedom of scientific research   157
                 2. Patriotic duty   158
                 3. Defence of one's political beliefs
                     or economic interests   158
                 4. The "slippery slope" argument   159
                 5. Belief in self-defence, deterrence, or the
                     concept of a contained nuclear war   159
                 6. Belief that nuclear weapons control "small
                     wars" and prevent big ones   160
                 7. The futility of individual protest   160
                 8. Culpability and responsibility lie
                     with the decision makers   162
                 9. Superior orders   162
                10. Lack of official position   162
                11. Economic necessity   163
             Some Ideological Objections   164
             a) The neutrality of science   164
             b) The worthiness of the scientific endeavor   165
             c) The truthfulness and rationality of science   165
             d) The openness of science   166
             e) The unpredictability of scientific consequences   166
             f) The misapplication of science by others   167
             Some International Declarations
                 on Scientific Responsibility   167
             Unilateral Scientific Abstention   172
             Current Ethical Concerns Among Scientists   174
             The Need for an Ethical Code for Nuclear Scientists   176

CHAPTER 10   Consequences of the Thesis advanced in this Book.......... 182

             Conclusion: Practical Advantages of Underlining
             Scientific Responsibility   182
                 1. Clarification of the issues for scientists   182
                 2. Sharpening of the scientific conscience   182
                 3. Creation of a climate of scientific opinion   183
                 4. Evolution of codes of ethical conduct
                     for nuclear scientists   183
                 5. International declarations   183
                 6. Greater public awareness   184
                 7. Reinforcing of anti-nuclear moral sentiment   184

8.	Strengthening the wall of resistance to the use of nuclear weaponry	184
9.	Clarifying the distinction between destruction and war	185
10.	Reliance on existing principles rather than future treaties	185
11.	More affirmative use of the legal system	186
12.	Channelling science towards peace	187

APPENDIX A The Nuclear Winter according to Lord Byon, 1816

APPENDIX B The Fallacy of Star Wars

APPENDIX C Einstein's Letter to Roosevelt, 1939

APPENDIX D Niels Bohr's Memorandum to Roosevelt, 1944

APPENDIX E Extract from 'Franck Report' to the Secretary of War, 1945

APPENDIX F The Russell-Einstein Manifesto, 1955

APPENDIX G Declaration of the Canadian Pugwash Group, 1982

APPENDIX H For the Species and the Planet: A Statement in Support of the Five Continent Peace Initiative, 1985

APPENDIX I Resolution of Human Rights Committee on Illegality of Nuclear War

APPENDIX J Principles Formulated by the International Law Commission

APPENDIX K Proposed U.N. Declaration of Scientific Responsibility in Relation to Nuclear Weaponry

CHAPTER ONE

The Beginnings

The President of the United States was at lunch aboard the U.S.S. Augusta with members of the crew. Truman was returning home from Potsdam after his meeting with Stalin and Churchill. Captain Frank Graham, White House Room watch officer, handed the President a note:

> TO THE PRESIDENT
> FROM THE SECRETARY OF WAR
> Big Bomb dropped on Hiroshima 5 August at 7:15 p.m. Washington time. First reports indicate complete success which was even more conspicuous than earlier test.

The President said to the sailors around him, "This is the greatest thing in history. It's time for us to get home."[1]

At Los Alamos, where the scientists had been making the bomb, a terse announcement was made of the "successful combat drop" of one of the laboratory's "units". Cheers re-echoed through the laboratories and "The place went up like we'd won the Army-Navy game" according to the secretary of Robert Oppenheimer, the scientist who had masterminded the research. The scientists assembled in the auditorium and Oppenheimer strode down the aisle "making no effort to calm the clapping, foot-stomping, yelling scientists. They broke into their demonstration as Oppie entered and continued for a long time after their leader clasped his hands together overhead in the classic boxer's salute and mounted the podium. Hiroshima was their sweet victory."[2] There were many celebration parties that night.

An enormous scientific effort, representing years of concerted work by hundreds of scientists, had achieved its goal. Whatever else the statesmen, the generals and the scientists had intended, on that day their cumulative efforts had resulted in the instantaneous death of 80,000 people and the obliteration of a city of 400,000 people. In its ruins, the skin of the survivors was hanging in shreds; their flesh ripped open, their eyeballs melted away, they scurried to relief

1

centers which could no longer offer relief. Tens of thousands were yet to die, and the full enormity of the catastrophe had yet to dawn upon the Japanese people and the world. To this day, forty-two years later, the sad tales consequent on the nuclear explosion have been pouring in. The President was right that a new historical era had dawned, though his description of this event as "the greatest thing in history" was singularly infelicitous.

*   *   *

The story goes back to the discovery of nuclear fission in 1939 and even further beyond to the Einstein equation of 1905 which linked matter and energy. Certainly, from 1939 onwards the destructive potential of fission was discernible to the physicists working in this field. But not all of them reacted alike, and not all of those who worked on the bomb did so for the same reasons. Not all of them showed a like degree of concern with its political and social effects.

Once the proposition advanced in this work becomes an accepted principle of international law, as the author believes it will, collaborative work between scientists and lawyers will need to be done to draw distinctions, to circumscribe limits of responsibility, and to outline principles of exemption. That is a formidable task which lies beyond the limits of this book. All that the present work seeks to establish is the central proposition that a scientist who knows that the object of his work is the manufacture or improvement of nuclear weaponry, and nevertheless deliberately participates in such activity, is personally accountable under international law for the consequences of his work.

In the forty-two years that have elapsed since the Hiroshma bomb, mankind has, despite its demonstrated effects, produced the equivalent of three such weapons every hour. Who is responsible? Certainly the statesmen and the generals of the bomb-producing countries carry a heavy load of blame. The citizens of those countries must also take a share of the blame for having permitted their politicians to indulge in such policies. But it is certain also that these three Hiroshima-equivalents per hour could not have been produced without the scientists. This book attempts to concentrate on the legal implications of the manufacture and use of nuclear weapons and on the part which is played by scientists in the creation of them.

2

The legal and political complexion of the arms race in the nuclear age separates it from the arms races of the past. Conventional war had at least this element of rationality: that its purpose was not to destroy but to dominate politically. Nuclear war, by which nations are destroyed rather than subjugated, deprives war of any rationality it may have had. The role of the scientist in contributing to the possibility of such massive and indiscriminate destruction needs to be reviewed.

*   *   *

By April 1941, with nuclear fission already an achievement of two years' vintage, physicists at Germany's Kaiser-Wilhelm Institute of Physics were calculating the quantities of the isotope uranium 235 needed to create sufficient critical mass for an explosion. Professor Fritz Houtermans was writing a report which "for the first time made explicit calculations on fast-neutron chain reactions and the critical mass of uranium 235, i.e. that mass which, when assembled, would result in a spontaneous fast-neutron chain reaction and a violent explosion."[3]

Yet, the nuclear program did not have the enthusiastic support of the German High Command. Most on the Command thought that many technical breakthroughs needed to be made before the supreme weapon could become a practical possibility. Flushed with their current military successes, they anticipated that the war would end before the bomb could be created.

It is true that not all members of the High Command were prepared to give low priority to the nuclear effort. Albert Speer, for example, summoned Germany's outstanding physicists to a conference at which Nobel Laureate Werner Heisenberg explained to the general staff how nuclear fission could be used to produce an atomic bomb. According to Heisenberg, the Americans would be able to produce the bomb in two years; the Germans would need at least that much time to produce it, and could do so only if the administration provided full financial support for the project.

The time-span mentioned by Heisenberg was not attractive to the general staff, and although Hitler was briefly informed by Speer of the project on June 23, it received neither the enthusiastic support nor the top priority it needed. The project did proceed, but not "full steam ahead". The High Command's enthusiasm for the project may

3

have been dampened by the fact that its theoretical basis rested on "Jewish physics"—the discoveries of Albert Einstein. To the distorted reasoning of the Nazis, this meant that the value of his discoveries could not be publicly acknowledged.

The project also suffered physical setbacks, for in January 1943 a taskforce of Norwegian saboteurs destroyed the hydrogen electrolysis plant at Vernoek and drained half a ton of heavy water from its eighteen cells. The German uranium research program was thereby delayed for several months.[4]

Eventually the Germans gave up altogether the idea of making a bomb, thus raising various problems of conscience for some allied scientists, whose sole motivation in working on the bomb had been to beat the Germans to it. Other scientists saw value in making the bomb as a means to reduce the death toll and to shorten the war. Others were scarcely concerned with the moral issues but were guided by the mere delight of pursuing scientific knowledge and achievement. There were also those for whom it was merely another field of employment.

*   *   *

Unknown to the Allies, the Japanese were also busy on the bomb. Takeo Yasuda, Director of the Aviation Technology Research Institute of the Imperial Japanese Army, had come to the conclusion by April 1940 that nuclear fission was a field that the Japanese could not afford to neglect. He commissioned studies of the subject, and responsibility for the Japanese nuclear effort came to rest on the shoulders of Professor Yoshio Nishina, who had studied in Copenhagen under Niels Bohr. Nishina divided his team of brilliant young physicists into four research groups: the cyclotron atomic nucleus group, the cosmic ray group, the theoretical group, and a group which studied the effects of radiation upon living organisms. Fired with patriotic enthusiasm, the young men knew that the purpose of their work was to supply the Imperial Japanese Army with an atomic bomb.[5]

It was known to the Japanese team that Japan faced the problem of insufficient access to uranium ore. They were determined to go ahead, however, with whatever was available to them—Korea and Burma were considered possible sources. Nishina himself disapproved of the war, but his philosophy was, "We are all aboard a sinking ship, a ship called Japan. We must do what we can to save it."[6] As with the Germans, the need for immediate results weighed heavily on the High Command. Nuclear research was extremely expensive and consumed valuable resources at the very time when the war in the Pacific was becoming steadily more disastrous. The Nishina group redoubled its efforts, however, and reported that it was possible for Japan to produce an atomic bomb.

At a plenary session of the Diet in May 1943, Professor Aikitsu Tanakadate informed the legislators that it was now possible "to produce a bomb the size of a matchbox which has the explosive power to sink a battleship." The legislators were not sufficiently impressed, and the immense sums necessary for the research were not forthcoming.

The research still continued, however, and when two young scientists, Kigoshi and Ishiwatari, achieved in January 1944 the tremendous breakthrough of producing crystals of sexa-uranium fluoride, they danced for sheer joy in the bitter cold of a midwinter night.[7]

As Japan's fortunes sank in the far-flung theatres of war, the nuclear scientists worked ever harder, hoping for the magic breakthrough which would give them the bomb before their enemies landed on Japanese soil. They knew the hope was almost forlorn, but certainly did not suspect that the enemy's own research was so far advanced.

* * *

Among the Allies, a galaxy of great scientific minds was at work— both upon the scientific and the ethical aspects. By a quirk of destiny Hitler (and his ally Mussolini) unconsciously stimulated the assembling of that galaxy. C.P. Snow has described this as "the greatest emigration of intellectuals since the collapse of Byzantium, and one far more dramatic and influential than that."[8] Among the migrants were Einstein himself (who had renounced German citizenship at a very early age), Enrico Fermi of the Physics School in Rome (who though not himself Jewish, had a Jewish wife), Niels Bohr from the Institute of Theoretical Physics in Copenhagen, Edward Teller and Leo Szilard from Hungary, Josef Rotblat from Poland, and Otto Frisch from Austria. To unlock the secrets in the atom, they joined with those of American birth, such as J.R. Oppenheimer, and with men of Anglo-Saxon descent, such as James Rutherford, J.J. Thompson, Mark

5

Oliphant, James Chadwick and J.D. Cockroft. Many of the migrants had done important pioneering work before they moved. Even at the time the war clouds were gathering, most physicists realized that the latest researches meant that it was possible to unlock nuclear energy, and that explosives of stupendous power could be made.

The issues of conscience surfaced immediately, for the unadulterated thrill of pursuing scientific knowledge, which the physicists had hitherto enjoyed, became clouded by the fear that further research could well unveil a tool which in unscrupulous hands could lead to domination of the world. To some physicists like Josef Rotblat, still happily with us,[9] this was like an evil dream which they pushed back into the recesses of their minds, feeling themselves unequal to the task of grappling with the issues involved. To others, not so perceptive, it was simply the greatest of all intellectual challenges and one that had to be met; the question of application, they thought, could be left to others whose business it was to handle practical affairs.

While confusion reigned among the scientists on the question of the uninhibited pursuit of knowledge, Hitler himself provided enough incentive for many of the scientists to overcome their moral scruples. Reports filtered in that his scientists were at work on the bomb, and it was thought that he was a leader who would have no scruples at all in using the weapon if he had it. For the limited purpose of forestalling Hitler's world domination, Allied scientists went hard to work to beat him to the punch.

In an unused squash court at the University of Chicago on December 2, 1942, Fermi produced the world's first sustained nuclear chain reaction by using a pile of uranium, uranium oxide and graphite blocks. A team of engineers charged with reporting to the War Office on whether actual construction of the bomb should be undertaken saw Fermi control the reaction he had set in motion and bring to a halt the growing rattle of the Geiger counters registering the neutrons from the reactor. A year after it had decided to embark on "the greatest scientific gamble in history," the United States was beginning to see very specific achievements on the road to the bomb.

Los Alamos, selected for its secrecy and remoteness, became the center for the new project. General Leslie Groves of the army engineers was the supremo in charge, while Robert Oppenheimer headed the team of scientists. At other centers, thousands of people were engaged in various related activities. For example, 60,000 people were involved in the production of plutonium at Hanford, Washington. The entire project required a total of 539,000 man-years of effort and was described by Secretary of State Stimson as the greatest scientific project in the history of the world.

The scheme of operations raised various questions pertinent to the issue of responsibility. Several thousands of those engaged were at or near the level of semi-skilled or routine labor, and had no way to appreciate the overall nature of the project on which they were working. Even for many who were higher up, heavy secrecy inhibited the formation of an overall perspective regarding the nature and purpose of the enterprise. Only those "at the heart of the enterprise" really knew what was going on.

Here is the record of the reaction of one man, a researcher at Berkeley who worked in artificial radioactivity. "I was all in favor of making a bomb. And I want you to know that I have no guilt about it. I would do it again and for this reason: as I appraised the situation at that time, there was not for a long time in history any worse aberration of human conduct and human monstrosity than the Nazi regime in Germany. And the idea of an atomic bomb that could win the war against Germany was highly attractive to me. While nothing required me to work more than eight hours a day, I spent at least sixteen in the average day on the bomb project. I was very highly motivated simply because I thought it was important to win the war against Germany."[10]

But the Germans were losing the war. The bomb had not yet been produced. The defeat of the Germans occurred. The research came to acquire a very different complexion.

What started as a determined effort to defeat a specific monstrous enemy personified in Hitler became converted into the production of a weapon to use against whatever enemies the United States might have. In the context of the prevailing situation, that meant Japan. The qualms that might have assailed some of the scientists seemed to have little effect on General Groves, the director of the project. "It was always difficult for me to understand," he records, "how anyone could ignore the importance of the effect on the Japanese people and their government of the overwhelming surprise of the bomb."[11]

A useful contrast to this is the following note by Leo Szilard, one of the foremost physicists involved in the development of the bomb. In his memoir on the bomb he writes: "During the war, while we worked on the bomb, we scientists thought for a while that we were in a neck-and-neck race with the Germans and that getting the bomb first might make the difference between winning and losing the war. But when Germany was defeated, many of us became uneasy about the proposed use of the bomb in the war against Japan. Many of us were uneasy about how the existence of the bomb would affect the position of the United States after the war.''[12]

Szilard was in fact seeing even beyond the use of the bomb against Japan. Specificity of objective was getting blurred. The specific target of ''Hitlerite Germany'' had broadened into ''the enemies of the United States.'' Could it extend to the defence of the economic interests of the United States? If the United States could use it in this fashion, could not other powers that succeeded in making the weapon also argue its legitimacy for such purposes? Could this mean a confrontation of nuclear weapon with nuclear weapon? With arsenals containing bombs of even greater destructive power than the Hiroshima bomb, was there a danger of global holocaust?

The military, of course, were not attuned to see such factors. Nor did some scientists then see them, though the events that have occurred since then have made them plain for all to see.

Szilard prepared a manifesto, to which Einstein added his signature, recommending that the atomic bomb should not be used against Japan. A growing number of scientists who had worked on the bomb were of the same opinion; among them was Niels Bohr. Secretary of State Stimson passed on to President Roosevelt the information that the scientists differed widely on this issue. At the time, Roosevelt was far from well and nearing his death. ''I went over with him,'' wrote Stimson, ''the two schools of thought that exist in respect to the future control after the war of this project, in case it is successful, one of them being the secret close-in attempted control of the project by those who control it now, and the other being the international control based upon freedom both of science and of access. I told him that those things must be settled before the first projectile is used...''[13]

After Roosevelt's return from Yalta it was believed that the U.S. and the U.S.S.R. had entered into a secret military agreement. Niels Bohr and some other scientists feared that the postwar era was likely to be hazardous to the future of mankind if a nuclear arms race should result or if, through continued secrecy, there should be a confrontation with the Soviet Union. With remarkable prescience Bohr realized the importance of giving the Soviets some inkling regarding the bomb. He saw this as a means towards building up international confidence and control. He pressed his views upon the establishment and obtained interviews with both Churchill and Roosevelt.

His encounter with Churchill has been described by C.P. Snow as one of the "black comedies of the war."[14] Churchill was most reluctant to see Bohr, despite the latter's pre-eminence as one of the greatest scientists of the century. He was treated with discourtesy during a short half-hour interview.[15] Churchill was in fact very suspicious of Bohr. Churchill's memorandum to Lord Cherwell, his science advisor, reads: "How did he [Bohr] come into the business? ...He said he is in close correspondence with a Russian professor, and old friend of his in Russia, to whom he has written about the matter and may be writing still. The Russian professor has urged him to go to Russia in order to discuss matters. What is this all about? It seems to me Bohr ought to be confined or at any rate made to see that he is very near the edge of mortal crimes."[16]

When Churchill received Bohr, the invasion of Europe was only three months away and absorbed most of his energies. Bohr was unable to build up his argument step by step, given the tension and the short time allowed him. The conversation strayed into extraneous matters. Bohr was unable to communicate that Roosevelt had personally told him he would welcome British suggestions for the international control of atomic energy. Churchill thought his time was being wasted. In the words of a recent writer: "Much more than the meeting of two minds had been at stake. A course was set for decades to come. It was one of the few truly fateful turning points in history. A breakthrough towards disarmament had been possible for a moment. The opportunity to avoid the outbreak of an arms race had been missed. No better chance would ever come again."[17]

Bohr had had a very different response from Roosevelt, who had received him with warmth and cordiality,[18] but this could lead nowhere in the face of Churchill's opposition. Having regard to the fact that the Manhattan project was now employing 500,000 people, directly or indirectly, and spending a billion dollars a year; that Roosevelt was a sick man; that Churchill had taken a violent dislike to Bohr,[19] and heartily opposed the concept of internationalization; that many scientists had relatives in the armed forces and were anxious to get the war over and done with; and that many of the scientists did not have the same ethical scruples as Bohr—there was probably not much that could have been done at that stage to stop an arms race.

Some scientists urged that before dropping the bomb on Japan there should be a demonstration at sea or in an unpopulated area. Nobel Laureate Josef Franck and some others sent this request to Washington and a small group of Manhattan scientists—Oppenheimer, Fermi, Ernest Lawrence and A.H. Compton—were asked for their opinion. They divided, two on each side. Oppenheimer and Fermi were in favor of dropping the bomb without any preliminaries; Lawrence and Compton were against it.[20]

The trial of the bomb at Alamogordo in the New Mexican desert proved that its power even exceeded expectations. There was jubilation among the scientists. The decision was taken to drop two bombs: the uranium 235 bomb (the kind dropped on Hiroshima) and the plutonium bomb (the Nagasaki bomb). The second was dropped within three days of the first. Why two bombs? Grave moral and legal responsibility attaches to these decisions taken by the statesmen and the generals.

What were the reasons for the use of the bomb on an inhabited target? The following are among the more commonly advanced arguments:

1 . There were only three bombs available—not a vast arsenal. These had been produced at a cost of billions. The Americans could not afford the luxury of "wasting" a bomb.

2 . If there were an advertised demonstration and the bomb did not work, the blow to American prestige would have been too great. It would have been worse in the result than if the demonstration had not been made.

3 . There was the possibility of a Japanese attack upon the plane carrying the demonstration bomb. If the plane had been attacked, the consequences might have been very hazardous, especially since the bomb was still in the developmental stage.

4 . The Japanese High Command in Tokyo may not necessarily have been impressed by a remote demonstration of the power of the bomb. Japanese tenacity was so great that a more immediate demonstration was required of its power.

5 . The advantage of surprise would have been lost.

6 . Tens of thousands of American lives would have been lost if the

10

bomb were not used and Japan had had to be taken by physical invasion.

7 . The war needed to be ended as early as possible, for every month of delay meant that Soviet influence in the Eastern theatre would increase. Without dropping the bomb, there was a greater likelihood of Soviet occupation of large areas of Asia and even of Japan itself.

Convincing replies could be made to all of these arguments. Suffice it to say here that by this time Japan had virtually lost the war. Its capacity to produce military hardware had been almost entirely destroyed; as a target for air attack it was completely exposed; and it was facing an acute fuel and food crisis. Public morale was deteriorating rapidly.

It is a difficult question—but certainly one worth asking— whether the scientists could have halted or delayed the deployment of the bomb through a broadbased protest based on reasons of conscience. Perhaps they could have; but one will never know, because such an opposition did not develop. At most the opposition was confined to a determined few.

*   *   *

A glimpse now behind the iron curtain. On October 12, 1941, a leading Soviet physicist, Piotr Kapitza, addressed an international "anti-Fascist" meeting in Moscow. In his speech he stressed the military importance of atomic energy. Another physicist, G.N. Flerov, wrote to Stalin shortly thereafter urging that it was "essential not to lose any time in building the uranium bomb."[21]

The Soviet Government moved into action and appointed Academician Igor V. Kurchatov to head a project for making the bomb. Kurchatov's staff was small but high powered, numbering not more than 50 until 1945. However, after Hiroshima and Nagasaki it expanded. Stalin had sensed the growing urgency of the problem. He ordered Kurchatov and the Commissar of Munitions: "A single demand of you, comrades, provide us with atomic weapons in the shortest possible time. You know that Hiroshima has shaken the whole world. The equilibrium has been destroyed...Provide the bomb—it will remove a great danger from us."[22]

The Soviet effort gained momentum. A chain reaction was achieved on Christmas Day, 1946. "Investigations of nuclear problems were conducted at the highest pitch. Scientists understood the importance of achieving completion of the Soviet atomic project; they knew its significance in ensuring the safety of the Soviet Union. The necessity to create an equal atomic weapon prior to the time when its production would be developed in the U.S.A. dictated the fast tempo of the work."[23] The first Soviet atomic bomb was exploded on August 29, 1949.[24]

*   *   *

How do we assess the responsibility of scientists in these circumstances? It is a tangled skein which cannot be fully unraveled here. Each case needs to be examined individually in the light of the facts, and possibly all relevant data have not yet come to light. But the overall drama of events does highlight the importance of evolving general guidelines—at least from now, 42 years late—that need to be followed.

The story of the development of the bomb, of course, does not stop with the Hiroshima and Nagasaki bombs. In no time at all, the question arose of multiplying the destructive power of those bombs. Fission was not the only path to explosive power; fusion was another. If hydrogen nuclei could be fused, energy would be liberated in the process, and a bomb made along these lines would exceed the Hiroshima type a thousandfold in explosive power.[25] Robert Jungk, the author of *Brighter Than a Thousand Suns,* recaptures some of the heady spirit of those days. "At the University of California at Berkeley, most of the University's undergraduates were already on vacation or away on military service. The scientists—seldom more than seven—participating in the discussions had practically the whole campus to themselves. It was there, on a green lawn among high cedars, or in one of the many-windowed lecture rooms, to the accompaniment of the regular chiming of the hours from the campanile, like music of the spheres, that for the first time the conversation turned to the idea of man-made suns. Those were days, as Teller later recalled, filled with 'a spirit of spontaneous expression, adventure, and surprise'. The deep thrill at the discovery of the new dimensions of human knowledge and power made most of them forget that they had really met to design an instrument of death."[26]

In regard to the hydrogen bomb, the scientists had another

decision of conscience upon their hands. Many, as before, were unconcerned. Some were resigned to the inevitability that political forces would desire the new weapons. Others used what influence they had to prevent it. Oppenheimer opposed it and so, of course, did Einstein. On the Soviet side, Kapitza, intensely patriotic and much-admired by Stalin, refused to collaborate in the making of the hydrogen bomb. He was placed under house arrest but still continued his other researches. But large numbers of scientists on both sides were prepared to go ahead with the creation of the new superbomb— Edward Teller being a leader on the American side and Andrei Sakharov on the Russian. Within four years, the hydrogen bomb was a reality on both sides of the Atlantic. When the 1950s dawned, the world was closer to Armageddon than it had ever been before.

REFERENCES

1 Harry S. Truman, *Years of Decision*, Doubleday & Co., Garden City, N.Y., 1955, p. 421.

2 Peter Wyden, *Day One: Before Hiroshima and After*, Simon and Schuster, N.Y., 1984, pp. 289-290.

3 Elliott Roosevelt, *As He Saw It*, Duell, Floan and Pearce, N.Y., 1946, pp. 131-132.

4 David Irving, *The German Atomic Bomb*, Simon and Schuster, N.Y., 1967, pp. 164-165.

5 *The Day Man Lost*, ed. Pacific War Research Society, Kodansha International, 1972, pp. 19-20.

6 *Ibid.*, p. 23

7 *Ibid.*, p. 43

8 C.P. Snow, *The Physicists: A Generation that Changed the World*, Macmillan, 1981, p. 79.

9 See his reminiscences on the fortieth anniversary of the Hiroshima bomb in (1985) *Bulletin of the Atomic Scientists*, vol. 41, no. 7, August 1985, pp. 16-19.

10 John W. Gofman in Leslie J. Freeman, *Nuclear Witnesses: Outsiders Speak Out*, W.W. Norton & Co., 1982, p. 83.

11 Leslie R. Groves, *Now It Can Be Told: The Story of the Manhattan Project*, Harper & Bros., N.Y., 1961, p. 266.

12 "A Personal History of the Bomb," *The University of Chicago Roundtable*, September 15, 1949, p. 14, also reproduced in The Pacific Way Research Society, *The Day Man Lost*, Kodansha International Ltd., 1972, p. 104.

13 Henry L. Stimson and McGeorge Bundy, *On Active Service in Peace and War*, Harper & Bros., N.Y., 1947, pp. 615-616.

14 C.P. Snow, *op.cit.* p. 112.

15 For the most recent version of this, see Josef Rotblat's article in *Bulletin of the Atomic Scientists*, 1985, vol. 41, no. 7, August 1985, pp. 16-19.

16 Peter Wyden, *op. cit.* p. 124.

17 Peter Wyden, *op.cit.* p. 113.

18 C.P. Snow, *op.cit.* p. 113.

19 C.P. Snow, *op.cit.* p. 115.

20 C.P. Snow, *op.cit.* p. 120.

21 Herbert F. York, *The Advisors: Oppenheimer, Teller and the Superbomb*, W.H. Freeman, San Francisco, 1976, pp. 30-31.

22 A. Lavrent'yeva in "Stroiteli novogo mira" ("Builders of a New World"), *Vmireknig* ("In the World of Books"), No. 9, p. 4, quoted in David Holloway, "Entering the Nuclear Arms Race: The Soviet Decision to Build the Atomic Bomb 1939-45", *Social Studies of Science*, Vol. 11, 1981, p. 183.

23 V.M. Khaitsman, *The USSR and the Problem of Disarmament 1945-1959*, Nauka, Moscow, 1970, p. 94.

24 On the Soviet nuclear program see Arnold Kramish, *Atomic Energy in the Soviet Union*, Stanford University Press, 1959.

25 For an interesting account of the dilemmas of conscience which some of the scientists faced, see Chapter 17, "Dilemmas of the Conscience," in Robert Jungk, *Brighter than a Thousand Suns: A Personal History of the Atomic Scientists*, Penguin, 1982, pp. 249-266.

26 Robert Jungk, *op.cit.* p. 240.

CHAPTER TWO

The Cold War

Since the occasion of its first use, nuclear weaponry has hung like the sword of Damocles over a human race fearfully glancing at the slender thread on which its fate depends. Over the past 41 years, that thread has often come close to breaking. The Berlin Crisis (1948), the Korean War (1953), the Quemoy-Matsu Crisis (1958), the Cuban Missile Crisis (1962), and the Fourth Arab-Israeli War (1973) are all occasions when the United States threatened to use the weapon. The Soviet Union threatened China with its use during the Ussuri clashes (1969). On numerous other occasions, false alarms have brought the world to the brink of nuclear war. There have been miscalculation, misperception, malfunctioning of command systems, and sheer accidents, and as the arsenals increase numerically, so do the possibilities for disaster. Indeed, the U.S. Department of Defence has listed no less than thirty-two serious accidents between 1950 and 1980 involving various types of nuclear weapons.[1]

The risks of unintentional nuclear war have attracted concentrated study.[2] These risks have been broadly classified as: (a) nuclear war initiated independently of explicit decision by legitimate study; (b) nuclear war initiated on false assumptions; and (c) a conventional war unexpectedly escalating into a nuclear war.[3]

A more specific analysis of this problem leads to the identification of at least 24 possibilities, which include the following:[4] (a) technical failure or malfunction; (b) nuclear accidents due to human failure; (c) misinterpretation of nuclear accidents by opponent; (d) multiplication of risks due to nuclear proliferation; (e) catalytic effects of regional nuclear war; (f) nuclear terrorism; (g) loss of control due to "logic of events"; (h) crisis stress leading to misperception and misbehavior; (i) failure of rationality; (j) unexpected collateral damage in "limited" nuclear war; (k) misunderstandings due to differing strategic concepts in East and West; (l) arms race undermining C3 stability (C3 = Command, Control, Communications).

Despite these obvious dangers, mankind has been able to construct various ideologies—indeed, a "folklore" relating to nuclear weaponry—enabling it not merely to live with the weapons but to build them in increasing quantities. Some reference to these ideologies is essential if we are to address the question of scientists' responsibility, for scientists are part of society and as such absorb its ethos and folklore. The "folklore" of nuclear weaponry has provoked a substantial literature analyzing the transformation of traditional attitudes and beliefs regarding war and weapons in the light of the unprecedented nature of the nuclear bomb.[5]

Such thinking needs to be considered in two distinct periods: that which prevailed when the U.S. was the sole possessor of the bomb, and that of the period when the monopoly was lost forever.

The first period saw the emergence in America of a self-righteous attitude towards the possession and development of the bomb. The U.S. saw itself in the role of a knight in shining armor who had rescued the world from one form of totalitarianism and was now shielding it from another. There was no danger to the world so long as America alone possessed the bomb, for America would never use it for aggressive purposes. America was a democracy dedicated to concepts of justice and freedom; it had no expansionist designs. The bomb could enable it to rest comfortable in the assurance that its morally righteous role in the world would not be disturbed by those with a less worthy ideology. Moreover, its sole possession of the bomb enabled America to assume the role of world leadership which, in American eyes, it alone had the strength and the moral calibre to discharge. It also fitted into America's perceived destiny as a leader in the movement towards a just world order.[6]

These were all comfortable assumptions which made it seem proper to develop and improve upon the bomb. Moreover, the expense involved was not on such a scale as to interfere substantially with the other services which the American government was expected to discharge both to its own people and to the world. It was even thought that with the bomb, the military budget could be spared the expense of maintaining a large standing army.

Many American scientists were no doubt sustained and carried forward in their work by this comfortable set of assumptions; but there were some clouds darkening the horizon which the more perceptive among them would have noted. The most important was the knowledge that the nuclear monopoly could not last forever. Sooner or later, by "fair" means or "foul",[7] other major powers, particularly the Soviets, would achieve nuclear capability, thus triggering off an arms race which could spiral uncontrollably and which could lead the world to the brink of nuclear disaster.

Another factor making for qualms of conscience was the secrecy shrouding the manufacture and use of the bomb, a secrecy which ran counter to the principle of open government running through the American tradition. There was an element of abdication of civilian control over warfare, accentuated further by the contrast between the continuing nature of conventional war and the "one-shot" nature of the decision to use nuclear weaponry. The enormous destructiveness of the weapon also placed a moral question mark over even its possession.

When the Soviets became a nuclear power, the underlying bases of the "folklore" concerning the bomb were destroyed. The bomb was no longer a symbol lying in a locked closet and never intended for use. The U.S. was no longer unchallengeable in its position of world dominance and had to climb down from its role of lofty and detached idealism into a world of real power confrontation. "In the real world the United States was no longer morally exceptional—especially after Vietnam—but was a superpower pursuing interests, not ideals."[8]

At this stage, even if there had been justification for scientists being carried forward earlier on the tide of popular "folklore", the time had arrived for the re-evaluation of their position regarding the bomb. The brightness of the idealistic approach towards nuclear armament had visibly dulled, even from the viewpoint of the casual observer. Those who actively participated in the making of the bomb were arguably in a position of greater responsibility to give thought to the altered position.

Indeed, moves had been afoot internationally from the commencement of the United Nations to curb and, if possible, eliminate the dangers of nuclear weaponry, and scientists engaged in work on the bomb must necessarily have followed these moves with the greatest concern. A brief recapitulation of those moves will follow in this chapter in order to show how, in contrast to the rather euphoric "folklore" upon the subject, those really involved with decisions regarding the bomb were alive to its deeper implications. Scientists, too, could not justifiably avoid this concern.

Both the resolve to do something about it and the feeling that something could be done gave way gradually, however, to a feeling

17

of resignation which dulled the senses of politician and scientist alike. This led to a situation in which the scientist relegated to the back of his mind the difficult questions of conscience involved and continued to function as a cog in the machinery rather than as a sentient, concerned individual. All became victims to a situation of drift which has led the world to its present impasse, in which scientists of both sides contribute their efforts without giving any thought to the moral and legal implications of their acts. They have helped to construct Minuteman III ICBMs with 350 kiloton warheads, Soviet SS-18 ICBMs with 500 kiloton warheads, U.S. Trident C-4 SLBMs with 100 kiloton warheads, and Soviet SS-N-8 SLBMs with 200 kiloton warheads. The Hiroshima bomb, it will be remembered, was only a 13 kiloton weapon. Total warheads thus manufactured and now deployed range between 37,000 and 50,000 in number. The moral concerns are stilled. An intellectual paralysis has set in. It is all in a day's work.

Nor is it right to focus blame upon the scientist alone. The same intellectual paralysis has affected the lawyers as well. Like the general public and the statesmen, the lawyers were initially too severely taken aback by the power of the bomb to be able to contemplate the ramifications of its impact on international law. They were also too close to the event to assess its full significance. Thereafter, like the scientists, they absorbed some of the popular folklore about the bomb: that the bomb had saved lives in World War II and could prevent wars in the future, that the bomb was on the whole a weapon for the preservation of a righteous world order. American lawyers in particular were weakened in the enterprise of exploring the bomb's illegality by the circumstance that it was the U.S. alone which had used it in war.

Moreover, the outbreak of the Cold War, the Korean War, the Vietnam War, and the era of McCarthyism all helped to prevent what should have been a flood tide of critical examination of the legality of the bomb in all its aspects. What should have been a flood was but a trickle; only isolated works appeared, such as Schwarzenberger's *The Legality of Nuclear Weapons*[9] and Nagendra Singh's *Nuclear Weapons and International Law*.[10] Even this trickle of works dried up after a while, and the most momentous issue in international law scarcely attracted any serious writing for at least two decades. It was during this very period that the attitudes of passivity and resignation were building up on all sides, and which it was perhaps the task of

18

legal inquiry to prevent. The stream has now begun to flow, almost too late in the day.[11]

Perhaps a distinction may here be drawn between the lawyer and the scientist. If the lawyer did not pay sufficient scholarly attention to the bomb, this was a piece of inaction. The scientist who was actively engaged in making the bomb was engaged in an act of commission. Both disciplines were at fault, however, and the insufficiency of legal writing upon the illegality of nuclear weaponry[12] may well have contributed to the lack of concern about it.

These observations must now be placed in the context of the international moves afoot since the creation of the United Nations.

The very first resolution of the U.N. General Assembly, adopted unanimously on January 24, 1946, established an Atomic Energy Commission which aimed, among other objects, at eliminating from national armaments both atomic weapons and all other major weapons adaptable to mass destruction.[13] At the time of the resolution, however, America still had a monopoly over the bomb. On the one hand, the Soviet Union was not prepared to agree to inspection which would have prevented it from achieving the bomb; and on the other hand, the U.S. was not prepared to surrender the absolute advantage it then enjoyed. The plan for an international authority for the control of all phases of nuclear energy production and use throughout the world—called the Baruch plan after Bernard Baruch, the U.S. delegate to the Atomic Energy Commission—thus failed, and the Commission itself came to an end in 1952 without having achieved any success.

Other events complicated the picture. The Soviets exploded their first atomic bomb on September 23, 1949. The U.S. exploded its first hydrogen bomb in 1952. The Soviets followed suit in August of the ensuing year. Each superpower was becoming more intensely suspicious of the other. At home in the U.S., the fear of Communist conspiracy gripped popular attention. Overseas the Korean war was demonstrating how the U.S., having won the war to end all wars, could become embroiled in warfare again. Under the pressures of mounting fears on both sides, production of the bomb by the superpowers went on apace. Scientists and lawyers alike were diverted from considerations of immorality or illegality in regard to the bomb.

The years immediately following the creation of the U.N. were indeed years in which the possibility of a great legal initiative was lost. There was then the possibility of a compelling legal argument

19

that nuclear weapons were intrinsically illegal by their very nature—clearly their destructive power far surpassed anything that was permissible under the traditional laws of war. Many American lawyers in particular were somewhat wary of this argument, since it meant a rigorous examination of the legality of the use of the bomb on Japan. The argument went by default. It would also have been futile to expect the American government to accept such a position. With the argument for the pre-existing illegality of the bomb thus virtually abandoned, it became necessary to establish this position by treaty—by an international agreement that the use of the weapon would henceforward be illegal.

Such a sweeping declaration was, of course, difficult to obtain. Attempts in this direction were all doomed to failure. In consequence, the world has had to be content with piecemeal nibbling at the problem: partial disarmament, arms limitation, banning in certain areas (such as outer space, the Antarctic, and the seabed). The broad and fundamental argument became lost to sight in the midst of the minutiae, and the attention of all concerned, including scientists, was thus diverted from a consideration of the fundamental question of the bomb's inherent illegality. To this day, the world is a victim to this piecemeal attitude and has become conditioned by the belief that the general proposition somehow no longer holds true.

This general proposition did have a chance of asserting itself when, by an unforeseen conjunction of circumstances, the international climate began to thaw in 1953. The death of Stalin and the emergence of a new Soviet leadership, the ending of the Korean War, the election of President Eisenhower (who knew at first hand the horrors of war), the ending of French colonialism in Vietnam, Eisenhower's "Atoms For Peace" speech in the General Assembly—all these factors brought about a greater willingness to negotiate and compromise. Western proposals for disarmament drew an unexpectedly similar Soviet response on May 10, 1955. Instead of bringing the matter to a conclusion, however, the sub-committee of the Disarmament Commission adjourned for the summer recess; and when it resumed on August 29, the climate of opinion had changed. The folklore concerning the bomb was still powerful, and Eisenhower had come under pressure in the United States, particularly from the military-industrial complex. The latter had too much at stake, both professionally and financially,[14] and in his farewell address

Eisenhower later warned the American people of the power it could wield. At the same time, the Western allies were fearful of American concessions.[15] The U.S. withdrew its support. Another great opportunity was lost.

The Russians had also hardened their position in the meantime. In the East it was assumed that capitalism was now engaged in the grand design of preparing the liquidation of Communism, and the Communists believed that nuclear force was the only way to prevent this. As in the West, scientists became little cogs in the vast armaments machine, accustomed to a role of mechanically satisfying the demands of the war machine. In the days of Szilard and Kapitza, the scientists had been willing to question independently the purpose of the enterprises on which they were engaged; this kind of intellectual leadership was now lost. The attitude became one of conformity, not of examination of social responsibility.

The initiative for disarmament was lost. True, there were later attempts at comprehensive disarmament treaties, such as the McCloy-Zorin principles,[16] tabled at the U.N. on September 20, 1961, by the U.S. delegate John McCloy and the Soviet Deputy Foreign Minister Valerian Zorin. In November 1961 the U.N. General Assembly declared the use of nuclear weapons to be a crime against mankind and civilization.[17] But the international climate was worsening. In the clutching at straws on which there could be agreement, the broad raft of general principle receded from sight, and scientists, like all the others, were caught up in the confusion.

International disarmament now shifted to a lower key. Arms control and collateral measures have resulted in a large number of multilateral agreements (e.g. the Partial Test Ban Treaty, 1963; the Treaty on the Non-Proliferation of Nuclear Weapons, 1968; the Treaty on the Prohibition of the Emplacement of Nuclear Weapons on the Seabed, 1971). There have also been a number of bilateral U.S.-Soviet agreements: the Hotline Agreement, 1963; the U.S.-Soviet Nuclear Accidents Agreement, 1971; the SALT ABM Treaty limiting anti-ballistic missile systems, 1972; the Treaty on the Limitation of Underground Nuclear Weapon Tests, 1974; and the SALT II Treaty, 1979.

Yet these treaties, however useful, do not attack the heart of the problem. Nor have questions of scientific responsibility or the general principles of customary international law entered significantly into

21

the discussion. The U.N. continues to be active in discussing disarmament. At each regular session of the General Assembly, the First (Political) Committee spends about two months discussing disarmament. Between sessions there are sittings of the United Nations Disarmament Commission. The Conference on Disarmament meets continuously at Geneva. The Institute for Disarmament Research and numerous other expert groups are doing valuable work around the clock. Yet all this activity produces a comparatively minuscule result, for the general principles underlying international law in this area are no longer treated as having the potency to make an impact on the conduct of the superpowers. The stress upon those general principles must be revived. Those general principles must be pursued into their specific applications. The responsibility of scientists is one of the specific applications of those general principles—one which has been glossed over too long as the general principles have receded from the horizon.

The major nuclear powers conduct themselves with scant regard for established principles of international law, although they themselves have insisted that the principles be used and they have heavily underscored them when it suited their policies at the end of World War II. Their attitudes in the arms race and in strategic discussions regarding World War II have done more than any other single factor to spread the impression that the relevant principles of international law have been rendered inoperative by practice and have now fallen into desuetude.

If the powerful, who have more than ordinary obligations to the world community in the realm of international law, should act in this fashion, the less powerful may legitimately ask why abstentions and forbearances should be demanded from them in the very same fields in which the powerful show no restraint.

The Treaty on the Non-Proliferation of Nuclear Weapons, which entered into force in 1970, came up for its five-yearly review in 1985, the fortieth anniversary of Hiroshima. The Treaty was acceded to by no less than 128 States and is the world's only major disarmament treaty. It is hence one of the greatest bulwarks against the spread of nuclear capability to non-nuclear states, and it is a safeguard against the multiplication of possible occasions for the use of nuclear weaponry. Nuclear weaponry, once used anywhere even by a minor power, has great potential for embroiling the greater powers in an

22

all-out nuclear war, for power vacuums do not exist in the international world. A non-nuclear nation, once totally destroyed in a conflict with a nuclear nation, will attract others to share what is left of its territory and airspace, if not of anything else. Two nuclear nations, destroying each other like Kilkenny cats[18] will inevitably suck supporters into the conflict. The importance of the Treaty is thus quite obvious.

The Treaty not only prohibits the transfer and control of nuclear weapons to non-nuclear States, but also imposes a prohibition on the non-nuclear States to manufacture or acquire such devices. The vast majority of the non-nuclear States have voluntarily accepted this prohibition. Articles I and III of the Treaty, which impose limitations upon the non-nuclear powers, were initiated by the nuclear powers, particularly the U.S. and the U.S.S.R., which wrote the original draft. Articles IV to VI, which were pushed by the non-nuclear powers, were in a sense the quid pro quo in return for which they agreed to the limitations upon themselves. Article VI in particular was an undertaking to pursue negotiations in good faith towards a treaty on general and complete disarmament.

The question was raised in 1985, and continues to be raised, as to why the non-nuclear powers should place fetters upon themselves, while the nuclear powers display an apparent lack of commitment to the obligations they assumed under Article VI. The non-nuclear nations will not be content to disqualify themselves forever from membership in the nuclear club. If they should reverse their course and repudiate the Treaty, a substantial roadblock on the highroad to nuclear Armageddon will have been removed.

Realizing the importance of the Treaty, concerned international observers and groups directed their best energies towards strengthening the Treaty and removing the difficulties in the way of its continued acceptance. A notable effort in this direction was made by Prince Sadruddin Aga Khan, former United Nations High Commissioner for Refugees, in sponsoring the Colloquium of the Groupe de Bellerive in Geneva in June 1985. It examined in advance of the U.N. session the arguments likely to be offered for and against the Treaty.

At the Six Nation Summit on Nuclear Disarmament held in Delhi in January 1985, Prime Minister Rajiv Gandhi pointed out that although the U.N. Charter could not obviously refer to nuclear weapons, the General Assembly had unequivocally declared that the use of such weapons is a crime against humanity. Yet the five permanent members of the U.N., who have a monopoly on nuclear weapons, claim a kind of legitimacy for their possession of them. They continue to produce nuclear weapons of an increasingly sophisticated nature. "Existing compacts," Gandhi stated, "deny to non-nuclear weapons States the right to conduct experiments even for peaceful purposes, while placing no restraint on nuclear weapons powers in the matter of multiplying their arsenals. This is a discrimination to which we have objected."

There is also another dimension to this problem: the aspect of the human right to self-determination. It is among the most important of all human rights, for without it no other human right can be said to be complete. If nations lack autonomy, all civil and political rights, and all social, economic and cultural rights, are circumscribed and hemmed in by those who are in a position of dominance. The late Prime Minister Olof Palme of Sweden drew attention to this at the Delhi Summit. "The principle of self-determination," he said, "must mean that we, the non-nuclear weapon states, have an equal right to be masters of our own destiny. This right is being circumscribed by the threat of use of weapons which would bring death and destruction to all peoples. Our message today is that we can never accept an order which in any way resembles a colonial system where the ultimate fate of other nations is determined by a few dominant nuclear powers. We, the non-nuclears, must also have a say."

A review of the Cold War and the succeeding years brings into relief two outstanding facts—that arms escalation has proceeded uninterruptedly for the past forty-one years and that nuclear weapons have not been used during this period. Is there a linkage between these two all-important facts? Have deterrence and the strategy of the "bargaining chip" worked?

In the first place, it should be noted that nuclear weaponry has not prevented the world from being drawn to the brink of nuclear war on more than one occasion.

Secondly, it is the contention of this book that reliance on escalation is yet another instance of the survival into the nuclear age of the thought processes of the past. The strength to cause grievous harm to one's enemy is a powerful means of bringing him to the negotiating table. The strength to destroy him gives even more telling force to one's argument. But there the validity of the argument ceases.

Once a party has the power to destroy his opponent totally, any power beyond that is surplusage. Bargaining power is not increased when the power to destroy mounts from 10 times total destruction to 20 times or indeed to a hundred or a thousand times. If this argument were correct, a protagonist who can destroy his opponent a thousand times must carry more weight than one who can destroy his opponent only one hundred times. Such an argument is unacceptable. Beyond total destruction there stretches a void where all additional power is meaningless. Deterrence theory will be more fully examined later in this book.

Statesmen who have reached their political maturity in the prenuclear age may well have been convinced of the need to add strength to the national biceps so as to terrify opponents with the prospect of a "knock out" blow. However, just as muscular power is rendered irrelevant when both parties possess firearms, further fire-power becomes irrelevant when both parties have long since reached the ability to destroy each other more than a hundred times over. Statesmen of the post-Hiroshima age have no justification for military thinking which is as outmoded as reliance on physical strrength was against firearms.

Nearly a quarter century ago, President Kennedy addressed himself to the question of the alleged megaton gap between the U.S. and the Soviet Union in a radio/television interview on December 17, 1962. He was asked for his reaction to a newspaper advertisement of the Douglas Company urging a 2.5 billion dollar program for a nuclear delivery system. The President detailed the existing missile systems and said: "There is just a limit to how much we need, as well as how much we can afford to have a successful deterrent. I would say when we start to talk about the megatonnage we could bring into a nuclear war, we are talking about annihilation. How many times do you have to hit a target with nuclear weapons? That is why when we are talking about spending this 2.5 billion dollars, we don't think we are going to get 2.5 billion dollars worth of security."[20]

In the quarter century that has passed we are still counting weapons as a former generation counted tanks and torpedoes, oblivious of the fact that this is an exercise in futility once the threshold of annihilation is passed. The U.S. is today targeting all of the 200 largest Russian cities, and 80 per cent of the 886 cities with populations over 25,000. Many of them would receive more than 10 hydrogen bombs.

Moscow alone would receive 60, resulting in such severe pressures that not a building or tree would be left standing.[21] Likewise, the Soviets make no secret of the fact that they would massively target all U.S. command control and military installations, all Government centers and centers of political leadership, all major economic and industrial facilities, all power stations including the 73 or more nuclear reactors, strategic raw material stocks, oil refineries, and storage operations.[22]

Yet the spiral of escalation still goes on.[23] It cannot go on forever. At some point frayed tempers and jangled nerves, depleting psychological resources and increasing tensions, must find an outlet. Escalation cannot keep the lid on the cauldron indefinitely. The increasing pressure it causes must lead to an explosion.

As the current escalation of the arms race takes us to a level at which further escalation is a greater burden than even the U.S. economy can bear, perhaps a new opportunity presents itself for the nuclear powers to review their current practices and attitudes. The change in the Soviet leadership, the growing groundswell of popular protest, unprecedented famine and loss of life in Africa, the firm anti-nuclear stand of countries like New Zealand and India—all these are demonstrating that we cannot walk along the nuclear road much farther, and that we need to re-examine our basic premises. We have just completed the fourth decade of the post-Hiroshima era; it is time to take stock.

REFERENCES

1 "U.S. Nuclear Weapon Accidents," *The Defence Monitor* (Washington), Vol. X, No. 5.
2 See Daniel Frei, *Risks of Unintentional Nuclear War,* United Nations Institute for Disarmament Research, Geneva, 1982; H. Roderick and U. Magnusson (eds.), *Avoiding Inadvertent War: Crisis Management,* Lyndon B. Johnson School of Public Affairs, Univ. of Texas, 1983.
3 Frei, *op.cit.,* p. 216.
4 For the full list see Frei, *op.cit.,* p. 217.
5 See Alan Wolfe, "Nuclear Fundamentalism Reborn," *World Policy Journal,* Fall 1984, p. 87; Lawrence Freedman, *The Evolution of Nuclear Strategy,* St. Martin's Press, N.Y., 1981; Patrick Glynn, "Why an American Arms Buildup is Morally Necessary," *Commentary,* Vol. 77, No. 2 (February 1984); Joel Kovel, *Against the State of Nuclear Terror,* Pan Books, London, 1983. For the political and psychological case against nuclearism, see R.J. Linton & Richard Falk, *Indefensible Weapons,* Basic Books, 1982.
6 See generally Wolfe, *op.cit.,* especially pp. 90, 92.
7 There was a widely prevalent belief in the U.S. that the only way in which the Soviets could acquire the know-how to make a bomb was by theft of secrets or kidnapping personnel from the U.S.
8 Wolfe, *op.cit.,* p. 93.
9 Stevens and Son, London 1958.
10 Praeger, N.Y., 1959.
11 See Richard Falk, Lee Meyrowitz and Jack Sanderson, "Nuclear Weapons and International Law," *Indian Journal of International Law,* Vol. 20, 1980, pp. 541-595; World Order Studies Program, Princeton University Center for International Studies, Occasional Paper No. 10, 1981. A non-legal work that has acted as a powerful catalyst for many lawyers is Jonathan Schell, *Fate of the Earth,* Knopf, New York, 1982.
12 See Richard Falk, et al., *op.cit.,* p. 543
13 GA Resolution 1(1).
14 Sir Mark Oliphant, the Australian scientist who worked on the bomb before it was used at Hiroshima, relates how during this period he and Niels Bohr were shown over an armaments factory by the chairman of the board of the company. "Noting the preponderance of arms manufacture, we asked what the factory would do if peace broke out. Our guide replied that the possibility of such an event gave him many sleepless nights." —"The Social Responsibilities of Scientists" in J. Rotblat (ed.), *Scientists, the Arms Race and Disarmament: A UNESCO/Pugwash Symposium,* Taylor & Francis, 1982, p. 193.
15 See Alva Myrdal, *The Game of Disarmament: How the U.S. and Russia Run the Arms Race,* Pantheon, N.Y., 1976, pp. 82-83.

16 See Allan McKnight and Keith Suter, *The Forgotten Treaties*, Law Council of Australia, 1983, pp. 25 et seq.

17 Resolution 1953(XVI).

18 The reference is to the legendary fighting cats who eat up each other, commencing with their tails, till nothing is left of either.

19 Ralph Lapp, *The Weapons Culture*, Penguin Books, 1968, p. 140.

20 Helen Caldicott, *Missile Envy*, Bantam Books, 1985, p. 214.

21 *Ibid.*, p. 212.

22 For a definitive study and comparison of the different perceptions of each other held by the U.S. and Soviet governments, in consequence of which the arms escalation goes on, see Daniel Frei, *Assumptions and Perceptions in Disarmament*, United Nations Institute for Disarmament Research, United Nations, New York, 1984.

CHAPTER THREE

The Distinctiveness of Nuclear Weapons

International law does not outlaw most classes of conventional weaponry, even though some of them are capable of producing very devastating effects. Entire cities have been fire-bombed or flattened, and large numbers of non-combatants have been killed by non-nuclear bombs, but such weapons have not been treated as illegal. Why then declare nuclear weapons illegal?

The answer is that they have certain distinctive characteristics which set them apart. It is true that various other weapons have been declared illegal in the past, such as the dum-dum bullet; they have been condemned by treaty or otherwise as inflicting unnecessary suffering. The nuclear weapon, however, combines within itself more principles of illegality than almost any other, as will be demonstrated in Chapter 6. Indeed, only biological weapons offer a comparative degree of illegality.

In order to lay the foundation of the argument concerning the illegality of nuclear weaponry, it is necessary to explore the scientific and factual consequences of nuclear weapons in the light of the latest research upon the subject. Recent studies regarding "nuclear winter" provide a useful focus for summarizing the results.

THE NUCLEAR WINTER

In 1982 P.J. Crutzen and J.W. Birks suggested[1] that massive fires ignited by nuclear explosions could generate quantities of sooty smoke that would reduce the sunlight reaching the earth's surface and adversely affect climate. Other scientific papers published around the same period suggested that dense clouds of soil particles may have played a major role in the mass extinction of certain life forms on earth, such as the dinosaurs.[2] Following up on these lines of thought, scientists used new data and improved models to investigate what effect the dust and smoke clouds generated in a nuclear war might have upon the global environment.[3] (These are, of course, effects entirely apart from the short-term effects of blast, fire, and radiation.)

They found that the smoke cloud obscuring the solar rays would be due principally to the high soot content from urban and industrial

29

centers. Forest fires and the smoke and dust generated from ground-level explosions would also be significant, but lesser causes.

Those familiar with the dark clouds blotting out the sunlight caused by bush fires, such as the Ash Wednesday fires of 1983 in Australia, will readily understand the darkening effect of even a very moderate forest fire extending over a few hectares of forest. In a nuclear war the ground temperatures would be 3,000°C and above, and hundreds of thousands of hectares of forest would burst into flame, producing the Ash Wednesday effect several times over. If the heavy soot of industrialized areas were added to this, one could well image the magnitude of the effect.

Historical records also afford some insights into what would happen. According to Russian records, the huge forest fires of 1371 produced thick smoke clouds which blotted out the sun for two months. Wild animals lost their sense of smell and wandered among people, while birds lost their orientation and fell to the ground.[4] In 1815 the eruption of the Tambora volcano in Indonesia produced an abnormal summer in North America, where snow fell in June.[5] In Bengal the harvest was poor because of cold weather, and the shortage of food resulted in starvation and an epidemic of cholera which later swept through Europe and North America.[6] Giant fires in Siberia in 1915 caused cereal grains to ripen two weeks late, yielding abnormally puny seeds of grain.[7]

A significant result of the new line of inquiry into smoke clouds was reported in a paper by R.P. Turco, O.B. Toon, T.P. Ackerman, J.B. Pollack, and Carl Sagan called "Nuclear Winter: Global Consequences of Multiple Nuclear Explosions"[8] (often referred to as the TTAPS study after the initials of the authors.) The study assumed that a majority of the world's population would survive the immediate consequences of a nuclear exchange; it went on to investigate the fate of those survivors in the post-war environment. The paper dramatically demonstrated that the long-term global effects of nuclear war could prove to be as devastating as the immediate consequences.

The bomb dropped on Hiroshima was a 12.5 kiloton weapon, i.e. the equivalent of 12,500 tons of TNT high explosive. Today's weapons are measured in megatons, i.e. the equivalent of millions of tons. At the time the TTAPS study was conducted, there was a total of 12,000 megatons of yield in the world's arsenals—the equivalent of one million Hiroshima bombs.

Studies of the climatic effects of a nuclear war are based on differing scenarios of how many weapons would be fired and where they would be fired. As a baseline, many project an exchange of about 5,000 megatons; this represents less than half the weaponry available in 1983 and probably represents about a third of the weaponry now available. Most of the scenarios are based on the initial injection of smoke and dust into the atmosphere of the Northern Hemisphere, since this is where most of the exchanges are likely to take place.

Widespread fires would occur after most nuclear outbursts over forests and cities.[9] Scientists have calculated by weight the amount of combustible material likely to be consumed by fire, taking into account the area of forests in the Northern Hemisphere as well as other combustible material likely to be consumed in the cities. Wildfires would consume about 500,000 square kilometers of forest, brush and grassland, and 24,000 square kilometers of urban area.[10] Smoke weighing up to 225 million tons would thereby be injected into the atmosphere in a matter of days, as compared with the 200 million tons now released annually. After being confined initially to the Northern Hemisphere, the clouds would drift into the Southern Hemisphere after a few days. By obstructing sunlight, the dust clouds would significantly alter global temperature.

The TTAPS study drew several tentative conclusions, among which were the following:

1. A global war would produce a significant surface darkening over many weeks and generate sub-freezing land temperatures. There would be large perturbations in global air circulation patterns and dramatic changes in local weather and precipitation rates, producing a harsh "nuclear winter" in any season.

2. Relatively large climatic effects could result even from relatively small nuclear exchanges (100 to 1,000 megatons) if urban areas were heavily targeted, because as little as 100 megatons is enough to devastate and burn several hundred of the world's urban centers.

3. Unlike soil dust, smoke particles absorb sunlight and their atmospheric residence time is great, since they are extremely small.

4. Exposure to radioactive fallout may be more intense and widespread than predicted by models which neglect intermediate fallout extending over many days and weeks. In a 5,000 megaton exchange, whole-body gamma-ray doses of up to 50 rads are possible in the mid-latitude area of the Northern Hemisphere.

Larger doses would accrue within the fallout plumes of radioactive debris, which would extend hundreds of kilometers downwind of targets.

5. The situation would be aggravated by the destruction of medical facilities, food stores and civil services, which would lead to many extra fatalities.

The report concluded by observing that the magnitudes of the first order effects are so large and the scientific implications so serious that they require vigorous examination by all concerned.

The TTAPS scenario of "nuclear winter" has been tested, confirmed and refined by later studies, which have used three-dimensional models in place of the one-dimensional ones used by TTAPS.

Through its Scientific Committee on Problems of the Environment (SCOPE), the International Council of Scientific Unions (ICSU) has conducted a major review of the entire issue of the environmental consequences of nuclear war. This is the SCOPE-ENUWAR (*Environmental Consequences of Nuclear War*) project, which was commissioned to study "biological, medical and physical effects of the large-scale use of nuclear weapons" and to prepare a report for wide dissemination that would be an "unemotional, non-political, authoritative and readily understandable statement of the effects of nuclear war, even a limited one, on human beings and on other parts of the biosphere." ENUWAR was strictly enjoined by the Secretary General of ICSU "to restrict the examination to scientific issues and eschew policy questions or matters of advocacy."

SCOPE-ENUWAR conducted a series of meetings over a period of two years in Europe, Asia, North and South America, and Australia. Scientists from 16 countries, including the Soviet Union, Japan, and India, participated in these studies, and centers of research included the Computing Center of the USSR Academy of Sciences in Moscow, the National Center for Atmospheric Research at Boulder, Colorado, and the Lawrence Livermore Laboratory. Non-governmental channels as well as governmental ones were used to marshall this great mass of scientific information.

The report of this study, *The Environmental Consequences of Nuclear War* (SCOPE publication 28), was released at the Royal Society, London, on January 6, 1986.[11] This 2-volume study, perhaps the most comprehensive on the subject, deals with the physical and atmospheric effects (volume 1) and the ecological and agricultural effects (volume 2), and represents in the main a consensus among the distinguished scientists from many nations who were involved in the research. Great weight attaches to it as the first attempt by an international scientific group to bring together what is known about the possible global environmental effects of nuclear war. The ensuing discussion hence draws upon this study.

Although the report admits to some uncertainties owing to the unprecedented nature of nuclear war, it concludes that there is a considerable probability that a major nuclear war could gravely disrupt the global environment and world society. It draws the following general conclusions:

1. Multiple nuclear detonations would result in considerable direct physical effects from blast, thermal radiation, and local fallout. The latter would be particularly important if substantial numbers of surface bursts were to occur, since the lethal levels of radiation from local fallout would extend hundreds of kilometers downwind of detonations.

2. There is substantial reason to believe that a nuclear war could lead to large-scale climatic perturbations involving drastic reductions in light levels and temperatures over large regions within days and changes in precipitation patterns for periods of days, weeks, months or longer. Episodes of short term, sharply depressed temperatures could also produce serious impacts—particularly if they occur during critical periods within the growing season. There is no reason to assert confidently that there would be no effects of this character and, despite uncertainties in our understanding, it would be a grave error to ignore these potential environmental effects. Any consideration of a world after a nuclear war would have to consider the consequences of the *totality* of physical effects. The biological effects then follow.

3. The systems that currently support the vast majority of humans on Earth (specifically agricultural production and distribution systems) are exceedingly vulnerable to the types of perturbations associated with climatic effects and societal disruptions. Should those systems be disrupted on a regional or global scale, large numbers of human fatalities associated with insufficient food supplies would be inevitable. Damage to the food distribution and agricultural infrastructure alone (ie., without any climatic pertur-

bations) would put a large portion of the Earth's population in jeopardy of a drastic reduction in food availability.

4. Other indirect effects from nuclear war could be serious both individually and in combination. These include disruptions on an unprecedented scale of communications, power distribution, and societal systems. In addition, potential physical effects include reduction in stratospheric ozone and, after any smoke had cleared, associated enhancement of ultraviolet radiation; significant global-scale radioactive fallout; and localized areas of toxic levels of air and water pollution.

5. Therefore, the indirect effects on populations of a large-scale nuclear war, particularly the climatic effects caused by smoke, could be potentially more consequential globally than the direct effects, and *the risks of unprecedented consequences are great for noncombatant countries also.* [12]

It is to be noted also that the December 1984 issue of *Scientific American* reported that if anything, the initial TTAPS predictions on "nuclear winter" appear to be understated. [13] One measure of the importance attached to the question is the decision by the Reagan Administration to launch a large-scale research project, at a cost of $50 million, to clarify the issue. Also significant is the fact that the "nuclear winter" theory has stimulated "a surge of research activity" [14] and that this activity now embraces a much larger range of concerns.

Research falls into four broad groups: atmospheric, agricultural, medical, and social impact. A word about each of them will assist in providing the factual basis for the legal propositions which will be discussed in the later part of this book.

Atmospheric Effects
Appended are two maps from the latest studies on smoke dispersion. They are based on research done in 1985 by Starley Thompson of the SCOPE/ENUWAR project at the National Center for Atmospheric Research in Boulder, Colorado. They examine a 180 million metric ton injection of smoke into the atmosphere (the amount that would result from a 6,500 megaton war).

34

The first map shows the smoke injection regions for a baseline scenario in which 180 million tons of smoke are injected between 0 and 7 kilometer altitudes. The second shows the resulting distribution after 15 days, assuming a July injection. The numerals on the second map indicate smoke absorption optical depth. It will be observed how the cloud has crept southwards, intercepting the sun's rays in the southern hemisphere as well.

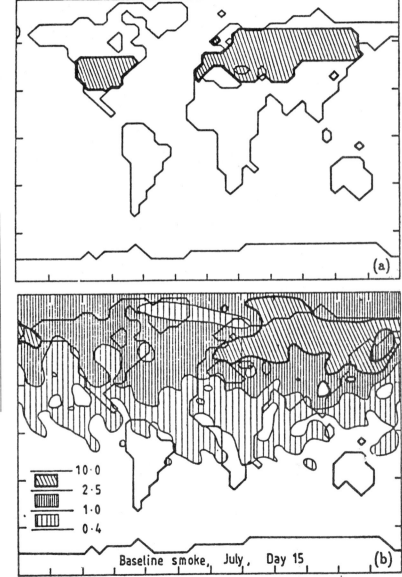

10·0
2·5
1·0
0·4

Baseline smoke, July, Day 15

(a)

(b)

The obstruction of sunlight caused by such an injection of smoke would result in a dramatic reduction of surface temperatures such as is shown in the following map:

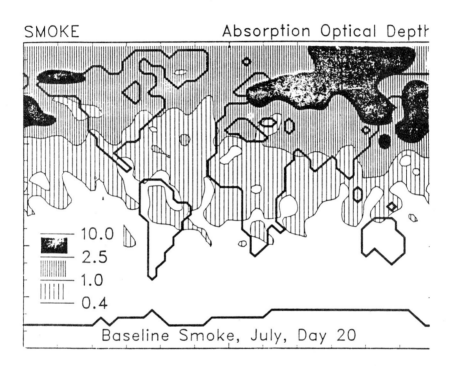

SMOKE   Absorption Optical Depth

Baseline Smoke, July, Day 20

Surface temperatures in °C on day 20 after smoke injection for the July baseline case of Thompson (1985).

Source: *Environmental Consequences of Nuclear War*, Vol. 1, p. 175.

The effects of these differences on agriculture are discussed in the next section.

Agricultural effects

The ENUWAR Agricultural Effects Workshop held at Essex University on January 16-18, 1985, added much to scientific understanding of the effects of nuclear war upon climate and the impact of resulting climatic changes on agriculture. The workshop concluded that large temperature changes were not needed for crop damage to result. A mere drop of 2 °C during the growing season in Canada, for example, would eliminate wheat production in that country because of changes in the length of the frost-free growing season and the time required for wheat maturation.

Changes in the rate of precipitation would also affect productivity. Plants are far more dependent upon general precipitation than they are on rainfall alone, which is not always available.

The tentative conclusions of the Agricultural Effects Workshop were as follows:

1. Agricultural production in the Northern Hemisphere during the first growing season after a nuclear winter would be largely or totally eliminated because of climatic stresses alone.
2. Agricultural production in the Southern Hemisphere could be significantly depressed in the first growing season, depending on the extent of climatic stresses there.
3. Agricultural production would be significantly reduced by average growing season temperature reductions of 1-5 °C. The most sensitive crops would be affected by temperature reductions even at the lower end of that range.
4. Even in the absence of changes of climate, agricultural production would be significantly reduced because of the loss of fossil energy subsidies and human labor for agricultural systems. This kind of productivity reduction would be most important for non-combatant countries that have advanced agricultural systems.
5. Even assuming optimal distribution of food resources within a given country, lack of food would become a severe problem for many non-combatant countries, especially those with large populations such as India and China.
6. Recovery of agricultural production would take a very long time compared to the duration of food stores in most locations in the world.

7. Precipitation changes following a nuclear war may be as important for agricultural productivity as changes of a few degrees in temperature. For adequate analyses of the effects of nuclear war on natural systems, however, more work needs to be done in estimating the precise amount of precipitation likely in the first few years after a war.

Other agricultural effects include acid rain, which could multiply severalfold the acidity of the soil and the destruction of the ozone layer. Changes in the ozone layer would hamper photosynthesis and harm the bacterial flora of the surface layer of the soil.

With the publication of *Environmental Consequences of Nuclear War* we now have, in easily available form, an enormous volume of detailed information on the impact on agriculture of a serious nuclear exchange. This fresh information is sufficient by itself to remove any lingering doubts there might have been concerning the unique nature of the nuclear peril. The loss of one year's food production such as would probably ensue was analyzed for its impact on 15 representative countries, and summary effects were analyzed for 135 countries.[17] The study graphically indicated the extreme vulnerability of the Earth's human population. There would of course be areas of uncertainty. "What can be said with assurance, however, is that the Earth's human population has a much greater vulnerability to the indirect effects of nuclear war, especially mediated through impacts on food productivity and food availability, than to the direct effects of nuclear war itself."[18]

It is to be remembered that the human casualties from the direct effects of nuclear blast, thermal radiation and ionizing radiation are projected to be in the range of several hundred millions.[19] "The indirect effects could thus result in the loss of one to several *billions* of humans."[20]

The following presentation speaks for itself. The first chart shows the vulnerability of human population to loss of food production if food stores are at a minimum at the relevant time. The second shows the position if food stores are at a median level. The solid bars show the current population, and the striped bars the optimal number of survivors.[21]

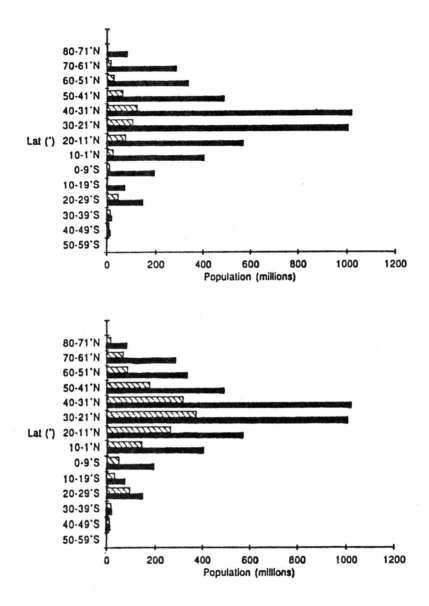

Medical effects

The report of the WHO International Committee of experts on the effects of nuclear war on health and health services points out that in addition to the effects of blast and heat, the radioactivity from a nuclear explosion would have devastating medical effects, both immediately and in the long term.

The Committee considered three war scenarios:

1. The detonation of a 1-megaton bomb over a large city, killing more than 1.5 million people and injuring as many.
2. A "limited" nuclear war fought with smaller tactical weapons totalling 20 megatons, aimed at military targets in a relatively densely populated area, exacting a toll of about 9 million dead or seriously injured, of whom more than 8 million would be civilians.
3. An all-out nuclear war, in which nuclear weapons totalling 10,000 megatons were used, resulting in more than a billion deaths and a billion injured.

The Committee observed that it was obvious that no health service in any area of the world would be capable of dealing adequately with the hundreds of thousands of people seriously injured by the blast, heat or radiation from even a single 1-megaton bomb. Even the death and disability that could result from an accidental explosion of one bomb from among the enormous stockpiles of weapons would overwhelm national medical resources. There would not be enough doctors and nurses to look after the victims of even one attack.

"It is difficult," reported the Committee, "to comprehend the catastrophic consequences and the human suffering that would result from the effects of nuclear explosions in the second and third of the above scenarios. Whatever remained of the medical services in the world could not alleviate the disaster in any significant way. To the immediate catastrophe must be added the long-term effects on the environment. Famine and disease would be widespread, and social and economic systems around the world would be totally disrupted."[22]

The following diagram from the WHO report indicates the area of destruction of nuclear weaponry.[23]

COMPARISON OF THE EFFECTS OF BOMBS

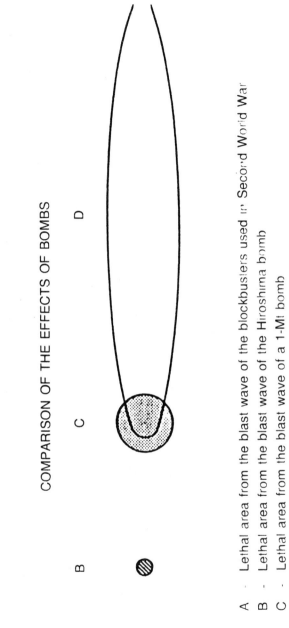

A — Lethal area from the blast wave of the blockbusters used in Second World War
B — Lethal area from the blast wave of the Hiroshima bomb
C — Lethal area from the blast wave of a 1-Mt bomb
D — Lethal area for fall-out radiation from a 1-Mt bomb

41

Gamma-ray exposure from fallout could reach the human body in a variety of ways. Externally, it could reach the body from radioactivity deposited in the ground. It could enter the body internally through inhaled radioactivity from the air, from consumption of contaminated food, and from inhalation of suspended radioactivity. The result of the exposure to gamma-rays would be radiation sickness, which has such symptoms as anorexia, nausea, vomiting, and diarrhoea.

In the case of an all-out nuclear war, the fallout would be on a global scale and would last for months or years. In the case of smaller exchanges, the period could range from a few weeks to a few days. Even in the case of a single local detonation, the place of deposition would extend hundreds of kilometers downwind.

The report of the Committee of Experts concluded as follows:

> As doctors and scientists, the members of the Committee feel that they have both the right and the duty to draw attention in the strongest possible terms to the catastrophic results that would follow from any use of nuclear weapons. The immediate and the delayed loss of human and animal life would be enormous, and *the effect on the fabric of civilization would be either to impede its recovery or make recovery impossible.* The plight of the survivors would be physically and psychologically appalling. The partial or complete disruption of the health services would deprive survivors of effective help.
>
> The Committee is convinced that there is a sound professional basis for its conclusions that nuclear weapons constitute the greatest immediate threat to the health and welfare of mankind. It is not for the Committee to outline the political steps by which the threat can be removed; but mankind cannot be secure until that is done.

World medical concern with nuclear warfare is manifest also through the activities of organizations such as International Physicians for the Prevention of Nuclear War (IPPNW).

Social effects

Social life as we know it would disappear after a nuclear war. The probability is that survivors, concerned only for their own survival, would revert to the law of the jungle, jealously guarding their meagre foodstuffs and possessions with their lives. A process of brutalization would be in operation, for central authority would have largely broken down and the will of the strongest in any local area would tend to be obeyed. Interlopers would be kept out of virtually closed local communities, and intruders would be killed. The local "head man" or "ruler" would enforce his will arbitrarily. Courts and legal procedures would have broken down.

Iron discipline would be needed to regulate the distribution of meagre food supplies, and in the initial days the distribution itself would be reduced to having vehicles drawn by draught animals. Overseas sources would not initially be available, as sea transport, dependent on fuel, would not be available.

Communication, which is essential to distribution as well as to linkage with the center, would have broken down. The electromagnetic pulse, one of the results of nuclear explosions, would initially destroy all communications. A surge of power in the powerlines would destroy the administrative infrastructure based on power-based communication. In the difficult initial days, all central authority would have broken down. There would be political chaos.

Public health and sanitary facilities would have broken down. Millions of unburied human and animal corpses would make conditions macabre. Insect population and flies would proliferate. What food and water supplies existed would have been at least partially contaminated. Those who would still be able to move about would not be able to lead normal lives, for they would be disfigured by monstrous keloids—enormous ghastly growths on the skin surface. (Many of these keloids, larger than saucers and more than an inch deep, have been surgically removed from Hiroshima survivors and are on display in the Hiroshima museum.) The survivors would also have festering burn injuries.

Families and groups would develop hostilities towards each other. Commerce would have been destroyed and whatever exchange there might be would be dependent on barter. Refrigeration and food preservation would be non-existent; pesticides would be unavailable; seeds for future crops would be difficult to come by.

The scenario of a return to the life of primitive man is nearly complete. There would be no one in control of nations anymore.

*   *   *

The facts set out in this chapter have been elaborated upon in many volumes. The SCOPE-ENUWAR report provides the most detailed and objective scientific assessment thus far. The first military evaluation of the nuclear winter theory appeared on February 28, 1985, when the Pentagon delivered to Congress a report entitled, ''The Potential Effects of Nuclear War on the Climate''. The report accepted as valid the theory that a nuclear war could create a cloud of smoke and dust thick enough to block out the sun and cause a devastating nuclear winter. While the study acknowledged that the effects of a nuclear winter could be equal to or even worse than the more direct damage caused by the explosion of nuclear weapons, it said that there was insufficient evidence to determine the length and severity of such a cataclysm.

The report maintained that the Reagan administration's policies would not be affected by the nuclear winter theory, nor would it alter plans for a ''Star Wars'' defence in light of the theory. Despite these statements, the probability of a nuclear winter inevitably has an important impact upon strategic planning and, consequently, upon the legal issues discussed later in this work. The strategic significance of the nuclear winter is examined in a series of articles in *Issues in Science and Technology,* Winter 1985.[24] Broadly speaking, there are only two ways to avoid a nuclear winter: complete nuclear disarmament or complete nuclear defence.[25] Since both of these are currently unattainable, various military strategies are being worked out to try to lessen the impact of nuclear winter—as if that were possible. These strategies are based on a limited strategic defence in which both the weapons used and the targeting would be more discriminating. However, none of these measures can reduce the danger of escalation once war begins, since nuclear war is not like a game of chess where each move can be calmly and objectively determined. Moreover, concentration on vast numbers of ''limited'' nuclear weapons is counterproductive. For instance, in the European theatre (where land warfare is also likely to take place) the weapons must either be used or fall into the hands of an advancing enemy. The tendency would be to use them, preferably in a first strike. What would be gained by reducing the firepower of individual weapons would be lost by the fact that the numbers of weapons would be multiplied.

There can, of course, be no finality about the nuclear winter findings. They may overstate the danger or understate it, for we are in an area beyond the pale of human experience.

In *The Nuclear Winter,* Dr. Carl Sagan has summarized the position in these terms: "Nuclear war is a problem that can be treated only theoretically. It is not amenable to experimentation. Conceivably, we have left something important out of our analysis, and the effects are more modest than we calculate. On the other hand, it is also possible—and, from previous experience, even likely—that there are further adverse effects that no one has yet been wise enough to recognize. With billions of lives at stake, where does conservatism lie—in assuming that the results will be better than we calculate, or worse?"

The following recent developments will also help to place it in perspective:

1. The U.S. National Academy of Sciences issued its long awaited report in December 1984 on "The Effects on the Atmosphere of a Major Nuclear Exchange". This was the result of a two-year study and concluded that nuclear winter is a "clear possibility". Nuclear war, it said, could result in "long-term climatic effects with severe implications for the biosphere." It said that nuclear winter would now be included in any analysis of the consequences of nuclear war, but called for additional scientific research to narrow the uncertainties. The report was prepared by a NAS committee of eminent scientists which was chaired by George F. Carrier of Harvard University.

2. On March 1, 1985, the U.S. Secretary of Defense submitted a report to Congress called "The Potential Effects of Nuclear War on the Climate." The 17-page report said that the climatic effects of a nuclear exchange may endanger human survival on "a scale similar to other horrors of nuclear war." The report did not address the biological and environmental aspects of nuclear winter.

3. Following a request by the Canadian Minister of the Environment, the Royal Society of Canada completed a comprehensive 309-page report on nuclear winter. The Royal Society found the nuclear winter hypothesis to be "plausible and results credible." It stressed that a drop in summertime temperatures of even 1-4 °C could sharply reduce or eliminate Canadian grain production and exports. Nuclear war could destroy Canada's forests and expose a large portion of the Canadian population to fallout.

4. The U.S. Office of Science and Technology Policy at the White House now has under consideration an American program for scientific research on the climatic effects of nuclear war.

5. On December 17, 1984, the United Nations General Assembly adopted Resolution 39/148 F, which recognized that the prospect of nuclear winter poses a significant new peril to all nations, even those far removed from a nuclear war zone. The resolution requested the Secretary General to compile documentation on recent national and international scientific studies on the climatic effects of nuclear war; this documentation was to be submitted to the General Assembly in the Autumn of 1985.[26]

It is fair to say, then, that we now possess enough knowledge concerning nuclear winter for it to be a factor in our attitude towards these weapons, including questions of their legality. As Dr. Carl Sagan observed at the 1985 Bellerive Colloquium, we now realize that even in the early 1950s the arsenals of the the U.S. were capable of triggering a nuclear winter. The Soviet Union reached that status—also without knowing it at the time—in the 1960s. At the present time France, Britain and China have, each of them, sufficient weapons to cause a nuclear winter. We do not know the exact point at which the nuclear winter would come about, but we do know, with certainty, that the arsenals of the world long ago passed that point. "It is simply not safe," said Sagan, "to have a planet in which nuclear winter can be triggered. We are vulnerable to computer malfunction, to misunderstood orders, to madness in high office, and it is fundamentally foolish to permit the world arsenals to be at this level." If there is no planetary safety at this level, the only course for survival is to turn the ascending curve steeply downward. Every additional nuclear weapon which scientists help to produce only delays the day we set foot upon the road to planetary safety.

It has been mentioned that nuclear weapons present a number of features which, separately and cumulatively, place them in a class apart from conventional weaponry. Among these features are the following:

1. Damage is necessarily caused to countries which are not parties to the conflict.
2. Nuclear war is fraught with danger to the entire eco-system of the planet.
3. Damage is caused to future generations and may affect the entire future of the planet.
4. It places the right to life of all citizens of the planet in the hands of those who control nuclear weapons.

5. It destroys the possibility of coexistence between the victors and the vanquished after a war. Since war is only a means to an end and not an end in itself, war would then become an act of total irrationality.

6. We shall never know for certain the results of nuclear war unless we try it. It is the one experiment we cannot afford to try.

7. Concepts of self-defense become entirely irrelevant in the case of nuclear war.

8. The attacker is in effect throwing a boomerang, since an all-out nuclear war would destroy the attacker as well.

9. With environmental pollution, we have reached a limit situation in which the seemingly infinite seas and atmosphere can take no more punishment. Similarly, nuclear war poses a limit situation in which the seemingly infinite human population would be able to take no more punishment.

10. Defence against nuclear weapons is impossible. No prior weapon has had this quality.

11. The military value once possessed by nuclear weapons, such as at the time of Hiroshima, has been neutralized by later developments. The ending of the nuclear monopoly, the proliferation of weapons, and the recent findings on nuclear winter render the weapon militarily useless.[27]

Einstein said that after the nuclear weapon, nothing would ever be the same again. Indeed, nothing regarding war is the same as it was before, but we still keep applying the outmoded logic of conventional war. We increase armaments and prepare for defence very much as statesmen and generals did in ancient Rome. The Roman maxim *si vis pacem para bellum* (if you wish peace, prepare for war), has been turned inside out by nuclear weaponry. Yet our military planners, like schoolboys, still mouth the Roman maxims. We must grow out of these outmoded beliefs if we are to survive.

In all, over a dozen worldwide studies, including two in the Soviet Union, have confirmed the results of the TTAPS studies.

It has become clear, from the evidence cited in this chapter, that there is a scientific and factual basis for the contention that nuclear war *can* result in the destruction of civilization—and perhaps of man himself, along with various other creatures that exist on this planet. The *possibility* is sufficient to sustain this thesis. *Certainty* is neither claimed nor required. While all forms of conventional warfare leave open the prospect of postwar recovery and a continuance of human civilization and the human species, nuclear war has the potential to eliminate recovery, shatter civilization beyond restoration, and destroy the human species and the human habitat.

The expressive words of President Jimmy Carter in his farewell speech of January 14, 1981 bear repetition: "In an all-out nuclear war, more destructive power than in all of World War II would be unleashed every second for the long afternoon it would take for all the bombs to fall. A World War II every second—more people killed in the first few hours than in all the wars of history put together."

It is important to note that all discussions prior to 1983 concerning the legal implications of nuclear war were conducted without any reference to the nuclear winter scenario. Even without reference to it, the legal evidence was strong enough. The dramatic new scientific facts now available must necessarily make a significant further impact upon discussions of the legal questions involved.

REFERENCES

1 *Ambio 11*, 1982, p. 114.
2 L.W. Alvarez, W. Alvarez, F. Asaro, H.V. Michel, *Science* 208, 1095 (1980); W. Alvarez, F. Asaro, H.V. Michel, L.W. Alvarez, *Science*, 216, 886 (1982); W. Alvarez, L.W. Alvarez, F. Asaro, H.V. Michel, *Geol. Soc. Am. Spec. Pap.* 190 (1982), p. 305; R. Ganapathy, *Science* 216, 885 (1982); O.B. Toon, T.P. Ackerman, C.P. McKay, R.P. Turco, *Science* 219, 287 (1983).
3 For non-technical presentation of these scientific findings, see Ehrlich, Sagan, Kennedy and Roberts, *The Cold and the Dark: The World after Nuclear War*, W.W. Norton & Co., 1984. See also London and White (eds.), *The Environmental Effects of Nuclear War*, Westview Press, Boulder, 1984.

4 E.P. Borisenkov and V. Pasetsky, *Extreme Natural Phenomena in Russian Chronicles of 11-17 Centuries*, Gitrometeorizdat Publ. House, Leningrad, 1983, p. 239.

5 See Appendix A.

6 H. and E. Stommel, *Volcano Weather: The Story of the Year Without Summer*, Seven Seas Press, 1983.

7 P.N. Lvov and A.I. Orlov, *Prophylactics of Forest Fires*, Forest Industry Pub. House, Moscow, 1984, p. 116.

8 *Science* December 23, 1983, vol. 222, p. 1283.

9 A. Broido, *Bull. At. Sci.* 16, 409 (1960); C.F. Miller, "Preliminary Evaluation of Fire Hazards from Nuclear Detonations," *SRI (Stanford Research Institute) Memo. Rep. Project IMU-4021-302* (1962); R.U. Ayers, *Environmental Effects of Nuclear Weapons* (HI-518-RR, Hudson Institute, N.Y., 1965), vol. 1; S.B. Martin, "The Role of Fire in Nuclear Warfare," *United Research Services Rep. URS-764 (DNA 2692F)*, 1974.

10 *Science*, 222, 1283 (1983).

11 SCOPE 28, *Environmental Consequences of Nuclear War*, published on behalf of the Scientific Committee on Problems of the Environment (SCOPE) of the International Council of Scientific Unions (ICSU) by John Wiley & Sons 1986. Volume I: *Physical and Atmospheric Effects* (ed. A. Barrie Pittock, et al.); Volume II: *Ecological and Agricultural Effects* (ed. Mark A. Harwell & Thomas C. Hutchinson).

12 Foreword to *Environmental Consequences of Nuclear War*.

13 *Scientific American*, December 1984, p. 60.

14 *Ibid.*, p. 60.

15 *Environmental Consequences of Nuclear War*, Vol. 1, p. 172.

16 *Ibid.*, p. 175.

17 *Ibid.*, chapter 5.

18 *Ibid*, p. 481.

19 *WHO Report* 1984; M.A. Harwell, *Nuclear Winter: The Human and Environmental Consequences of Nuclear War*, Springer Verlag, N.Y., 1984; Ambio Advisory Group, "Reference Scenario: How a Nuclear War Might be Fought, *Ambio 1*, 1982, pp. 94-99.

20 *Environmental Consequences of Nuclear War*, p. 490.

21 Both diagrams are from p. 480 of *Environmental Consequences of Nuclear War*.

22 *World Health Organization, Effects of Nuclear War on Health and Health Services*, Geneva, 1984, p. 6.

23 *Ibid.*, p. 15.

24 *Issues in Science and Technology*, Winter 1985, pp. 114 et seq.

25 *Ibid.*, pp. 120 et seq.

26 Taken from *March 1985 Update* issued by the Center on the Consequences of Nuclear War.

27 It is noteworthy that as early as the 1950s there was much debate in Sweden as to whether that country should go nuclear. Nuclear capability was well within the reach of Sweden, but it decided not to take the nuclear road. Prime Minister Tage Erlander said, "That which should be our protection could equally well be transformed into the greatest threat to our neutrality and our peace."

CHAPTER FOUR

The Arsenals

The question of the legal responsibility of those who make nuclear weapons, as with all legal questions, needs to be considered in its factual context. An important element of that context is the current state of the nuclear arsenals. Progressive increases in those arsenals are clearly tilting the balance in favor of war. In the words of Lord Zuckerman, for many years science adviser to the British Government, "With every delay in reaching an agreement on the control of nuclear arms, nuclear weapons change and build up so fast that the best that can be achieved later is worse than the worst that might have been concluded a year ago."[1]

The arsenals of the superpowers, as of 1985, were as follows:

STRATEGIC NUCLEAR FORCES, 1985

Delivery System	United States — Weapon System			U.S.S.R. — Weapon System		
	TYPE	Number Deployed	Number in Stockpile	TYPE	Number deployed	Number in Stockpile
Land-based missiles	Minuteman II	450	480	SS-11 Mod 1	520	640 - 1280
	Minuteman III	550	1825	SS-13 Mod 2	60	60 - 120
	Titan II	30	50	SS-17 Mod 3	150	600 - 1200
				SS-18 Mod 4	308	3080 - 6160
				SS-19 Mod 3	360	2160 - 4320
Submarine-based missiles	Poseidon	304	3300	SS-N-5	42	42 - 60
	Trident I	312	3000	SS-N-6 Mod½	336	336 - 672
				SS-N-8	292	292 - 584
				SS-N-17	12	12 - 24
				SS-N-18 Mod ⅓	224	672 - 2510
				SS-N-20	60	360 - 432
Bombers	B-52 G/H	263	4733	Miya-4 Bison	45	90 - 180
	FB-III	61	360	TU-95 Bear	120	366 - 812
				TU-22M Backfire	130	390 - 780
Aerial refuellers	KC-135	615	—		125	—
ABMs				Galosh	32	32 - 64
		2585	13748		2816	9132 - 19198

Source: World Armaments and Disarmament. SIPRI Yearbook 1985. Stockholm International Peace Research Institute, pp. 44 and 58.

51

Over and above these strategic nuclear forces, both superpowers also maintain several thousand weapons each in their theatre nuclear forces. Delivery systems for these include land-based missiles, artillery, carrier aircraft and ship-to-air missiles.

In addition to their work on the maintenance of these enormous arsenals, scientists are deeply engaged in ongoing research. The following table of major U.S. weapon system programs indicates many items which will only become operational in the late 1980s and 1990s, such as the thousand Midgetman missiles scheduled for 1992 and 764 Trident II's scheduled for 1989.

[Chart: Major US Nuclear Weapon System Programs]

Major US nuclear weapon system programs

Weapon System	Total no. to be produced	First year operational
MX missile	223	1986
Trident Submarine	20-25	1982
Trident I	595	1979
Trident II	764	1989
B-1B	100	1986
Stealth	132	1990s
B-52 modifications	263	Ongoing
ALCM	1,739	1982
GLCM	565	1983
SLCM	4,068	1984
Advanced cruise missile	2,600	1988
Pershing II	325	1983
Midgetman	1,000	1992

Source: World Armaments and Disarmament, *SIPRI Yearbook 1985*, Stockholm International Peace Research Institute, p. 52.

On the Soviet side, the available figures are not as specific. Research is reportedly in progress, however, on such weapons as the solid-fuelled MIRV and SS-X-26 and on a large liquid-fuelled follow-up to the SS-18.[2]

The role played by scientists in research will of course be greatly enhanced if the Star Wars program continues.

ANALYSIS OF U.S. FIREPOWER

The U.S. has, first of all, its "strategic triad" of 1) land-based inter-continental ballistic missiles (ICBMs), 2) nuclear submarines equipped with long-range ballistic missiles, and 3) manned bombers and unmanned drone aircraft.

In 1982 the ICBM force had 1,000 Minuteman missiles. In 1985 it had over 2,000. Each carries between one and three bombs, with each bomb having a range of 12-120 H. Of this vast stockpile, nearly a thousand are already deployed and stand poised to attack the Soviet heartland. They have a combined firepower of over 100,000 Hiroshima explosions.

The second leg of the triad, the nuclear submarines, can deliver a blow no less devastating. One Polaris submarine can simultaneously attack Moscow, Leningrad, Kiev, Tashkent, Baker, Kharkov, Gorky, Novosibirsk, Kuibyshev, and Sverdlovsk; and these ten cities, each with a population of over one million, would be immediately destroyed. Nonetheless, only a small fraction of the total firepower of the submarine would have been used, for each Poseidon has 16 missiles and each missile has 10 or more warheads (each equal to three Hiroshimas) that can be separately targeted. In 1982 the United States had 31 such submarines. Five of the even more powerful Trident submarines were in operation by the end of 1984, and in 1985 the U.S. Navy requested $2.2 billion for further research on Trident II SLBM's.[3]

The third leg of the triad, the aircraft-borne attack, is always ready for immediate action, and is specially designed to penetrate Soviet air defences. In 1984, $7 billion was appropriated by Congress for the purchase of 34 BI-B aircraft.

To this fearsome catalog must be added a fourth element: the "tactical" bombs. Intended for "theatre" or "battlefield" use, some of them are only one-twentieth the size of a Hiroshima weapon.

This whole armory is able to deliver its attack within minutes of receiving the command. There is no recall once the command goes forth.

ANALYSIS OF SOVIET FIREPOWER

The vulnerability of the U.S. to Soviet firepower is not sufficiently appreciated. Some 25% of the American people are concentrated in ten metropolitan areas, and just as the U.S. can paralyze the major Soviet cities with a fraction of the firepower of one Poseidon submarine, so the Soviets can paralyze these ten urban centers using only a small part of their firepower potential. Having several thousand strategic warheads at their disposal, they need only a few dozen to flatten these ten urban centers. In an all-out nuclear war, there is no doubt that these centers would be carefully targeted dozens of times over. Even if it were possible to construct one, a Star Wars defence shield would only provoke further multiplication of the targeting missiles, and no more than 5% of such missiles would need to get through for the urban centers to be destroyed. With the destruction of the urban centers, all organized life in the United States would end.

The Soviet submarines may not be as silent or efficient as their American counterparts, but they are amply equipped for the purpose of destruction. The Soviet fleet of 62 submarines carried 966 missiles in 1985.[4] These missiles could deliver nearly 2,000 bombs varying between 16 and 80 H each. The Typhoon, launched in 1980, is equipped with 20 long-range ballistic missiles, each armed with 12 warheads. Over 200 U.S. cities could be struck by one Typhoon.

Long-range Soviet bombers (150 in number) can carry 400 nuclear bombs with an average yield of 80 H. In addition, intermediate-range weapons such as the 250 mobile SS-20 missiles have been available since 1982.

With a total inventory of over 20,000 bombs, the Soviets could flatten the United States several times over, even if only 5-10% of them got through.

A COMPARATIVE SURVEY

Let us look briefly at how the American and Russian arsenals compare with each other. Many of the facts have been provided by the 1984 Briefing Paper of the Union of Concerned Scientists titled, "The Balance of Forces: Strategic Nuclear Weapons."

Who is ahead?

There is no broad consensus as to who is "ahead". Much depends on what aspect is emphasized. Studies by the International Institute of Strategic Studies—considered by many experts to be the most authoritative, independent source of data on world military forces—suggest that the arsenals are roughly equal.

Intercontinental Ballistic Missiles (ICBMs)

The Soviets have a larger number of land-based missiles and warheads. This leads to the frequent assertion by the U.S. that the Soviets have a superiority in ICBMs and that America is handicapped by a "window of vulnerability." The U.S. also maintains a substantial ICBM force, however, and the U.S. missiles are more accurate and reliable. While Soviet ICBMs can deliver a great megatonnage, the U.S. weapons can strike closer to specific targets.

The missiles on both sides are equipped with multiple, independently targetable re-entry vehicles (MIRVs).

While the U.S. Minuteman missiles are solid-fuel rockets, all Soviet ICBMs except the SS-13 continue to use liquid fuel, which is highly corrosive and volatile. Therefore, more Soviet missiles than American missiles are sent down for repair or maintenance at any given time.

Submarine-launched ballistic missiles (SLBMs)

The Soviet Union has deployed four new classes of SLBMs and over 60 new missile-carrying submarines over the past 15 years, while the U.S. has built only two new types of submarine missiles. The U.S. missiles, however, are superior to the Soviet SLBMs. The Poseidon C-3 and Trident C-4 are each capable of carrying 8 to 10 warheads. Although the Soviet SLBMs can deliver a greater megatonnage, the American SLBMs are considerably more accurate and have solid fuel.

The U.S. keeps around 50 per cent of its submarines at sea at all times, while at any one time no more than 15 per cent of the Soviet submarines are at sea. Since the submarine is far less vulnerable to attack while at sea, this naturally gives the U.S. an advantage.

Robert C. Aldridge, a former Lockheed engineer who had been in charge of the Lockheed unit entrusted with designing the Trident submarine has pointed out that by 1988 there are expected to be nine Trident submarines, each carrying 24 Trident missiles. Each missile would have eight 100-kiloton warheads—about eight times the firepower of the Hiroshima bomb. Thus there would be a grand total of 1,728 warheads, each of which could be separately targeted, making a Trident commander "the third most powerful man in the world."[5]

Bombers

The Soviets have constructed 200 new Backfire bombers. Currently they lack the capability to fly an intercontinental roundtrip without refuelling. The advanced construction of the Backfires has led some U.S. strategists to assert an imbalance in this area; however, the U.S. has been upgrading its own B52 bombers with sophisticated electronic devices such as radar-jamming. About 60 of them also have been fitted with a load of 12 cruise missiles, and there are plans to equip as many as 200 of them in this way. The cruise missiles give the U.S. bomber forces the capability for unmanned penetration deep into the Soviet Union.

Launch on warning systems

One disastrous effect of the arms build-up is that it can operate as a kind of strategic boomerang, reducing rather than enhancing national security.[6] For example, the U.S.S.R. might respond to the U.S. Trident II's SLBM capability by adopting a "launch on warning" policy, which would guarantee that any incoming U.S. warheads targeted at silos would only strike empty ones. The U.S.S.R. is also building its own force of advanced SLBMs. By the same token, an increase of Soviet SLBMs would threaten the land-based component of the U.S. strategic triad, forcing the U.S. to adopt a "launch on warning" strategy. The result is a hair-trigger situation, in which either political or military leaders would have very little time to make the appropriate decisions. America will have perhaps ten minutes warning in the case of a Soviet attack—or what is falsely perceived to be a Soviet attack. In the case of Europe, there may be no more than one minute to analyze the threat and decide upon the right response. This means that a missile can probably reach its target in Europe before a sleeping leader could even be awakened and briefed on the situation. It is hardly any wonder, therefore, that more and more dependence is being placed on machines which are pre-set to launch on warning. The more each side refines its armaments, the more the superpowers are driven into situations in which the machines take over.

Launch on warning systems are considered in greater detail in chapter 7.

Weapons sites

The logistics of storage and deployment of weapons are complex, and the sites on which they are located need to be expanded as more weapons are produced. Bombers, ICBMs, interceptors, manufacturing sites, servicing stations, repair depots—all these will multiply and spread across each opposing nation. As they expand, however, there are more targets which the adversary needs to cripple at first strike. The consequence is that any given part of a country will have less chance of escaping total destruction. An indication of how nuclear weapons locations have spread in the U.S. is given in the appended map.

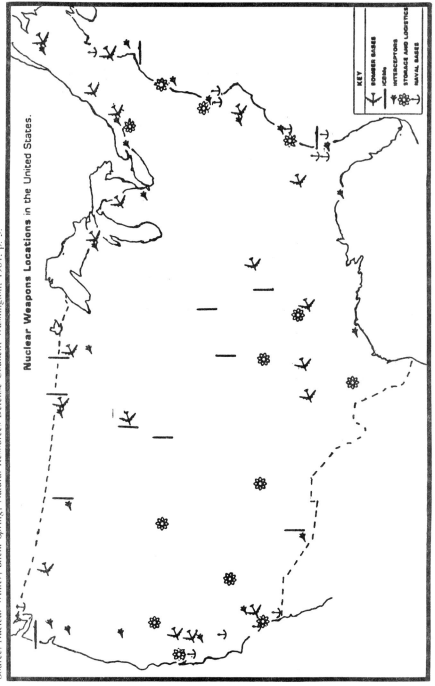

Source: *Nuclear Winter*, *Silent Spring*, Natural Resources Defense Council. Washington. 1984. p. 5.

Nuclear Weapons Locations in the United States.

Having said so much, it must nonetheless be stressed that the real question is not which arsenal is superior. Long ago that question became purely academic. An individual can die but once, and it does not matter whether one has the power to kill him or her ten times over or a hundred. So it is with nations: they too can die, and the question of how many times over is senseless.

The killing of nations has occurred before. Though many individual aboriginals have survived, the aboriginal "nation" of Australia was killed. Though many individual American Indians have survived, the "nation" of American Indians was killed. And what such systematic genocide has achieved in the past, nuclear weapons are designed to do in the future. Individuals might survive, but the nation—in the sense of a territorial group with its own lifestyle—will have vanished. Individual Americans or Russians may survive, but the American and Soviet nations will be dead beyond recall.

In this context, practicing the art of nuclear balance sheet accounting is profitable for only two parties: the nuclear arms manufacturers and the demogogues. Dr. Carl Sagan pointed out in *The Nuclear Winter* that "there are fewer than 3,000 cities on earth with populations of 100,000 or more. You cannot find anything like a million Hiroshimas to obliterate. As an exercise conforming to the normal human dictates of being directed to an end or being an end in itself, it is devoid of either value or sense." A recent study of the subject adds: "The problem facing strategic planners on both sides is not the lack of nuclear weapons, but a shortage of interesting targets. The United States and the U.S.S.R. would run out of cities and military bases worth destroying long before they ran out of bombs."[7]

*   *   *

THE OTHER WEAPON STATES

The overwhelming figures of superpower weaponry tend to divert attention from the strength of the arsenals of some of the other nuclear powers, particularly the U.K. and France. Each of them had upwards of 500 nuclear warheads in 1985. They also continue to be heavily engaged in research, with the French exploding test devices in the Pacific and the British sharing the Nevada Test Site. The figures for British and French nuclear weaponry are as follows:

British nuclear forces, 1985

Delivery system	Weapon System Type	No. deployed	Year deployed	No. in stockpile
Aircraft	Buccaneer 52	30	1962	60
	Jaguar A	36	1973	36
	Tornado GR-1	140	1982	280
Submarine-based	Polaris A3	32	1968	96
missiles	Polaris A3-TK	32	1982	64
Carrier aircraft	Sea Harrier	30	1980	30
ASW helicopters	Sea King	69	1976	69
	Wasp	16	1963	16
	Lynx	35	1976	35

French nuclear forces, 1985

Delivery System	Weapon System Type	No. deployed	Year deployed	No. in stockpile
Aircraft	Mirage-IVA	34	1964	75
	Jaguar A	45	1973	50
	Mirage-IIIE	30	1964	35
Air refuellers	C-135F	11	1965	—
Land-based missiles	S3	18	1980	18
	Pluton	42	1974	120
Submarine-based	M-20	80	1977	80
missiles	M-4	16	1985	96
Carrier aircraft	Super Etendard	36	1978	40

Source: *SIPRI Yearbook 1985*, pp. 65 and 67 respectively.

At the present time, China is estimated to have a stockpile of over 300 weapons. There are at least three other countries in which scientists are believed to be actively working on the development of nuclear weapons. Pakistan is reportedly on the verge of achieving them, while Israel and and South Africa are widely believed to have attained them already. This achievement of nuclear capability by previously non-nuclear states obviously adds tremendously to the risk of nuclear war. Those scientists contributing to this proliferation must be held responsible for consciously adding to the danger.

PROLIFERATION

The spread of nuclear weapons is usually described in terms of horizontal proliferation and vertical proliferation. Horizontal proliferation refers to the spread of nuclear weapons into the hands of previously non-nuclear powers. Vertical proliferation refers to the increase of nuclear weapons by those who already have them.

Although in the 1960s it was predicted that around 25 countries might have nuclear weapons in the next few decades, that fear has not been realized so far. Canada and Sweden, both countries well able to acquire this capability, have deliberately decided to refrain from going nuclear; the same probably also applies to a few other countries. India, though it acquired nuclear capability many years ago, has pursued the path of non-acquisition of nuclear weapons and does not regard itself as a nuclear power. The proliferation that has been taking place in the last two decades is thus primarily vertical proliferation rather than horizontal.

The discussion of proliferation in terms of either horizontal or vertical has tended to obscure, however, certain other species of proliferation which deserve attention. These include the deployment of weapons in new areas and the increase in the number of authorities with power to decide on the firing of nuclear weapons.

One form of this horizontal deployment of weapons in new areas is represented by the nuclear submarines, which travel in all the oceans of the world. Another form is the emplacement of nuclear weapons in Europe. With the launching sites in non-nuclear European countries, both the sites and the surrounding countryside thereby become targets for the opponent.

The deployment of nuclear weaponry in such non-nuclear countries as Greece, Italy, Turkey, Belgium, the Netherlands, and West Germany also means that the forces of those countries have access to nuclear weapons. Although the President of the United States is widely supposed to have the sole control over the nuclear button for the West, it is hard to see how this could be true in light of the fact that thousands of weapons are deployed in the various possible theatres of war. The very fact that decisions need to be made within a matter of minutes makes it impossible to have these weapons "locked in" until there is a command from the President. Authority must necessarily be delegated.[8] According to a 1975 Library of Congress report, the President has delegated the power "to subordinate officers in the chain of command virtually without limitation." One writer comments, "According to the report, delegation of authority to use nuclear weapons would be secret. Nevertheless, there is substantial evidence that others than the President have access to the nuclear button."[9] According to another report, "Sending thousands of locked weapons into the fog of war flies in the face of every known military tradition. The peacetime controls for preventing unauthorized use of nuclear weapons would then be swept away as irrelevant to the new condition of a real possibility of war."[10]

The electronic locks on these weapons are known as permissive action links (PALs), and it may well be that in peacetime the control over them is retained by the highest political authority. In a state of maximum alert, however, it is most unlikely that the weapons would be sent into the field locked against use until a Presidential finger presses the button within a minute or two of the launch of the attack. Such a situation seems even more unlikely when one considers the fact that a delay of a few minutes could mean that one's own weaponry would be destroyed on the ground or the centers of political control might be immobilized. In the words of Lord Zuckerman, it is "inevitable that if the concept of tactical warfare were to have any meaning at all, there would have to be authority for 'prior release' as soon as hostilities begin."[11] PALs must therefore be looked upon as essentially peacetime checks and balances which will inevitably be relaxed and removed as the tension mounts in the immediate pre-war period.

Nuclear missile submarines pose a further serious problem owing to the vulnerability of command channels to outside attack. This may mean that negative control measures may come into force, sometimes described as a "fail-deadly" command system. This means that power would be delegated to the submarine commander if headquarters fails to despatch at stated intervals a signal showing that it is alive and functioning.[12] In that event, "Every nuclear missile submarine amounts to an independent authority with untrammelled powers to launch their weapons."[13]

Proliferation is thus multi-dimensional rather than merely vertical and horizontal. While we may congratulate ourselves on the lack of horizontal proliferation, we must not fail to observe the dangerous horizontal spreads implicit in vertical proliferation.

REFERENCES

1 D. Ford, H. Kendall and S. Nadis, *Beyond the Freeze: The Road to Nuclear Security*, Union of Concerned Scientists, Beacon Press, 1982, p. 93.

2 *Ibid.*, p. 57.

3 *Ibid.*, p. 48.

4 *SIPRI Yearbook*, 1985, p. 58.

5 Robert C. Aldridge, "First Strike Breakout in 1988," *Ground Zero*, Dec. 83/Jan. 84, p. 1.

6 25 *Scientific American*, 1981, p. 64.

7 Ford, Kendall and Nadis, *op. cit.*, p. 12.

8 See Robert C. Aldridge, *First Strike*, Pluto Press, Boston, 1983.

9 *Ibid.*, p. 247.

10 Paul Bracken, *The Command and Control of Nuclear Forces*, Yale Univ. Press, 1983, p. 168.

11 *Dangers of Nuclear War*, ed. F. Griffith and J.C. Polyani, Univ. of Toronto Press, pp. 164-5.

12 Paul Bracken, *The Command and Control over Nuclear Forces*, Yale Univ. Press, New Haven, 1983, p. 229.

13 K. Subrahmanyam, "The Link Between Horizontal and Vertical Proliferation," Bellerive Colloquium, June 1985. This paper is worth consulting on this and other matters in this section.

CHAPTER FIVE

The Origin and Current Status of the International Law of War

DOES INTERNATIONAL LAW EXIST?

There is not the space in a work of this nature to address the important question of whether international law is in fact law. It will suffice to observe here that the system of international law is an ongoing system. The fact that it is sometimes violated does not necessarily imply that it is an invalid one; criminal law, for example, is recognized as a valid system despite the fact that there exist murders, bank robberies, and rapes. With international law violation is the exception and compliance the rule. Despite some outstanding instances in which it has been violated, nations of the world honor international law daily in a myriad transactions. There are respect for territory or airspace, the honoring of treaties, universal postal regulations, world health rules, freedom of the high seas, and diplomatic relations between states. Even though we are still in the era of nation states claiming national sovereignty, the current world order could not exist without international law.

Nations must, and generally do, comply with the rules of international law even though it may be against their immediate interests, for in the long term they could not survive without the system. It is true that there is often no enforcing mechanism, but law is something more than policemen and courts. The question is not whether international law is enforced but whether it is in fact observed and influences behavior. One should not ask whether there is an effective judiciary with power to enforce the law, but whether disputes are resolved in an orderly fashion in accordance with international law. In the words of a leading modern writer, it is probably true that "*almost all* nations observe *almost all* the principles of international law and *almost all* of their obligations *almost all* of the time."[1] If international law is difficult to make, it nevertheless keeps being made. If it is slow to grow, it nevertheless grows. While sometimes it has not deterred certain actions, it has often delayed them or limited them. It helps to determine the choice between alternatives. It influences international action.

If mankind is to survive, it can only do so by relying on international law. It is essential to take a positive view of it and to strengthen it, rather than to undermine the real force it already enjoys. The more one treats it as futile and ineffective, the more futile and ineffective it becomes.

The Charter of the United Nations and the new postwar regime of international law have taken international law well beyond any level of recognition it enjoyed in the past. In the area of the law relating to war, numerous international treaties and conventions have multiplied the breadth of its application as well as the depth of its penetration. It is accepted even across major ideological barriers, and all nations tend to relate their actions to international law. As with domestic law, international law must not be seen in terms of the traffic policeman but in terms of procedures, concepts, principles and habits of obedience. The law of war is a vital component of this very body of procedures, concepts, principles and habits.

It must not be thought that merely because the force to regulate it does not presently exist, the subject matter of the international law of war is beyond the scope of international law. The power to regulate is only one aspect of any rule; that which is illegal is illegal whether the power to regulate it exists or not. Both national law and international law afford many examples of this.

The analytical positivism of the nineteenth century, as taught by such exponents as John Austin, insisted that law is a command of the sovereign, and that every society has an identifiable repository of sovereign power strong enough to declare the law and enforce it. Under such theories international law would not exist, since there is lacking a source of sovereignty in the international community. However, these theories are inadequate even for dealing with the social realities within national legal systems. This has been demonstrated by anthropologists such as Malinowski[2] who show that in many customary societies, customary regulation of numerous details of communal life functions with all the precision and authority of law despite the absence of repositories of power or formal enforcement procedures.

In national law there is the further example of trade unions, many millions strong, that sometimes commit acts which are illegal and pronounced to be so by the court. The courts would not have the power to compel enforcement, but in most cases the court orders are obeyed. In international law there are instances of cases in which the decisions of international tribunals (whether arbitral or judicial) are respected, despite the absence of power to enforce them. Even if such orders are not respected, what is an illegality remains an illegality.

THE SOURCES OF INTERNATIONAL LAW

The sources of international law are stated authoritatively in Article 38 of the Charter of the International Court of Justice. They are:
1. International conventions (or treaties).
2. International custom as evidence of a general practice accepted by law.
3. The general principles of international law recognized by civilized nations.
4. Judicial decisions and the teachings of the most highly qualified scholars as subsidiary means for the determination of rules of law.

Given that rules may draw their validity from general recognition rather than from the power to enforce them, it appears then that there are several sources embodying this general recognition. Apart from treaties (where countries are bound by the fact of their express consent), there are custom, general principles recognized by civilized nations, judicial decisions, and the opinions of scholars. All must be consulted to determine whether general recognition exists. If it does, the norm in question is law, whether or not there is power or a mechanism for enforcement.

These very sources all point towards the illegality of nuclear weaponry. Treaties outlawing nuclear weapons regionally or imposing bans on proliferation or testing indicate widespread international sentiment against them. International custom contains numerous well-settled principles which, if applied, would render such weapons illegal. The same applies to the general principles of international law recognized by civilized nations. Finally, the judicial decisions and the writings of jurists contain numerous references to such principles as being essential parts of international law.

THE CHARACTERISTICS OF A LEGAL PRESCRIPTION

A recent analysis of the characteristics of international law which is particularly helpful in the context of nuclear weaponry is one written by the jurists Myres McDougal and Michael Reisman.[3] This analysis identifies three strands of expectation regarding a norm if it is to be considered as a legal prescription—namely, a policy content, an authority signal, and a control intention. These three strands have been likened to the coaxial cables of modern telephone communications.[4] In the context of nuclear weaponry, each of the three is satisfied, although there is neither the power of enforcement nor a central repository of such power.

a) Policy content

There is no dearth of pronouncements, at every level, that nuclear weapons should be considered illegal under international law. The U.N. General Assembly in its Declaration on the Prohibition of the Use of Nuclear and Thermonuclear Weapons has condemned the use of nuclear weapons as "a direct violation of the Charter of the United Nations."[5] Other pronouncements in this Declaration condemn their use as "contrary to the rules of international law and to the laws of humanity"[6] and "a crime against mankind and civilization."[7]

67

Moreover, there are numerous principles in the inherited body of international law which quite clearly render nuclear weapons illegal. These are considered in greater detail in the next chapter. They include:

1. Causation of indiscriminate harm to combatants and non-combatants.
2. Aggravation of pain and suffering.
3. Violation of laws of humanity.
4. Contradiction of the principle of proportionality.
5. Nullification of a return to peace.

b) Authority signal

We have seen that there are sufficient indicators from the international community that the use of nuclear weapons is considered contrary to generally accepted norms of international law. Communications of policy, however, are insufficient if they are unaccompanied by indications that the belief and value systems they embody are meant to be authoritative and not merely moral pronouncements.

It can be clearly demonstrated that the international intention is to make the norms relating to war subject to the exercise of international authority. The Nuremberg trials provide an outstanding illustration, for in them the norms relating to the treatment of non-combatants and captives and the conduct of the war itself were enforced by international authority. The Shimoda case in Japan held that the nuclear bombings of that country were contrary to international law in general and to the laws of war in particular.[8] This judgment examined the principles of military necessity, humanity and chivalry in relation to nuclear weaponry on the basis that those principles were authoritative in this field.

Perhaps the most important recognition of the authority of the international law relating to war, however, is the series of Four Geneva Conventions of 1949, together with the two 1977 Additional Protocols. These international agreements demonstrate quite clearly that the laws relating to the humane conduct of war are to be treated as authoritative in the nuclear era. Thus, "these and other communications express a far-flung community consensus that nuclear weapons and warfare do not escape the judgement of the humanitarian rules of armed conflict."[9] It is true that the United Kingdom and the United States registered their formal "understanding" that the rules established by the Additional Protocol I of 1977 would not regulate or prohibit the use of nuclear weapons; but that reservation is not binding on the other parties. It represents the reservations of only a small minority of the global community, a minority which in any event had signed the protocol and thus subscribed to its general principles.

There is also a clear indication of the illegitimacy of nuclear weapons in the Nuclear Non-Proliferation Treaty of 1968, which prevents states without nuclear weapons from achieving a nuclear capability. If these weapons are illegitimate for the non-nuclear states, they must be illegitimate for the nuclear states as well. The same act cannot be legitimate for some nations and illegitimate for others.

c) Control intention

In addition to the formulation of the norm and communication of its authoritative nature, there must be indications that the international community also entertains an intention of control. Such indications of intention come from nations as well as from the more informal multilateral organizations in the international community.

Numerous declarations of the United Nations bear witness to this control intention. Admittedly, declarations are not binding as such in international law; but a series of declarations, supported by the overwhelming majority of the international community, are evidence of the opinion and intention of the vast majority of mankind.

Among these declarations are the three Resolutions on Non-Use of Nuclear Weapons and Prevention of Nuclear War: those of 1979 (112 in favor, 16 opposed, 14 abstentions), of 1980 (113 in favor, 19 opposed, 14 abstentions), and of 1981 (121 in favor, 19 opposed, 6 abstentions).

Other expressions of international sentiment, even among the nuclear powers, are the Treaty on the Non-Proliferation of Nuclear Weapons and other Weapons of Mass Destruction on the Seabed and the Ocean Floor (1971) and the Anti-Ballistic Missile Treaty (1972). The regional treaty of Tlatelolco on the Prohibition of Nuclear Weapons in Latin America (1967) is an important example of a treaty expressing a regional consensus on the illegality of nuclear weapons.

The Nuclear Non-Proliferation Treaty is particularly significant, since in its preamble it spells out that there must be cessation of the manufacture of nuclear weapons, liquidation of all existing stockpiles, and the elimination of nuclear weapons from national arsenals. Article VI contains an undertaking by the nuclear powers to work towards a treaty on general and complete disarmament "under strict and effective international control."

Apart from such formal pronouncements, there are numerous informal expressions of the sentiment prevalent among the international community. For example, the 1978 Delhi Declaration on Disarmament for a Just World, adopted by participants at the International Workshop on Disarmament, called for a treaty "to renounce the possession and use of nuclear weapons forever and to join in a common effort to promote all measures to eliminate all nuclear weapons stockpiles."[10] The 1972 Stockholm Declaration of the U.N. Conference on the Human Environment, the resolutions of various international bodies of church organizations, human rights organizations, scientific organizations, and medical organizations are other indicia of a growing international sentiment concerning the control of nuclear weapons.

SWINGS TOWARD INTERNATIONAL LAW

As with all patterns of human behavior, the level of observance of international law is not uniform. At some periods in history there is a marked trend towards its observance, and at other times there seem to be marked departures. For example, in the aftermath of World War II there was a marked trend on the part of the world community to proclaim adherence to international law. The international lawlessness of the Hitler regime had created a climate of realization that adherence to the civilized norms of international behavior was essential if a better world order was to emerge. The Nuremberg Charter and trials— victors' procedures as they might have been—affirmed these principles, and in various international forums the great powers reaffirmed the binding nature of international law.

Four decades have passed since that period, and a new terror stalks the world. The proliferation of nuclear weapons has reached such proportions that each superpower—plus each of the other three nuclear powers—already has several times the weaponry necessary to cross the threshold of a nuclear winter. A succession of crises is increasing international concern. We have reached the stage when the dangers are again such that a renewed commitment is necessary to international law. Unlike the last occasion, when Hitler threatened the liberties of the world, war is not available as a means for restoring the balance; indeed, civilization can only survive by averting such a war. A principal means of restoring the balance is the commitment to international law, a commitment which will only come about by the efforts of individuals. There are signs of that effort at many levels of society; perhaps most important is that among the scientists themselves, from whom the intellectual leadership should emerge. If the pendulum of respect for international law has swung some distance away from the spirit of 1945, this is the opportunity to help swing it back. The alternatives—the destruction of mankind or the adherence to international law—never before have stood in such stark contrast.

THE FRAMEWORK OF THE LAW RELATING TO WAR

The body of international law relating to the law of war is present in many cultural traditions—Hindu, Judaic, and Islamic, to mention but a few. In the case of Islamic law, systematic treatises on international law, such as the treatise of Al Shaybani, were being written as early as the eighth century; this was eight centuries in advance of the first European textbooks on the subject, which were written by such scholars as Grotius and Vitoria. In this discussion we shall, however, concern ourselves mainly with the European law, for it is that system which has generated the largest volume of contemporary writing relating to the war of law.

In the European tradition, the law relevant to war can be considered in two main segments: that of Just War (*Jus ad bellum*) and that of the Just Conduct of War (*Jus in bello*). The first analyzes the circumstances in which it is justifiable to go to war. The second analyzes, in the context of a war already underway, what constitutes just conduct of the parties in that war. The body of learning in regard to the Just War goes back as far the fifth century, starting with the writings of St. Augustine. Treatments of Just Conduct in War go back to the mid-twelfth century, the era of Gratian's *Decretum* (which systematized the canonical writings) and the Second Lateran Council.

The law of Just Conduct in War represents, in a sense, an attempt to resolve the tension that exists between the polar opposites of military necessity and humanitarianism.[11] Georg Schwarzenberger, a seminal writer on international law, describes the tension as a tug-of-war

71

between military necessity and civilization.[12] Unless one is prepared to say that considerations of civilization (or humanity) are totally irrelevant in regard to war, an effort must be made to find the boundary lines of each within a military situation. The law of war tries to do this, and to fail to recognize this law is to abandon one's humanity.

Both the *jus ad bellum* and the *jus in bello* contain important principles that bear on the issue of nuclear war. In recent years, especially since World War II, human rights treaties and principles have also grown to such a volume that human rights law has become an important discipline in its own right. Many principles of human rights law overlap with some of the principles of the *jus in bello*, for such issues as the humanitarian treatment of prisoners of war and civilian populations are issues both of human rights and of the law of war. A field called international humanitarian law has grown up to cover this overlapping segment. As far as the law of war is concerned, however, this is a subsection of the traditional *jus in bello*, and in this book it will be discussed in conjunction with the latter.

THE JUS AD BELLUM

General legal principles regarding the right to go to war remain the same whether the force to be used is conventional weapons or nuclear weapons. Nonetheless, the total destructiveness of nuclear weaponry requires that certain distinctions be made on the basis of which type of force is to be used. Moreover, the question of whether a nation is entitled to use nuclear weapons for a first strike needs separate consideration, even if the nation is entitled to use force in the first instance.

The current law relating to the commencement of war is to be found in the U.N. Charter. Article 2(4) requires all members to refrain in their international relations from the threat or use of force against the territorial integrity or political independence of any state. The only occasion when the use of force is permissible is when a state is under armed attack, in which case the right of self-defence is recognized, within very severe limits, under Article 51.

Reference should also be made to the Kellogg-Briand pact (The General Treaty for the Renunciation of War of August 27, 1928), where there is express condemnation of having recourse to war as an instrument of national policy. By 1939, the year of the outbreak of World War II, the treaty was binding on 63 nations, including Germany, Italy, and Japan.

The Definition of Aggression Resolution of 1974 defines aggression as the use of armed force by a state against the sovereignty, territorial integrity or political independence of another state or in any other manner inconsistent with the Charter of the United Nations. It goes on to state, in Article 5(1), that no consideration of whatever nature—whether political, economic, military or otherwise—may serve as a justification for aggression.

The present writer submits that the nature of nuclear weapons, as discussed earlier in this book, renders the use of them impermissible, even if there is a right to use force in terms of the U.N. Charter and the Definition of Aggression Resolution. The justification of self-defence is more fully discussed in the next chapter. It will be sufficient to observe here that it means *defence* of *oneself,* not total destruction of one's enemies, oneself, and innocent neutrals. If these latter results are even a reasonable possibility, the concept of self-defence cannot justify the taking of such a risk.

The Soviet Union has made a unilateral declaration that it will not use nuclear weapons in a first strike, and it has called upon the U.S. to do the same. The U.S. is not prepared to do this; presumably it wishes to reserve the option of a nuclear reply to a conventional Soviet attack in Europe, where the U.S.S.R. has a superiority in conventional weapons. Such retaliation should not be permissible, not only because of its illegality but because of the certainty that it would provoke a nuclear reply.

What does the traditional law of war have to say regarding the just war?

The notion of the just war became particularly important to Christian Europe because in the first ten centuries of Christendom the Church combined both temporal and spiritual power. In its temporal capacity the Church could not shut its eyes to the necessity for war. In its spiritual capacity, it had to be guided by the non-violent tenets of Christianity. This was an opposition that the pre-Christian Roman Empire had not faced, for the spiritual authority of the Roman state was in fact subordinate to the temporal and tended to rubber stamp the latter's decisions to go to war. When Christian Europe faced the problem, it needed to work out a reconciliation of war with Christianity. Hence the doctrine of the "just war."

As the most influential Church theologian until St. Thomas Aquinas, Augustine's writings in the fifth century had an enormous influence upon European concepts of the legitimacy of war. While war was not outlawed, the justice of a given war was made strictly dependent upon certain conditions. These were right authority, a just cause, right intent, the prospect of success, proportionality, and that war should be a last resort.

In addition to drawing upon Roman customs and traditions relating to war, St. Augustine used certain concepts already established in Greek philosophy; the principal influences were Aristotle and Cicero. To these Augustine added Biblical and early Christian materials. In his writings, Augustine did not address himself directly to the question of just conduct in a war that already had been commenced.

It is interesting to notice that even by the standards laid down by St. Augustine, nuclear war would not be permissible. It fails to satisfy at least two of his requirements: the prospect of success and proportionality. No nation can succeed in a nuclear war, and the damage inflicted would be out of all proportion to the provocation, even if the provocation were very great.

The writings of St. Augustine remained the most authoritative formulation until St. Thomas Aquinas elaborated upon them seven centuries later. In these elaborations the requirement of proportionality of ends and means also figures prominently.[13]

These ancient theological requirements, the subject of numerous theological and legal commentaries over the centuries, are still invoked in contemporary discussions of justifications for possible superpower conflicts.[14]

It should be pointed out, however, that in the past it was possible to invoke the doctrine of a just war for the purpose of offensive or aggressive war, such as a religious war. This is no longer possible under current international law, for Article 2(4) of the U.N. Charter prohibits the threat or use of force against the territorial integrity or political independence of any state. Current international law permits the use of force in only one circumstance: individual or collective self-defence.

Hence the relevance of just war doctrine to contemporary war must necessarily be confined within the limits of the concept of defence. Indeed, "the nuclear weapon states admit to no other rationale for their arsenals, and the question ultimately before us must be whether any *defensive* use or threat of use of nuclear weapons—'first strike' or 'second strike', 'strategic' or 'tactical'—may be considered contrary to international law, hence prohibited."[15]

Applying a combination of just war doctrine and defence to the superpower confrontation, one writer, Professor W.V. O'Brien, states: "In practical terms, this task of evaluating the substance of just cause leads inescapably to a comparative analysis of the characteristics of the politics or political-social systems posed in warlike confrontation. Specifically, one must ask whether the political-social order of a country like the United States is sufficiently valuable to warrant its defence in a war against a country like the Soviet Union, which, if victorious, would impose its political-social order on the United States."[16] The slogan "Better Dead Than Red" itself invokes the just cause requirement. Professor O'Brien continues:"Whether the negative goal of not being Red is sufficient to justify a war that may leave many dead and still not ensure a political-social order of very high quality (a continuing probability in most of the Third World) is a most difficult question and has divided many men of goodwill in the post World War II era. Any just war analysis that does not face the question of the comparative justice and character of contending political-social orders is not offering responsible answers to the just war ends/means dilemmas of the modern world."[17]

With all due respect, there are several answers which may be given to the claim that just war doctrine permits nuclear war as a means of resolving conflicts between different political-social orders. Among these are:

1. The nuclear winter findings show that the choice is not between one way of life or another, but rather a choice between life and death. Communist ashes and capitalist ashes will be indistinguishable from each other, which is not much of a way to "save" a given lifestyle.

2. The argument that one lifestyle is better than another is dangerous, for each side may be convinced of the superiority of its own philosophy. Self-righteousness on either side precludes all negotiation.

3. By considering another political-social order as so manifestly imperfect as to justify war against it, a society is arrogating to itself an unacceptable degree of international authority and setting itself up as an international judge between social orders.

4. We have long passed the stage, represented by the philosophy of Clausewitz, in which it is believed that each state is entitled to advance its national interests by such force as it can command. The present stage, based on the Grotian system of international law, believes in the co-existence of different national orders, however much their central philosophies might be at variance. Invoking the just war doctrine to attack another state represents the antithesis of international law and a reversion to a world order which mankind has left behind.

5. No one system has the answer to all the socio-political problems of the world. It is a naive world view that sees only black and white instead of shades of grey on the world political scene.

6. In the words of the Pastoral Letter on War and Peace of the National Conference of U.S. Bishops, "One of the criteria of the just war tradition is a reasonable hope of success in bringing about justice and peace. We must ask whether such a reasonable hope can exist once nuclear weapons have been exchanged."

Is it the case, then, that the right of self-defence must be abandoned, and any aggression suffered without protest? Yes, if it is a matter of using nuclear weapons. Self-defence in the nuclear age must be limited to such non-nuclear weapons as pass the test of legality. This may be impractical in such cases as the European theatre, where Soviet conventional weapons are alleged to be superior; but it is even more impractical to resort to nuclear weaponry and thereby destroy in its entirety the very lifestyle and set of values one wishes to preserve. We have to come to grips with this reality or perish.

Even were it to be fought with conventional weapons, the only case in which an aggressive war might be permissible is one waged for purposes of humanitarian intervention. An example would be the attempt to end genocide in a neighboring state. The opinion of scholars is divided on this issue, but the majority of juristic opinions seems to be against even this.[18]

To sum up, the *jus ad bellum* doctrine is not available for offensive war in the modern age, whether it is waged with nuclear weapons or conventional weapons. The doctrine is still theoretically relevant for defensive wars waged with conventional weapons, though the danger of escalation into a nuclear war makes even this kind of self-defence problematical. In regard to the latter, it is instructive to note how different the position of the modern church is from the position of Augustine and Aquinas. In his speech to the U.N. General Assembly in 1965, Pope Paul VI denounced the "massacres and fearful ruins" of the immediate past and called for the vow "never again war, war never again."[19]

THE JUS IN BELLO

It has already been mentioned that in his writing St. Augustine devoted little attention to the question of how a war already begun could be conducted justly. The development of this aspect of the law of war commenced in the mid-twelfth century with Gratian's *Decretum,* in which this scholar of the Church sought to assemble the vast amount of canonical material that had appeared over the centuries. His systematic and analytical treatment of a Christian just war doctrine provoked much discussion concerning the just moral and legal limits of war.

In 1139 the Second Lateran Council banned the crossbow and siege machines from warfare among Christians. The ban was not very successful, but it was an indication that at least some thought was being given to the question of what kinds of weapons might be legal in warfare.

In regard to the issue of the limits of just war, an important turning point was the thought of the Spanish theologian Francisco de Vitoria, who wrote two works on war: *De Indis* ("On the Indians") and *De Jure Belli* ("On the Law of War"). At the time Vitoria was writing, the accepted European thinking was that it was just to make war for religion. The standard doctrine was "There is no warre in the world so just and honorable as that which is waged for Religion."[20] Moreover, holy war in the name of religion tended to become total war, with no moderation in regard to the military means. Vitoria maintained that "Difference of religion is not a cause of just war." He also raised the question of the rights of the non-Christian population—a matter which hitherto had not been seriously discussed. It had been assumed that since the war against them was a just war, they, as non-Christians, had no rights. Vitoria advanced the then-revolutionary view that their lives had to be respected. He maintained that they could not legally be tortured or treated inhumanely.

77

Once the just war aspect of the foreign conquests was removed, it became natural to deal with the limitations on the conduct of war. Vitoria gathered together, in a comprehensive doctrine, the various strands of thought concerning what these limitations should be. Traditions of chivalry already existed, governing knightly warfare among Christians. Moreover, Thomas Aquinas had already worked out a well-developed doctrine on non-combatant immunity. He had also examined, in less detail, the allowable means of warfare and the rights of the conquerors over the conquered. Vitoria argued that such codes were to be applicable to all wars and not merely to wars among Christians.

After Vitoria the law relating to the *jus in bello* came to be elaborated much further, most notably by Grotius, who is generally looked upon as the father of international law. Reaching back to classical learning to support his arguments on the proper conduct of humanity in warfare, Grotius completed the secularizing process. His principles were drawn not from the teachings of religion but from the collective experience of mankind in an enormous range of civilizations and cultures. He emphasized both the absolute binding nature of the restrictions on war (the *jus in bello*) and the considerations of equity and proportionality, thereby laying the foundations for the modern humanitarian law of war.[21] Grotius laid down the rule that captives should not be put to death and declared in categorical terms that non-combatants were not to be killed. He rejected theories of retaliation and the argument that it was necessary to strike terror. "The advantage which is expected by striking terror," he wrote, "cannot give a right to kill men. Those who have violated the laws of war may be put to death, but loyalty to one's cause or country is not a cause for punishment when captured." He also maintained that revenge is not a justification for killing one's opponents. "It is also most true," he said, "as some theologians have noted, that it is the duty of rulers and leaders, who wish to be reckoned Christians by God and men, to abstain from storming of cities, and other like violent proceedings; which cannot take place, without great calamity to many innocent persons, and often do little to promote the ends of war; so that Christian goodness almost always, justice mostly, must inspire a repugnance to them."

Many of the same laws of humanitarian warfare propounded by Grotius were anticipated in other cultures, notably the Islamic. At an early date Islamic culture had worked out rules of kindness and chivalry in warfare, including in its code injunctions against the use of incendiary projectiles, diverting the water supply or poisoning the wells of the enemy. Mutilation of prisoners and the killing of women and children was absolutely forbidden.[22] The existence of such standards of conduct in ''pagan'' nations weighed heavily upon Grotius when he compared them with the rules among Christian nations. He wrote: ''I, for the reasons which I have stated, holding it to be most certain that there is among nations a common law of Rights which is of force with regard to war, and in war, saw many and grave causes why I should write a book on that subject. For I saw prevailing throughout the Christian world a license in making war of which even barbarous nations would have been ashamed; recourse being had to arms for slight reasons or no reason; and when arms were once taken up, all reverence for divine and human law was thrown away, just as if men were thenceforth authorized to commit all crimes without restraint.''[23]

Since the time of Grotius there has been a very steady development of the *jus in bello*. One result has been the various conventions of the nineteenth and twentieth centuries; another has been the development of the principles of international humanitarian laws. The most important of these principles are set out in chapter 6; suffice it to say here that the principles have become so ingrained in the law of war that they find a place in current military manuals defining the duties of officers and men in the conduct of military operations.

THE HUMAN RIGHTS DIMENSION

In addition to the rules of customary international law that are pertinent to war, there is another section of international law which, in the postwar years, has assumed a place of increasing importance: the law relating to human rights. Many sections of this body of doctrine are entrenched in international law by treaty; others are part of the body of international customary law.

Many of these human rights norms support the proposition that nuclear war is illegal, but none more so than the fundamental human right on which all other human rights rest, namely the right to life.

Even the most absolutist political theories of the past, such as that of Hobbes, accorded this right to the individual; and John Locke.

a philosopher to whom modern human rights doctrine is greatly in debt, categorized the right to life as one of those fundamental rights which which no ruler could take away from his subject. More recently, the express formulation of this right is found both in the Universal Declaration of Human Rights (article 3) and in the International Covenant on Civil and Political Rights (article 6). Although the Universal Declaration of Human Rights is only a declaration, common acceptance has elevated it to the level of international customary law. The Covenant on Civil and Political Rights is binding on its signatories as a treaty.

By these standards the actual use of nuclear weapons is an obvious illegality, in that it would violate the inalienable right of human beings to live. Its illegality is also manifest under the Genocide Convention, which declares that under international law it is a crime to commit acts with intent to destroy, in whole or in part, a national, ethical, racial or religious group as such. One could also easily make a catalogue of those other human rights—social, cultural, economic, civil and political—which would be violated by the launching of a nuclear attack.

In a less obvious way, the arms race itself is a violation of human rights, not least of all because it represents an action totally inconsistent with the recognition of the right to live. But it also leads to the undermining of many other human rights.

For example, the tight security surrounding the manufacturing of nuclear weapons necessarily places severe restrictions on the rights of workers to freedom of movement, freedom of speech, and freedom of association. The growing militarization of society at all levels which accompanies the arms race spreads this denial of rights through all levels of the population.

Economic rights also become violated by the arms race. The billions of dollars pumped into armaments represent a substantial section of current global resources; all these resources are thereby diverted from serving to eradicate global poverty, poor medical care, unemployment, and world hunger. It has been rightly said that "even if the arms are not ultimately used in war, they 'kill' indirectly by diverting scarce economic resources from basic development such as nutirition, medical care, housing and education."[24] This link between the arms race and underdevelopment is now an established part of human rights doctrine. In the expressive words of President

Eisenhower, "Every gun that is made, every warship launched, every rocket fired, signifies in a final sense a theft from those who hunger and are not fed, from those who are cold and are not clothed."

A great number of other human rights are violated directly or indirectly through the arms race. One class of them that is violated irreparably is the group dependent on the environment; such rights range from the right to life itself to such human rights as the right to food and the right to aesthetic enjoyment of the environment. In connection with this it should be noted that the 1972 Stockholm Conference on the Environment resolved "to call upon States intending to carry out nuclear weapons tests to abandon their plans to carry out tests, since they may lead to further contamination of the environment."[25]

REFERENCES

1 Louis Henkin, *How Nations Behave, 2nd Edition,* Columbia Univ. Press, 1979, p. 47.
2 B. Malinowski, *Crime and Custom in Savage Society,* Kegan Paul, 1926.
3 Myres S. McDougal and W. Michael Reisman, "The Prescribing Function in World Constitutive Process: How International Law is Made," 6 *Yale Stud. World Public Order,* 1980, pp. 249-56, 268-84.
4 W. Michael Reisman, "International Law Making: A Process of Communication," 75 *Proc. Am. Soc. I. L.,* 1981, pp. 101, 108.
5 G.A. Res. 1653, 16 U.N.G.A.O.R. Supp. (No. 17) 4, U.N. Doc. A/5100 (1961) para. 1(a).

6 *Ibid.*, para. 1(b).

7 *Ibid.*, para. 1(d).

8 1964 *Jap. Ann. Int. L.*, p. 212 (English translation)—judgment of the District Court of Tokyo, December 7, 1963,

9 Burns H. Weston, "Nuclear Weapons versus International Law: A Contextual Reassessment," 28 *McGill L.J.*, 1983, 542 at 563.

10 4 *Alternatives, A Journal of World Policy*, 1978, p. 155.

11 See McDougal and Feliciano, *Law and Minimum World Public Order*, Yale Univ. Press, 1961, pp. 72-76.

12 G. Schwarzenberger, *Manual of International Law, 5th Edition*, ed. Stevens, 1967, pp. 197-199.

13 See St. Augustine, Book LXXXIII q. *Super Josue* and Aquinas, *Summa Theologica secunda secundae Q 40*. See also D'Entreves, *Aquinas: Selected Political Writings*, tr. J.G. Dawson, Oxford: Blackwell, 1948.

14 For example in Professor William O'Brien's treatise on *The Conduct of Just and Limited War*, Praeger, 1981, pp. 33-35.

15 Burns H. Weston, *op.cit.*, p. 549.

16 William O'Brien, *op.cit.*, p. 20.

17 William O'Brien, *op.cit.*, p. 21.

18 In favor of intervention, see Lillich, "Intervention to Protect Human Rights," 15 *McGill L.J.*, 1969, pp. 205-219; McDougal and Reisman, "Rhodesia and the U.N.: The Lawfulness of International Concern," 62 *Am. J. of Int. Law*, 1962, p. 1; contra, see Brownlie, "Humanitarian Intervention," in *Law and Civil War in the Modern World*, ed. John Norton Moore, Johns Hopkins Univ. Press, 1974, pp. 218-227; Thomas M. Franck and Nigel S. Rodley, "After Bangladesh: The Law of Humanitarian Intervention by Military Force," 62 *Am. J. of Int. Law*, 1968, pp. 275-305.

19 Pope Paul VI, *Never Again War!*, U.N. Office of Public Information, N.Y., 1965, p. 37. See further Jim Castelli, *The Bishops and the Bomb: Waging Peace in the Nuclear Age*, Doubleday, 1983. The volume contains the text of the American Bishops' 1983 Pastoral Letter on War and Peace, which has also been separately published as *The Challenge of Peace: God's Promise and Our Response*, Publication No. 863, Office of Publishing Services, U.S. Catholic Conference. For the joint Pastoral Letter of the German Bishops, see *Out of Justice, Peace: The Church in the Service of Peace*, Irish Messenger Publications, 1984. See also *Peace and Disarmament*, Documents of the World Council of Churches and the Roman Catholic Church, 1982.

20 Allen, *A True, Sincere, and Modest Defence of English Catholics*, p. 103.

21 See generally on this topic J.T. Johnson, *Just War Tradition and the Restraint of War: A Moral and Historical Inquiry*, Columbia Univ. Press, 1981.

22 See Perry Bordwell, *The Law of War between Belligerents: A History and Commentary*, Callaghan & Co., Chicago, 1908, p. 12.

23 Grotius, *Prolegomena*, Para. 28 (tr. Whewell).

24 *SIPRI Yearbook*, 1981, p. 117.

25 Stockholm Declaration of the U.N. Conference on the Human Environment (1972), 11 *I.L.M.*, p. 1416. To be noted also is the 1977 Geneva Protocol I Additional prohibiting means of warfare which may cause "widespread, long-term and severe damage to the natural environment."

CHAPTER SIX

Is the Use of Nuclear Weapons Illegal?

WHAT PRINCIPLES OF INTERNATIONAL LAW RENDER THE USE OF NUCLEAR WEAPONS ILLEGAL?

This chapter first seeks to establish the proposition that the use of nuclear weapons is illegal and a crime against humanity. It then argues that whether or not it be a crime under international law, it is an international delict or tort—that is, an act which is wrong, whether or not it be criminal.

International law consists, as we have seen, not merely of treaties. Among the sources of international law enumerated by Article 38 of the Charter of the International Court of Justice are international custom, the general principles of law recognized by civilized nations, judicial decisions, and the opinions of outstanding jurists, all of which strongly establish the illegality of nuclear weaponry.

The absence of a specific treaty banning the use or manufacture of nuclear weapons means that only one of the sources of international law is absent. All the others—international custom, general principles of law recognized by civilized nations, judicial decisions and juristic writing—can be strongly invoked in support of this proposition. The advent of the nuclear bomb and the manufacture of nuclear weaponry in several countries have not displaced this principle. There is also a strong body of international declarations which, although they do not have the force of law in themselves, do strongly indicate the sense of the international community on this issue and reinforce the contention that such a principle now forms part of customary international law.

It is sometimes argued that nuclear weapons do not come within the scope of laws of war which were formulated before their invention. This is a spurious argument, for the same could then apply to the dum dum bullet and chemical warfare. What is important is the principle underling the rule. Specific applications of the general principle occur in the light of events and circumstances that only arise later. Nearly every piece of legislation and nearly every Constitution (that of the U.S. is the best example) must be applied to situations that were not envisaged when they were formulated. These sources of law would only be inoperative if they had no general principle which would cover the new situation. In the case of nuclear weapons, those general principles do exist.

There are a number of reasons why nuclear weaponry should be included in the category of weapons forbidden by customary international law and general principles of law recognized by civilized nations. They include:

Reason 1. Causation of indiscriminate harm to combatants and noncombatants.

India's celebrated pre-Christian classic, *The Ramayana,* tells us that the use of a weapon of war which would destroy the entire race of the enemy was forbidden by the virtuous prince Rama. The reason given is that the weapon would destroy even those who did not bear arms; such destruction en masse was forbidden by the ancient laws of war even though Rama's adversary was fighting an unjust war.[1] So strong was the ancient tradition that historians record that in the face of invading armies Indian peasants would pursue their work in the fields, confident of the protection afforded them by the tradition that war was a matter between the combatants.[2] This is an ancient principle in several other cultural traditions; Hindu law, Chinese law, Jewish law, Islamic law, and ancient European tradition regarding the law of war join in acknowledging this principle, and make it a generally accepted rule of customary international law.

We have seen in the preceding chapter that the early European origins of this rule go back to the thirteenth century. In the nineteenth century and in the years immediately preceding World War I, this principle received such wide approval that it came to be embodied in the Military and Naval Manuals of the Great Powers. For example, a standard Manual of Military Law issued by the British War Office in 1914 states: "It is, however, a universally recognized rule of International Law that hostilities are restricted to the armed forces of the belligerents, and that the ordinary citizens of the contending States, who do not take up arms and who abstain from hostile acts, must be treated leniently, must not be injured in their lives or liberty, except for cause or after due trial, and must not as a rule be deprived of their private property."[3]

It is true that civilian casaulties incidental to an attack upon a military target have been regarded as legitimate and part of the necessary incidents of warfare. A distinction must be made, however, between the incidental causation of such casualties and their deliberate and direct causation. Noncombatant sick and wounded cannot legally be attacked, nor can religious institutions, cultural institutions, or hospitals.

Article 6 of the Nuremberg Charter declared that the extermination of the civilian population, whether in whole or in part, constituted a "crime against humanity." Lest it be thought that the Nuremberg principles reflected merely victor's justice after the event, it should be pointed out that the prior existence of such principles can be demonstrated from pronouncements of the nations which were ranged against each other in World War II. Thus, the U.S. protested against the Japanese bombing of Nanking in 1937 in these terms: "The Government holds the view that any general bombing of an extensive area wherein there resides a large population engaged in peaceful pursuits is unwarranted and contrary to the principles of law and humanity."[4] The Supreme Court of Japan in the Shimoda case likewise affirmed this principle in great detail, although the claim of the plaintiffs against the Japanese Government concerning injuries suffered from atomic bombs was dismissed for other reasons.[5]

In the postwar period, the Proclamation of Teheran, adopted by the General Assembly in Resolution 2442 (XXIII) by 115 votes to none against and 1 abstention, affirmed that the right of belligerent parties to adopt means of injuring the enemy is not unlimited and that it is prohibited to attack civilian populations as such. This is one of many such resolutions. Singly they do not have the force of law, but their cumulative effect is evidence for a generally accepted body of customary international law. They certainly provide evidence that there has been no abrogation in the postwar years of such rules as were undoubtedly part of customary international law in earlier times.

Further confirmation of this is provided by the Protocols to the Geneva Conventions. The 1977 Protocol I (Additional) affirms in Article 48 that parties to the conflict shall at all times distinguish between the civilian populations and the combatants.

Of the four Geneva Conventions of 1949, one relates specifically to the protection of civilian persons in time of war. Embodying principles recognized earlier, the Convention places the belligerents under the obligation to spare those parts of the population that take no part in the fighting. To this end it provides a whole series of practical measures including the establishment of safety zones, civilian hospitals, and relief supplies, and provisions for child welfare and the circulation of family news. Civilians are protected from ill treatment and pillage, and are declared entitled in all circumstances to respect for their person. They are to be humanely treated and protected against all acts of violence.

The opinion of eminent jurists also provides confirmation of the existence of such a principle in the postwar years. The meeting of the Institute of International Law in Edinburgh in September 1969 declared in article 6 of its conclusions that ''Existing international law prohibits, irrespective of the type of weapon used, any action whatsoever designed to terrorize the civilian population.'' Article 6 also stated, ''Existing international law prohibits the use of all weapons which, by their nature, affect indiscriminately both military objectives and non-military objects, or both armed forces and civilian populations. In particular, it prohibits the use of weapons the destructive effect of which is so great that it cannot be limited to specific military objectives or is otherwise uncontrollable...''

It is thus sufficiently established that weapons which cause indiscriminate harm to combatants and noncombatants alike are contrary to international law, and that this principle has not been abrogated by contrary practice.

The proportion of civilians affected by war seems to be steadily rising owing to the destructiveness of modern weapons. Of those killed in World War I, some 5% were civilians. In World War II the number was 50%.[6] In the Vietnam war, it is estimated that 70% of the deaths were deaths of civilians.[7] In World War III, should it occur, the percentage will be the total proportion the non-combatant population bears to the combatant.

If it is a valid law that civilians are entitled to protection, then obviously the use of nuclear weapons is illegal, since there is no way for civilians to be protected. Indeed, the damage which a nuclear war would inflict goes far beyond even the scope of genocide, which has been declared a crime against humanity. Genocide is the extermination of only one group of human beings. Nuclear war would exterminate not only defined groups but *all* human beings both combatant and noncombatant, without regard to any principle of selection. It

86

destroys all living things and the environment as well. Therefore it has sometimes been described as "omnicide" as opposed to the "mere" crime of genocide. Should nuclear war occur, the culpability for this kind of killing would go far beyond the already enormous culpability attaching to genocide.

An interesting test of whether the mass killing resulting from the use of nuclear weaponry would qualify as a crime against humanity is the test of role reversal suggested by Professor Richard Falk and others.[8] If the Germans or the Japanese had used atomic bombs against North America and Europe (and had still been defeated), there is little doubt that the use of these weapons would have been looked upon as international crimes "of signal magnitude." Professor Falk observes, "To adopt this perspective of role reversal is helpful in orienting our understanding of the present status of nuclear weaponry and strategic doctrine. The use of this weapon against Japanese cities was of course shielded from immediate legal scrutiny because of the outcome of the war; there was no disposition to self-judge the legally dubious military policies of the victors."[9]

Reason 2. Aggravation of pain and suffering.

It is illegal to cause needless aggravation of pain and suffering. The first support for such a principle comes, again, from the ancient traditions of many cultures. The cross-bow and siege machines were outlawed by the Second Lateran Council on this ground in 1139. The mainstream of nineteenth-century European international law pursued this principle in regard to specific cases as increasingly cruel weapons of war were made available by modern technology.

When the dum-dum or expanding bullet was invented, the 1868 Declaration of St. Petersburg affirmed that the right of a nation state to injure a belligerent was not unlimited. It also affirmed that the only legitimate object of war is to weaken the military forces of the enemy; that this object would be exceeded by the employment of arms which uselessly aggravate the sufferings of disabled men or render their death inevitable; and that the use of such arms would be contrary to the laws of humanity.

The Hague Declaration of 1889 regarding Asphyxiating Gases declared that if a projectile has the sole object of diffusing such gases, it is so heinous and odious as to be unequivocally illegal. This declaration extends to *production, possession, threat or use* of *any* poisonous substances or emissions as weapons of war. (Would this not extend to radioactive devices?)

The British military manual issued by the War Office in 1914 is interesting in this connection as representative of widely accepted principles. It reads: "It is expressly forbidden to employ arms, projectiles or material calculated to cause unnecessary suffering. Under this heading might be included such weapons as lances with a barbed head, irregularly-shaped bullets, projectiles filled with broken glass, and the like; also the scoring of the surface of bullets, the filing off the end of their hard case, and smearing on them any substance likely to inflame a wound."[10] There can be little doubt that by the end of the nineteenth century this principle could clearly be described as "a general principle of law recognized by civilized nations."

The 1925 Geneva Gas Protocol prohibited the use of gases and bacteriological means of warfare. The protocol applies not only to gases, but to "all analogous liquids, materials and devices," whether solid, liquid or gas.

The 1980 Convention on Prohibitions or Restrictions on the Use of Certain Conventional Weapons which may be Deemed to be Excessively Injurious or to have Indiscriminate Effects agreed, *inter alia*, to ban fragmentary weapons which inflict wounds with particles which are not detectable by X-rays. It also agreed to limit the use of air-delivered incendiary bombs.

It is to be remembered that while the laws of war permit actions which further the aims and purposes of war, the infliction of suffering *per se* does not fall within these purposes. Hence the prohibition of "unnecessary suffering" and "superfluous injury". Nuclear weaponry by all accounts causes so much suffering to the survivors as to make them envy the dead. The sufferings of the *hibakusha* (atom bomb victims) of Japan are well documented. A visit to the Hiroshima museum will more than suffice to provide evidence of their suffering to anyone with the courage to bear it. For those unable to make the trip to the museum, some idea of the horrors is given in John Hersey's *Hiroshima*. Other works worth consulting are *Hiroshima: In Memoriam and Today* (ed. H. Takayama, The Support Society of Hiroshima), which contains the stories of Hiroshima survivors, and M. Hachiya, *Hiroshima Diary: The Journal of a Japanese Physician* (tr. W. Wells, Univ. of N. Carolina Press, 1955). The leukemias, the keloids, the cancers, the retarded babies, and the lifelong physical and social sufferings need to be appreciated in detail if one is to understand the full horror involved.

Reason 3. Violation of the laws of humanity.

International law has always contradicted the proposition that "all is fair in love and war." One cannot massacre prisoners, or deliberately destroy hospitals, or refuse treatment to enemy sick and wounded. Such principles stem from considerations of humanity, which are part of the inheritance of civilization. Numerous historical documents, such as the 1868 Declaration of St. Petersburg and the 1925 Geneva Protocol prohibiting chemical weapons, represent another strand of humanitarian concern woven into the law.

European attention came to focus on humanitarian law when Henry Dunant, a young Swiss banker, wrote his book *A Memory of Solferino* in 1862. Dunant had been in Solferino in northern Italy by chance when the famous battle was fought against Austria by France and Italy, resulting in over 40,000 dead and wounded. Dunant concerned himself mainly with lessening the suffering of the military personnel involved, but his efforts helped to concentrate attention on the horrors of war in general. His work led to the foundation of the Red Cross and to the Geneva Convention of 1864, the precursor of many other Conventions which did not limit themselves only to combatants.

With the progressive increase in the destructiveness and cruelty of military weapons in the nineteenth century, feelings of conscience led to the banning of certain categories of weapons (as in the 1868 Declaration of St. Petersburg) and the formulation of the customary rules of war (such as the Hague Rules of 1899). These feelings intensified in the twentieth century when the two World Wars demonstrated how destructive modern conditions of warfare could be. Clearly the wars of law promulgated in the nineteenth century needed even more precise formulation, amplification and development. With the formation of the United Nations and the proliferation of international committees and agencies, which set the stage in turn for a series of conventions, declarations and resolutions, more clarity and substance were given to the broad general principles previously formulated.

Particular reference should be made to the "de Martens Clause" in the preamble to the Hague Convention IV on the laws of land warfare. This provides that in cases not covered by the Regulations, inhabitants of occupied territories and belligerents "remain under the protection and the rule of the principles of the law of nations, as they result from the usages established among civilized peoples, from the laws of humanity and the dictates of the public conscience." This was a specific recognition of the significance of the laws of humanity in international law. The Parties to the Geneva Conventions of 1949 expressly recognized the de Martens clause as a living part of international law.

The sufferings induced by nuclear weaponry clearly make these weapons illegal by the laws of humanity.

Reason 4. Contradiction of the principle of proportionality.

We have dealt briefly with the principle of proportionality in the context of the just war doctrine. The principle is one of the most ancient and respected rules of warfare, and many traditions besides the European tradition recognize it. Thus in the *Mahabharatha*, it is recorded that the warrior Arjun refrained from using a hyperdestructive weapon because the fight was restricted to ordinary conventional weapons.[11] Moreover, sword was to fight against sword, a horseman was to fight against a horseman; swords were not to fight against clubs, or horsemen fight against footsoldiers. And if the opponent was mounted on a horse, it was contrary to the laws of war to fight against him on an elephant.

The Islamic law of war had similar principles, and the laws of chivalry prescribed no less. They required complete equality of weaponry and equipment, especially where duels were involved.

The principle of proportionality becomes relevant both in attack and defence. In attack it prevents the causing of harm which is disproportionate to the military objective. It also prevents the causing of suffering to civilians which is disproportionate to the military objective sought. In defence the principle means that the retaliatory force must be proportionate to the nature of the attack. This principle has its analogue in the principle of self-defence in criminal law. One does not use a sledgehammer to kill a fly. Criminal law acknowledges, of course, that grades of force cannot be weighed on fine scales: but there must be no obvious disproportion between the suffering inflicted in defence and that which is necessary for the purposes of defence.

A war fought with nuclear weapons would violate proportionality not only in causing unprecedented suffering, but in other ways also. If war is fought to avert an evil, the means must be proportionate to the evil to be avoided. With nuclear weapons this is not possible. One writer states: "Who are we, beings with a life expectancy of decades, to discuss the entire future of the planet in terms deriving exclusively from our concerns, concerns which may be expected to count for nothing in a few millennia, with or without nuclear war. There is megalomania, madness, in supposing that we can be important enough to make the judgment..."[12]

Reason 5. Nullification of a return to peace.

As formulated by Aristotle in universally accepted terms, the proper object of war is the establishment of conditions which are intended to bring about a just and lasting peace. This is to say that war is never an end in itself. Moreover, once a victory is achieved by one side or the other, the object and interest of both sides is the return to peace.

Unless one wishes to speak of the "peace" of a graveyard, there is no chance for a return to peace after a nuclear war. All that will be left of both victors and vanquished is a virtually dead mass of territory. To speak of "peaceful coexistence" in such a context would be a mockery.

It is true that there have been wars in the past which have come close to decimating the population of the vanquished country. However, even this devastation bears no comparison with the destruction of persons, property, and life-support systems that would take place in a nuclear war.

It is worth recalling that St. Augustine stipulated that "reasonable chance of success" was one of the prerequisites without which a Christian should not make war. Such success cannot exist when, as in a nuclear war, there is no chance for a return to peace afterwards.

Immanuel Kant wrote in 1797 that in war there should be no resort to acts which make the return to peace difficult. Perfidy and treachery are traditional examples, for they obstruct the re-establishment of harmony. Nuclear war would be an infinitely stronger example.

In 1830 Carl von Clausewitz, the Prussian General and military writer, wrote his famous work *On War,* which became so important to political thinking between the Napoleonic era and World War I that the whole period has been described as the Clausewitzean century. One of his three basic propositions was that the goal of all states is to increase their power at the expense of other states. The interests of nations being therefore always in a state of conflict, the power contest was the normal condition and war its manifestations. The struggles for power, colonies and markets were all driving forces which led naturally to war.

Yet even Clausewitz stressed that war is meaningless when divorced from political intercourse. He stated: "War can never be separated from political intercourse, and if, in the consideration of the matter, this is done in any way, all the threads of the different relations are to a certain extent broken, and we have before us a senseless thing without an object."[14]

Reason 6. Destruction of the eco-system.

Like the general rules of international law, the laws of war cannot stand still. They must take account of fresh developments in weaponry and international affairs. The nuclear age began more than 40 years ago, and it is more than time that international law adapts to the unprecedented change.

Since the rate of change is so rapid in modern times, the rules of international law must change at a similarly rapid pace; one can no longer wait the long periods which it took in former periods for principles to be settled. We need new concepts and principles; the consequences of nuclear war cannot possibily be handled adequately with the conceptual legal tools we have inherited. Among the new principles needed is a law which would make the destruction of the eco-system a crime. It should be realized that if and when the eco-system has no future, humanity doesn't either.

Some provisions for the preservation of the eco-system are made in Protocol I Additional to the Geneva Convention of 1949. In Article 55 on Protection of the Natural Environment, it says in paragraph 1: "Care shall be taken in warfare to protect the natural environment against widespread, long-term and severe damage. This protection includes a prohibition of the use of methods or means of warfare which are intended or may be expected to cause such damage to the natural environment and thereby to prejudice the health or survival of the population." Paragraph 2 states: "Attacks against the natural environment by way of reprisals are prohibited."

Since nuclear weapons have the power to cause permanent destruction to the environment, this should be enough per se to outlaw these weapons; and if traditional international law does not embody such a principle, the laws need to be created. In fact, there has been a foreshadowing of the creation of such a principle both in the Geneva Conventions and in international documents such as the 1967 Treaty of Tlatelolco. The latter spelled out that nuclear weapons, through the persistence of the radioactivity they release, constitute "an attack on the integrity of the human species, and ultimately may render the whole earth uninhabitable." It may be argued, therefore, that this new principle has already engrafted itself upon the existing principles of customary international law.

It is also interesting to note that the General Assembly, in Resolution 3264 (XXIX) of December 9, 1974, emphasized the necessity "to adopt, through the conclusion of an appropriate international convention, effective measures to prohibit action to influence the environment and climate for military and hostile purposes."

Reason 7. The extermination of populations and the decimation of mankind

As we have seen, the Nuremberg Charter did not, for the most part, make new law in declaring the extermination of a civilian population, in whole or in part, to be a crime against humanity. Even if the tribunal be criticized on the grounds that it was the creation of victors, it cannot be denied that to a great extent it merely clarified and applied pre-existing principles. However, it did put these principles in sharper relief than ever before. This was the case in the clarification of the notion that duty towards the international community overrides an individual's duties towards his own state. The specific case of the attempted extermination of the Jewish people provided the occasion for the formulation of the crime of genocide as a crime against humanity. The formulation was new in referring to the extermination of a group identified by such factors as race and religion, but the underlying humanitarian principles were of course ancient.

Even if the prior existence of such principles be contested, there is no doubt that by the acceptance of the international community they are now part of the recognized body of international law. It is particularly significant that they are accepted by the victorious powers, since it is the victorious powers, not the vanquished, who have made and are making nuclear weapons. Consequently, they at least will not be able to deny the binding nature of the Nuremberg norms in international law. President Truman himself, appearing before the General Assembly of the U.N., commended and affirmed the Nuremberg principles; and the resolution to make these principles a permanent part of international law was brought before the U.N. by the American delegation. This resolution[15] was adopted unanimously by the General Assembly on December 11, 1946. It covered both the norms laid down in the Nuremberg Charter and the norms contained in the Nuremberg judgment. The international community has further endorsed this aspect of the Nuremberg principles in the 1948 Convention on the Prevention and Punishment of the Crime of Genocide.

Reason 8. The possibility of extinction of the human race.

Throughout its history mankind has had to endure the thought of death. In the past there was always the possible consolation that if the individual perished, his family remained; if his family perished, his group remained; if his group perished, his nation remained; if his nation perished, his species remained. At times the individuals, families, groups, and nations have perished together; still the species has remained. Now for the first time in history even the extinction of the species itself is possible—perhaps even probable. In the past the killing of an individual has been considered a heinous crime; the killing of a family, even worse; the killing of a group, even worse; the killing of a nation, even worse. For each of them traditional law has had words to describe how great an offense they are. But we have no words that even begin to describe how grave an offense the killing of the species would be.

Some say that even if a nuclear war were to take place, that ultimate offense will not have been committed. They say that no matter how many bombs are exploded, there will always be some who will survive, and that life will be started afresh. Perhaps it is so—though it boggles the mind to imagine what kind of human life could start

94

afresh in a nuclear winter. The real point is that even if the chance of extinction were a slight one, it is not a chance which, under any standards, we are entitled to take. Nor is it a chance which we can afford to take. New principles of international law must arise to see that that chance is taken by no-one—not by individuals and not by nations, not for any consideration. To take that chance would not only be criminal but criminally insane.

Reason 9. Intergenerational damage.

In Western legal systems there is a tendency to tailor legal concepts only in relation to the needs and desires of the current generation. There is usually little attention paid to problems, such as those of the environment, which do not affect the current generation but would affect future generations. By way of contrast, such legal systems as the customary ones of Africa and Melanesia and the legal tradition of China respect the rights of future generations. In customary African law, the community participating in the legal system is thought of as being not only the living but those who have gone before and those who are yet to come. The rights of both forebears and posterity must be protected under the law. The introduction of this mode of thinking into Western jurisprudence is long overdue.

The explosion of nuclear weaponry would affect generations yet unborn, even if mankind should survive the holocaust. Genetic damage, global pollution and the extinction of various species of fauna and flora are all necessary consequences of nuclear war. International law needs to develop laws that would outlaw the causing of intergenerational damage.

Reason 10. The express prohibition of asphyxiating gases and analogous materials.

In discussing the principle regarding aggravation of pain and suffering, we referred to two international instruments, The Hague Declaration of 1889 regarding Asphyxiating Gases and the Geneva Gas Protocol of 1925. Besides illustrating that principle in a general way, it is arguable that they constitute in more specific terms a prohibition of nuclear weaponry.

The phraseology of the first extends to the use of *any* poisonous substances or *emissions* as weapons of war. Radiation is arguably a poisonous emission. Indeed, it can be an emission fatally poisonous to entire populations if it is on a sufficient scale.

In regard to the Gas Protocol, the General Assembly Resolution 2603A of 1969 interprets it to mean that any chemical agents of warfare—whether solid, liquid, or gaseous—which might be employed because of their direct toxic effects on man, animals or plants would be "contrary to the generally recognized rules of international law."

A large number of States, including the Soviet Union in 1928 and the United States in 1975, have become party to the Gas Protocol. It lends itself to a similar argument, for it prohibits not only gases but "all analogous liquids, materials, and devices," whether solid, liquid or gas. Radiation may not strictly be a gas, but it is an analogous destructive agency. It was not contemplated at the time, the only categories of agencies then under consideration being solids, liquids and gases, but the general tenor of the instrument clearly shows an intention to cover injurious agencies of this sort.

By showing a strong resentment at allegations of violation of either of these instruments, the international community has demonstrated the intention to make them effective. In fact they have been, on the whole, remarkably well observed. This strong international consensus of a control-intention can reasonably be extended to nuclear weapons.

There have been many reservations by States in regard to the exact scope of the Gas Protocol, but this does not alter the general principle of interpretation advanced above.

Reason 11. Destruction and damage to neutral States.

We have already examined the well-accepted principle that deliberate damage to civilian populations of belligerent States must be avoided in time of war. That principle must apply *a fortiori* to the destruction of the populations of neutral countries. In nuclear war this would occur on an unprecedented scale, and there is no conceivable means by which such damage could be avoided. Since this is known and certain, any decision to engage in nuclear war implies a deliberate decision to destroy other nations not engaged in the conflict. If international law means anything at all, it means that neutral nations cannot be *destroyed* merely to further the interests of the belligerent nations, however powerful the belligerents might be and however essential such destruction might seem to them.

96

THE DELICTUAL DIMENSION

The eleven reasons just discussed all establish that the use of nuclear weaponry is illegal and a crime against humanity. Using the analogy of municipal law, they are reasons which would bring the case within the ambit of criminal law.

In municipal law, the same act can constitute both a crime and a civil wrong (described in some legal systems as a tort, in others as a delict). For example, reckless driving can lead to both a criminal prosecution and a civil suit for damages. Similarly, in international law a single act can be both an international crime and a delict. The proven potential of nuclear weaponry to damage the human habitat causes their use to fall into both categories. This delictual dimension of the use of nuclear weapons, then, is a second head of liability, both cumulative and alternative to the liability incurred by the commission of an international crime. Indeed, even if warring powers were not committing a crime in using nuclear weapons, they would be guilty of a delict through poisoning the atmosphere and in other ways damaging the environment of countries which are not party to the conflict.

This delictual dimension of the use of nuclear weapons can be seen best through an analogy with municipal law. In municipal law it is a civil wrong to cause loss to one's neighbor by doing an act whose foreseeable consequence is to cause damage. Thus no one is entitled to release from his property a deleterious substance which can enter his neighbor's property and cause damage to him. The same principles carry over into international law. In the *Trail Smelter Case*[16], Canada was held responsible for polluting the air with sulphur dioxide fumes emitted by a smelter plant at Trail, British Columbia; the air pollution caused damage in the State of Washington from 1925-1937. Canada was directed to pay an indemnity and halt the pollution. The Tribunal observed, "Under the principles of international law, as well as of the law of the United States, no state has the right to use or permit the use of its territory in such a manner as to cause injury by fumes in or to the territory of another or the properties or persons therein, when the case is of serious consequence and the injury is established by clear and convincing evidence." Nuclear pollution and devastation must attract the principle *a fortiori*.

97

ALLEGED JUSTIFICATIONS AND THEIR INADEQUACY

Justification 1. Abrogation of international law by contrary practices.

It is true that principles prohibiting the indiscriminate slaughter of civilians and non-combatants have often been violated when large centers of population were destroyed from the air during the great wars waged in this century. For example, they were violated in the fire bombings and the aerial bombardments of World War II, not to speak of the devastation of Hiroshima and Nagasaki. For this reason some might argue that the international law on the matter has been abrogated by contrary practice.

In response to this, it should be pointed out that even if there have been consistent violations through the manufacture and use of weapons that flatten cities and indiscriminately destroy civilian populations, those violations have been carried out by a very small group of powerful nations. This small group can be counted on one's fingers, while the world community of nations exceeds the level of some one hundred and fifty States. Once it is accepted by the world community, customary international law cannot be abrogated in this day and age by the wishes or the conduct of less than 10% of the world's nations. We are past the stage when a small body of powerful nations could dominate international law and dictate its rules. If these rules are an established part of international law and if they still command the unqualified support of the vast majority of the world's nations—and this is certainly the case—those rules cannot be abrogated by the wishes or conduct of a small minority.

In any event, this specific point has received consideration in the Nuremberg judgment on *The Hostages Case*[17] in the following terms: "It has also been stated in the evidence and argued to the Tribunal that the rules of war have changed and that war has assumed a totalitarian aspect. It is argued that the atom bombings of Hiroshima and Nagasaki in Japan and the aerial raids upon Dresden, Germany, in the final stages of the conflict afford a pattern for the conduct of modern war and a possible justification for the criminal act of these defendants. We do not think the argument is sound."

It may also be argued that there has been a more general acceptance of the principle of indiscriminate slaughter in the dozens of smaller wars that have plagued mankind in this century. Yet, while it is generally accepted that the pursuit of a military objective may

98

incidentally involve civilian deaths and that therefore aerial bombardment per se is not intrinsically illegal, there has never been any general acceptance in principle or in practice of the proposition that one is entitled to wipe out entire cities merely for the military advantage this might bring.

Moreover, as we have seen, the relevant principles have been reaffirmed time and again both by the international community and by eminent international jurists. Even powers which have in practice violated these principles have reaffirmed them in the Nuremberg Charter and by their acceptance of the principles set out in the Nuremberg judgment.

Justification 2. The necessities of war.

In the view of some jurists, necessities of war constitute a ground on which the rules of international law can be overridden. According to this argument, there are certain dire and immediate urgencies in the life of a nation in which a statesman or general is compelled to protect his country from destruction by whatever means available. An example sometimes cited is the position of Britain when Hitler stood poised for the attack in 1940. As the Bomber Command argued, carrying death and destruction indiscriminately to the enemy population seemed the best means of halting the attack.

If this argument is to carry any weight at all, however, it must be proved that the danger is both imminent and supreme.[18] Was this the case with Britain? When by 1942 the bombing campaign, following Lord Cherwell's minute of 1942, made working-class residential areas in Germany the prime targets, the two factors of imminence and supreme danger no longer co-existed. Even if it had been at any stage legitimate to direct attacks at civilian targets or at cities as such, the enormous injuries inflicted on Germany and its army and the presence at Britain's side of the United States, with all its resources, had certainly removed the imminence of the danger.

In fact a group of scientists objected to the calculations on which the Cherwell minute was based. Their objection was apparently not formulated in moral terms,[19] but there were moral objections from professional soldiers.[20] The raids on German cities continued nonetheless, and this was certainly a situation for which "supreme emergency" no longer provided an arguable justification. Bombs were dropped on the city of Dresden, killing 100,000 people, as late as

1945. Even less justification was available under the doctrine of "supreme emergency" when the bombs were dropped on Hiroshima and Nagasaki.

Is the situation in which nuclear bombs are used for a first strike one of "supreme emergency"? Do imminence and supreme danger come together? Even if they do, can one then proceed in such a manner as to annihilate civilians by the million—far in excess of the Dresden or Hiroshima attacks—with the certain death of millions of one's own people as well? It is submitted that the "supreme emergency" is insufficient reason for the deliberate act of killing millions of innocent people.

The argument of "necessities of war" is not a generally accepted rule, for if it were to be accepted without limitation, most of the other rules of the international law relating to war would be reduced to a cipher.

The governments participating in the 1868 Declaration of St. Petersburg foresaw that new technologies (such as the newly invented dum dum bullet) could heighten the conflict between the necessities of war and laws of humanity. Such weapons tend to promote the idea that if one could terminate a war merely by using them, hundreds of thousands of lives could be saved. As we have seen, this argument was used in regard to Hiroshima and Nagasaki. The condition, in every case, is that the laws of humanity be temporarily overlooked.

In cases where new technology was leading towards new developments in armaments, the participants in the St. Petersburg Declaration reserved the right "to come to an understanding...in order to maintain the principles which they have established, and to conciliate the necessities of war with the laws of humanity." This decision was approved by legal experts advising their governments at the 1973 International Committee of the Red Cross (ICRC) Conference of Government Experts. They recommended restraint or prohibition in respect of new weapons that may be inhumane or indiscriminate, such as incendiary and fragmentation weapons.

The rule that even military necessity does not override international law was upheld in the judgment of the U.S. tribunal which tried Field Marshall List. It declared, "The rules of international law must be followed even if it results in the loss of a battle or even a war."[21]

Justification 3. Practical military strategy.

Since the first use of the bomb, a great deal of strategic theory has been constructed concerning its possible uses. In the 41 years during which these theories have been evolved and elaborated, moral considerations relating to the slaughter of hundreds of millions of people have been pushed aside in the name of a relentless "logic" of strategic needs. The philosophy has been that practical tactical planning should not be clouded over by moral considerations which are an obstruction to clarity of military thinking. As in pre-nuclear days, when commanders calmly calculated their military losses in a given operation in terms of tens of thousands of men (as though they were pawns in a game or entries in a balancesheet), so also in the nuclear age it is thought that generals must coldly calculate strategy without being unduly moved by loss of human lives.

This attitude is a supreme example of the dominance of traditional thinking and the failure to realize that the entire set of assumptions underpinning that thinking has fallen away. One may operate freely within a framework only so long as the terms of the operation do not exceed the scale of the framework itself. For example, one could discharge waste from ships into the ocean indefinitely if the discharge were on the scale of the eighteenth century, for the ocean had a relatively infinite capacity to absorb such wastes; or one could discharge pollutants into the air indefinitely before the Industrial Revolution, for the atmosphere had a relatively infinite capacity to absorb them. Since neither ocean nor air has an infinite capacity in today's context, an entirely new strategy needs to be devised for discharging waste and pollutants. So it is with war. When conflict was a matter of sacrificing tens or hundreds of thousands of men, or even a few million as in World War II, the reservoir of mankind was still large enough to take the blow and survive. But when the magnitude of the sacrifice would be hundreds of millions or billions of people, the operation would exceed the scale of the framework within which military strategy has traditionally been devised. When that happens, the "practical" strategy really has no relation to practicalities at all. In the planning for nuclear war, this attempted divorce of practical planning from morality has reached this limit situation and its unreality stands starkly exposed. As with pollution, an entirely new framework of reasoning must be devised, in which some of

101

the most basic assumptions of past military reasoning must be discarded.

Justification 4. The concept of a just war.

The origin and history of the just war concept have been dealt with in the previous chapter. Let me just add here that if nuclear weapons are illegal, they are illegal whether the war in which they are used is legal or illegal, just or unjust. Even their use in a war of self-defence would be illegal by this criterion.

Reference should be made in this context to General Assembly Resolution 1653 (XVI) of November 24, 1961. This Resolution condemned the use of nuclear weapons in *any* situation as being a crime against mankind and civilization.

That the general principles relating to violation of the laws and customs of war are not limited to illegal wars appears clearly from Protocol 1 Additional to the Geneva Conventions of August 12, 1949. Article 35 of that Protocol contains the following provisions:

> 1. In *any* armed conflict, the right of the Parties to the conflict to choose methods or means of warfare is not unlimited. 2. It is prohibited to employ weapons, projectiles and material and methods of warfare of a nature to cause superfluous injury or unnecessary suffering. 3. It is prohibited to employ methods or means of warfare which are intended, or may be expected, to cause widespread, longterm and severe damage to the natural environment.

Justification 5. Self-defence.

Reference has already been made to Article 51 of the U.N. Charter and its mention of self-defence. Should not a nation be entitled therefore to use nuclear weapons in retaliation if it is attacked with nuclear weapons?

Retaliation needs to have a logical justification, and it is hard to see what logical justification there could be in such a case. The nuclear attack from the enemy would be delivered by weapons several times the firepower of the Hiroshima bomb, and it would in all probability be a multiple attack, causing many towns and cities to be blasted out of existence. Should that be the case, national security considerations could not be a logical justification. The society of the country attacked would be destroyed; its survivors would be either too severely injured or dazed to constitute anything like a civic society. If therefore the retaliatory button were pushed, it would not be for victory, or for a balance of power. All such pre-nuclear concepts would be meaningless. Whether the retaliation were to come as a result of feelings of revenge or from panic, hysteria, or terror, the result would be the same: the probable annihilation of the human race and its life support system. In a word, the attempt at retaliation would be irrational.

In a recent issue of *Time Magazine*,[22] the President of the United States is reported as discussing just a scenario. He said, ''The word comes that they [the enemy missiles] are on their way. And you sit there, knowing that there is no way, at present, of stopping them. So they're going to blow up how much of this country we can only guess at, and your response can be to push the button before they get here so that even though you're all going to die, they're going to die too.'' The President went on to observe: ''There is something so immoral about it.'' Here the word ''illegal'' should be added to ''immoral'', since it would attract to itself the illegalities of destruction of the environment and annihilation of non-combatants we have already discussed.

The elevation of self-defence to a high level of recognition in international law is not to be wondered at. It has represented the highest moral justification of a soldier's calling, going deep into the roots of the human desire to cherish and protect one's territory, traditions, and national integrity. People of the highest moral stature have often experienced no qualms about taking up arms and inflicting death upon those who threaten these values. Indeed, it was a noble thing to do. *Dulce et decorum est pro patria mori* (''it is sweet and seemly to die for one's country'') was the classic expression of this view.

As with so many other concepts of war, however, this concept has been outmoded by the advent of nuclear weapons. When the nuclear powers fight a nuclear war, they will not be fighting for the defence of their country, which in any case will be destroyed by the conflict. What they will be seeking to achieve will be the destruction of their enemy's country rather than the defence of their own.

From the standpoint of international law, such retaliatory or revengeful slaughter of enemy populations would not be covered by the justification of self-defence. Indeed, it is a concept totally different from self-defence in content, quality and objective. It takes much brashness to assert that it is sweet and seemly to slaughter one's enemies by the millions for the sake of revenge or retaliation.

There are other ways as well in which nuclear weapons have radically altered concepts of defence, rendering the traditional legal principles outmoded. Traditionally, a cardinal method of ensuring national security has been the strengthening of one's defence capabilities. In the nuclear age, nothing one can do internally is sufficient to protect one's country, despite the claims made for a Star Wars type defence. The only way for a nation to increase its military strength is to enhance its ability to penetrate into the territory of the adversary. The old concept of weapons for defence (and the justifiability of creating them) no longer holds. The nuclear weapons being created are therefore aggressive rather than defensive, a fact which needs to be remembered when it is a matter of assessing culpability in their creation.[23] This consideration leads naturally to the distinction between "offensive" defence and "defensive" defence.

In the 1980s the concept of offensive defence has given rise to a developing field of strategic research. This strategic research has special relevance to the nuclear situation and must considerably influence international law concepts relating to self-defence.[24]

An offensive defence would be the attempt to prepare one's defence by readying the means of waging an offensive within the attacker's territory. This is what the U.S. and the U.S.S.R. seem to be doing rather than preparing for defence by fortifying their internal defences.

The adoption of an offensive defence strategy, however, necessarily heightens the risk of nuclear war. For instance, suppose that nation A adopts this strategy, the requirements of which are identical to those of a war of aggression. In an international atmosphere of lack of trust, the strategic observers of adversary nation B would naturally view such activity as preparation for aggressive war, and must make their plans on a "worst case" scenario. Even if nation B's intention had been to plan a defensive defence, its countermove would be to achieve an offensive defence capability. Noting this, A's strategic observers would infer aggressive intent and step up A's offensive defence preparations. But seeing the escalation of A's preparations, B would escalate accordingly.

Once this type of arms spiral has begun, it appears that very little short of war can break it. The irony of the situation is that both nations, A and B, initially may have had purely defensive intentions. But in a world of distrust, both assume enormously aggressive postures, and there is no means known for reading the true intent behind the overt preparations.[25]

Nor does the danger end there. As the arms buildup occurs on both sides, the possibility of survival after an attack by even a fraction of the opponent's nuclear arsenal becomes more remote. In this situation, the concept of a pre-emptive strike becomes more attractive to military strategists. Each side, whatever its protestations to the contrary, is ready with the apparatus for this purpose. Even those whose public posture is one of pure defensiveness prepare and enhance their first strike capabilities. The United States, for example, is doing so in the European theatre.

In short, the self-defence argument is a self-serving justification masking the inherent illegality of nuclear weapons. International law and international lawyers themselves have to shoulder a substantial part of the blame for permitting such an argument to assume its current credibility. In the words of an eminent American international lawyer:

> International lawyers have not upheld the fundamental mission of their profession. The fundamental mission of international lawyers is to study the means whereby the power of the modern nation-state may be restrained by the rule of law. All too often, lawyers have allowed themselves to become 'co-opted geopoliticians'...With respect to nuclear weapons, the failure of international law has been most pronounced. After 1945 the United States possessed the nuclear advantage yet did little to control it. As the Cold War intensified, we simply came to accept these weapons with little effort expended to subject these weapons to the restraints of law. As time went on, we came to accept the premise that the main threat to peace was the aggressive nature of our major adversary. We engaged in self-serving declarations that our weapons were merely defensive.[26]

Justification 6. The preservation of one's way of life.

Democracy, free enterprise, communism, or the socialist way of life are objectives which may be sincerely and deeply cherished by those desiring their preservation. How much may legitimately be sacrificed for the preservation of such cherished ways of life? Clearly a great deal. But the use of nuclear weapons would not contribute to their preservation, only to their sheer destruction. As Professor John Kenneth Galbraith once said, it will be difficult to distinguish the ashes of capitalism from those of communism after the global incinerations that will characterize nuclear war.[27]

Justification 7. Preventing destabilization of areas of influence.

The prevention of destabilization of areas of influence is another pillar of traditional strategic planning which may seem realistic in the context of conventional warfare but is completely unrealistic in the context of nuclear warfare. The nuclear winter would see postwar survivors struggling for survival amidst freezing conditions and near lethal doses of radiation. As mentioned earlier, the threshold for major climatic consequences may be very low. Only 100 megatons detonated over major urban centers could create sub-freezing land temperatures for months.[28] A 5,000 megaton war would spread dust clouds and radioactivity from the Northern to the Southern Hemisphere, constituting a serious threat to the survival of all living beings.[29] It is hard to see how this chain of events is "preventing the destabilization of one's areas of influence."

* * *

A MORE HUMANISTIC APPROACH
TO INTERNATIONAL LAW

There was a time when the traditional lawyer working within a national framework was wedded to the inherited formalisms of his profession to an extent which obscured his social vision of the law. The American sociological lawyers showed how this could make law stray far from the needs of society, and the call went out to the legal profession to help make law conform more to its social purposes. The call was heeded, and law, society, and lawyers were its beneficiaries.

International law currently is positivistic and accords great deference to the realities of power, making it less responsive to the broader international purposes which international law should subserve. It is indeed a paradox that we can, in international law, shut our eyes to the central realities of the international scene by too much reliance on "realism." One of these central realities is, in the stark words of Jonathan Schell, that "if we are honest with ourselves we have to admit that unless we rid ourselves of our nuclear arsenals, a holocaust not only might occur but will occur—if not today, then tomorrow, if not this year, then next."[30] Another is that under the current regime of international law we are slowly but surely working towards the irreversible crippling of our eco-system, polluting our oceans, poisoning our atmosphere, and making our land a desert. There are other central realities of which the North-South cleavage and the conservation of the common heritage of mankind are important examples.

By "realism" is meant that attitude in international law which concentrates on the role of power, the practice of States— the world of *Realpolitik*. It is a philosophical stance that traces its roots all the way back to Hobbes, Machiavelli, and Kautilya.[31] For the realist, a true view of the goings on at the level of international politics must not be obscured by a naive reliance on morality or idealism. Such views rest upon rigid concepts of sovereignty and the acceptance of force as the main effective means for the resolution of international disputes. This conceptual framework unfortunately excludes visions of a world future built upon human dignity as its central value, and lowers the strength of emerging custom and of general principles of international law. Moreover, the elevation of state practice to a level of pre-eminence stifles the development within international law of an increased inventory of sanctions for compliance and of a more survival-oriented set of concepts and norms. It tends to reduce the flexibility of the international lawyer and makes him less sensitive to the urgency of devoting his skills to the central global concerns of our time. The spectre of nuclearism must be fought with all the legal weapons at our command, but through the influence of statism we are using only part of the repertory available to us.

It must be stressed that the realities of state practice and sovereign power do not mean a devaluation of the other well-recognized sources of international law. One of the best illustrations of the inadequacies of statism and force lies in the field of nuclear weaponry. In this field international law has permitted the general principles to be so obscured by state practice that even some international lawyers fail to perceive them in the absence of treaties.

At various crises in history, the need for a broader view of the law, free of the fetters of positivism and yet attuned to social realities, has been urgently felt. Grotius, the father of Western international law, perceived this acutely amidst the unprecedented devastation of the Thirty Years War, when the old international legal order had crumbled and a new basis of co-existence was needed if the law of the jungle were not to prevail internationally. His idealism, firmly anchored in reality and human experience, provided the answer, and international law was born. At a similar crisis in history, when the old international order based on force has crumbled before the realities of the bomb, we need a new vision. Already in existence and fully recognized by international law—but rusting unused—are the tools to construct the new order: international custom and the general principles of international law.

They are no less valid in international law today in the nuclear age than they were at any time in history and if anything their importance is growing. They need to be fostered more than ever before. World order models such as the World Order Models Project[32] need to be explored as offering structural and normative bases for an international order centered upon human beings rather than sovereign states, and human idealism rather than state selfishness. To attempt to do so is not visionary, alarmist, utopian, or salvationist. It is an approach solidly based on legal principle. What is more, if humanity is to survive, it is in fact more realistic than any of the "realism" of current international law.

We have briefly examined in this chapter the principles which render the use of nuclear weaponry illegal and the speciousness of the arguments adduced in support of such use. We have also touched on the reasons why the traditional arguments relating to attack and defence are inapplicable where nuclear weapons are concerned.

At the recent Six Nation Summit on Nuclear Disarmament (January 1985), President Alfonsin of Argentina encapsulated all these arguments in memorable words. He said:

> We have lost the right to life. Nobody demanded that we surrender it. We never renounced that right voluntarily. But almost without realizing it, the nuclear arms race between the superpowers took that right away from us....All rights and freedoms as well as all material goods that both men and nations possess have a common foundation: the right to life. This is such an essential attribute in itself that no civilization, no culture, has ever denied it. However, today we have lost it: in a few minutes a small group of people can destroy everything that each human being on the planet has—beginning with his own life and the life of his kin—and everything a nation has built over the centuries. And all this can be done without hearing our voice, without taking into account our will, without us even knowing about it...simply because the superpowers and the nuclear powers, minding the legitimate needs of their own defense, have applied traditional war criteria in a world armed today with new weapons completely different from the ones used before. The incongruency between the criteria being applied and the actual means has dominated the nuclear arms race ever since the first atomic bomb was detonated.

That incongruency is too vital for us to let it be submerged in the torrent of discussion regarding conventional concepts of war.

REFERENCES

1 Nagendra Singh, *Human Rights and the Future of Mankind,* Motilal Nehru Memorial Lectures, Vanity Books, 1981, p. 93. See also Nagendra Singh, *Nuclear Weapons and International Law,* Praeger, N.Y., 1959.

2 *Ibid*, p. 93.

3 HMSO 1914, p. 236.

4 See *Report of the Fortieth Conference, International Law Association*, 1939, p. 69.

5 See 1964 *Japanese Annual of International Law*, pp. 212-259.

6 G. Kewley, *Humanitarian Law in Armed Conflicts*, VCTA, 1984, p. 38.

7 *Ibid*, p. 38.

8 Richard Falk, et al., "Nuclear Weapons and International Law," 20 *Indian Journal of International Law*, 1980, pp. 541-595.

9 *Ibid*, p. 589.

10 HMSO, p. 243.

11 Nagendra Singh, *op. cit.*, p. 98.

12 *Ethics and Nuclear Deterrence*, ed. G. Goodwin, Croom Helm, 1983, p. 94.

13 Immanuel Kant, *Die Metaphysik der Sitten*, 1797, para. 57.

14 Roger Parkinson, *Clausewitz: A Biography*, Wayland, London, 1970, p. 316.

15 GA Res. 93, UN GAOR 1st sess. part I.

16 U.S. v. Canada, 3 *U.N. Rep. Int. Arb. Awards* 1911 (1941).

17 11 *Trial of War Criminals before the Nurnberg Military Tribunals under Control Council Law No. 10*, 1317 (1949).

18 See on this point the excellent discussion in Michael Walzer, *Just and Unjust Wars*, Penguin, 1978, ch. 16.

19 *Ibid.*, p. 257.

20 See also C.P. Snow, *Science and Government*, New American Library, N.Y., 1962, p. 48.

21 11 *Trials of War Criminals before the Nuremberg Military Tribunals under Control Council Law No. 10, 1272 (1949)*.

22 *Time Magazine*, Jan. 28, 1985, p. 11.

23 See V. Kortunov, *Limited Nuclear War: A Strategy of Global Suicide*, MEMO, Moscow, Pravda 1984, and the review thereof in 7 *Disarmament*, 1984, p. 180.

24 See A. Boserup, "Nuclear Disarmament: Non-Nuclear Defence," in M. Kaldor and D. Smith (eds.), *Disarming Europe*, Merlin Press, London, 1982, p. 186. See also M.A. Evangelista, "Offense or Defense: A Tale of Two Commissions," 1 *Journal of World Policy*, 1983, pp. 45-70.

25 See Andrew Mack, "Arms Control, Disarmament, and the Concept of Defensive Defence," 7 *Disarmament*, 1984, p. 109.

26 22 *Science*, 1983, p. 1283.

27 *Ibid.*, p. 1283.

28 See chapter 3, *supra*.

29 See chapter 3, *supra*.

30 Jonathan Schell, *The Fate of the Earth*, Knopf, N.Y., 1982, p. 183.

31 See Richard Falk, *The End of World Order*, Holmes & Meier, 1983, p. 3.

32 The World Order Models Project: Projections for the Future, Proc. 66th Ann. Meeting, American Society of International Law; 66 *American Journal of International Law*, 244 (1972).

CHAPTER SEVEN

Is the Manufacture of
Nuclear Weapons Illegal?

To extend the principle of illegality from *use* to *manufacture* requires a consideration of two further possibilities: that the weapons may be manufactured not for use but for deterrence, and that manufacture does not need to be for a war of total destruction but could be for a contained nuclear war. If either of these positions has validity, it would remove or reduce the culpability associated with manufacture. We need therefore to probe both the true intention that lies behind deterrence doctrine and the strength of the claim that nuclear war can be contained. If the true intention behind deterrence is use, however conditional it might be, then the manufacture of weapons becomes a manufacture *for use* and is therefore culpable for the reasons set out in the previous chapter. If it is a reasonable inference from the information available to us that a nuclear war cannot be contained, then the manufacture of weapons becomes a manufacture for a purpose of which the reasonable and probable consequence is all-out nuclear war. Those who knowingly commit an act cannot seek to be absolved from responsibility for its reasonable and probable consequences.

DETERRENCE

The position of the Reagan administration regarding the intentions underlying the doctrine of deterrence was explained in 1982 by National Security Adviser William Clark to the (US) National Conference of Catholic Bishops Committee on War and Peace. Clark stated, "Our decisions on nuclear armaments and our defense posture are guided by moral considerations as compelling as any which have faced mankind. The strategy of deterrence, on which our policies are based, is not an end in itself but a means to prevent war and preserve the values we cherish: individual liberty...respect for the sanctity of human life, and the rule of law through representative institutions."[1]

It is submitted that this claim does not pass the tests either of practicality or of legality. The argument against it, in brief, is as follows. Deterrence necessarily connotes a preparedness to use nuclear weapons if deterrence fails. This use is not a token but a substantial or massive use. Such a massive use must necessarily provoke a massive retaliation, which would mean all-out nuclear war. Since such an all-out war would mean the probable destruction of the U.S. with its lifestyles and cherished values, the result would be the destruction of the very values which it was sought to preserve. This circularity is illustrated in the diagram shown below.

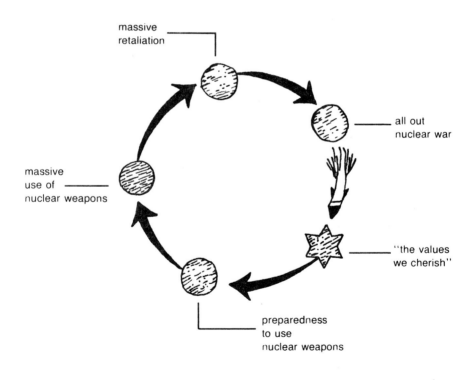

a) *The impracticality of deterrence.*

Assured mutual destruction is the very essence of the deterrence doctrine. As Mr. Robert McNamara observed in explaining the doctrine,[2] the potential aggressor (i.e., the enemy) must believe that this capability is actual and the will to use it is unswerving. This belief must be induced for the rest of time. It can only achieve success if the potential aggressor is permanently terrified into inaction. If there is a period of time in which one's opponent ceases to be terrified or calls one's bluff, deterrence has failed.

If one does not really want to use these weapons, one might deceive the enemy for some of the time by making him think that one means to use them. But one cannot expect to deceive him for *all* of the time from now to eternity. Hence deterrence strategists have sensed that deterrence cannot be achieved merely by empty threats. One must really mean the threat if one expects the opponent to be terrified by it.

As the late Olof Palme, Prime Minister of Sweden, recently pointed out,[3] deterrence involves not only technical capacity but political preparedness.

Deterrence then becomes not the storage of weapons with intent to terrify, but a stockpiling with *intent to use.* We straightaway come within the ambit of the prohibitions applicable to *use* of the weapon. We need to face squarely the fact that nuclear weapons are with us not only for deterrence, but for use; we should not allow the smokescreen of deterrence to cover up their inherent illegality.

The unacceptability of deterrence becomes obvious when we realize that once we are launched upon deterrence as a means of war prevention, we cannot afford to allow any abatement in its reign of terror. If it fails to terrorize even for a short time, a time-window of vulnerability would open up. Thus deterrence, like a massive dam, cannot afford to spring a single leak; but unlike the dam, which holds back a fixed quantity of water, the dam of deterrence holds back an ever-increasing reservoir of terror and destruction. The dam must thus keep growing on the scale of that which it seeks to confine. In the speech just mentioned, Olof Palme used the analogy that depending on deterrence is like addiction to a drug: you continually need a larger and larger dose.

Unreal in practical terms, the doctrine is also morally indefensible, since it perpetually links survival and security to terror. Churchill expressed this graphically to the House of Commons in 1955 when he said: "Safety will be the sturdy child of terror and survival the twin brother of annihilation." To commit humanity to a perpetual future where security is linked not to goodwill but to terror and intimidation is to invert and debase all human values. Such a course stands condemned by reality and morality alike.

Moreover, the implications of such a doctrine are too demoralizing to serve as a practical basis for ordering the future affairs of mankind. The doctrine means in effect that for all future time we must depend upon terror to survive. The future of the highest form of life known on this planet must be linked to the basest instincts of the jungle. The possibility of movement towards a better tomorrow, which has long been the aspiration of the human race, will be shut off. Just as love begets love, so terror begets terror. The perpetual fate of humanity will be an escalating spiral of terror which must explode when it can no longer escalate. If one thinks the doctrine of deterrence through to its logical conclusion, it not only plumbs the depths of human instinct on a time scale of perpetuity, but is a frustrating exercise in circularity from a logical point of view. If terror and security are in a symbiotic relationship with each other, then security must breed terror just as terror breeds security.

All civilization will then depend on intimidation for its continuance, and all the finer instincts and achievements of man will need to function within this framework of terror. At no stage in man's civilized history has the formula for survival been so ignominiously constructed.

One final aspect of deterrence is the vagueness of the concept. Not even the most vigorous exponents of deterrence will venture to tell us how much damage it is necessary to inflict in order for the concept to be credible to the enemy. Would it deter one's opponent to have 10 of its cities destroyed, or 100, or 1,000? Would it be a deterrent to destroy 50% of its population or 75% of its industrial capacity? This basic information is not known even by the superpowers. It is even more obscure how much weaponry would be required to produce the effect of deterrence. The whole concept is shrouded in more obscurity, therefore, than its advocates would like to admit. It means a licence to produce an unspecified number of weapons—when all the world knows that one-fiftieth of those in existence would "make the Soviet rubble bounce all the way from

Moscow to Vladivostock," to use the expressive phrase of Senator Edward Kennedy. It would also, of course, make the American rubble bound all the way from New York to San Francisco. Senator Kennedy also rightly said: "To suggest that we need to test and develop more weapons to maintain a credible deterrent is the kind of contorted logic which will guarantee a never-ending arms race in which both sides will be the losers."[5]

b) The illegality of deterrence.

The criteria of legality in the conduct of war have been discussed in chapter 5. Among the principles mentioned were the principles of proportionality, right authority, the need for a prospect of success, exhaustion of alternative methods and right intention. Each one of these principles is violated by the doctrine of deterrence.

Let us imagine that the doctrine of deterrence has failed and that, despite its terrors, an attack has been launched. Such an attack may be non-nuclear or nuclear. It may be counterforce (i.e., an attack on military targets and capability) or countervalue (an attack on non-military targets such as civilian populations or industry). It may be strategic (directed at the enemy's homeland) or theatre (directed at a particular theatre of war). Within each of these categories an enormous choice of weaponry is now available. There is a seemingly unending variety of forms, therefore, which a possible attack may take. The levels of intensity of the attack are also unpredictable.

While in previous non-nuclear wars there was time for reflection on the countermeasures to be taken, nuclear war will allow no such cushion of time. Decisions regarding the nature, the level and the targets of the deterrent strike must be taken within minutes if not seconds. Fine evaluations regarding proportionality will be impossible. An all-out nuclear retaliation will be a very likely response. More finely graded retaliations will be beyond the abilities of heads of state, and it may well be, as discussed in chapter 5, that field commanders will have to take these decisions. If so, there will be an infringement of the principle of right authority. From the start the concept of a just war has depended on the principle of right authority, and in the special case of nuclear weaponry there is common agreement among mankind that only a supreme political authority should make the decision to launch a nuclear war. In many species of attack, the retaliation will only be possible by violating this principle of right authority.

For reasons discussed elswhere in this work, the prospect of success does not exist in the case of nuclear war.

A retaliatory deterrent attack would also be difficult to justify on the grounds that all alternative peaceful methods have been exhausted. In point of fact, every one of the nuclear powers has violated its obligation, under the Nuclear Non-Proliferation Treaty, "to pursue disarmament by all available means." One look at the arsenals each of them has accumulated is enough to dispel any notion that they are fulfilling their obligation. The violations have been particularly flagrant in the last ten years, and the general world dissatisfaction with their performance in this regard was naturally the subject of acid comment at the five-yearly review of the Treaty in 1985.

The information now available regarding the consequences of nuclear war also precludes any pro-nuclear arguments based on the principle of right intention. As mentioned earlier, a nuclear war is more aptly characterized as the burial ground of all intentions, right or otherwise.

Other principles of war, namely the *jus in bello*, will also be violated, for there will be damage to non-combatants, to the environment, and to neutral nations—all of which goes far beyond what is permissible under the *jus in bello*.

In summary, the massive nuclear warfare which will follow from the first use of nuclear weapons will violate all the established principles of war. One writer on this topic says: "Where is the military necessity in incinerating entire urban populations, defiling the territory of neighboring and distant neutral countries, and ravaging the natural environment for generations to come...? If so, then we are witness to the demise of Nuremberg, the triumph of *Kriegsraison,* the virtual repudiation of the humanitarian rules of armed conflict...The very meaning of 'proportionality' becomes lost and we come dangerously close to condoning the crime of genocide, that is, a military campaign directed more towards the extinction of the enemy than towards the winning of a battle or conflict."[6]

A CONTAINED NUCLEAR WAR

There was much effort in the early 1980s to play down the effects of a nuclear war. Thus in the 1980 Presidential campaign, Mr. George

Bush expressed the view, in a much quoted speech, that a nuclear war was winnable. Later, widespread popular discussion raised the credibility level of assertions that nuclear war could be limited, that a protracted nuclear war could be won, and that civil defence measures for survival after a nuclear war could be effective. The belittling of the effects of nuclear war went so far that a Civil Defence Advisory Authority advised residents of Cambridge, Massachusetts to mount their automobiles in the event of a nuclear emergency and proceed 100 miles to the small town of Greenfield, taking their credit cards with them.[7]

If it were truly possible to contain a nuclear war, laws of war pertaining to such a conflict would more closely approximate those relating to a traditional war. Since total or near-total annihilation would not be the result, wars could even be fought to produce specific political effects.

The notion of limited nuclear war requires, in the first place, some analysis of the nature of war itself and of the concepts of victory and defeat. War is a means of resolution of dispute when all other means have failed. It is like a test of physical strength. The combatants draw upon their resources up to their very limits, and as long as any strength remains there is no surrender; the only exception is when the outcome is so obvious that there is capitulation to save lives and resources. History provides no examples of a surrender by a nation on its own soil while it still had the physical resources to inflict a crushing blow upon its adversary. To use the Clausewitzean analysis, war is violence pushed to its utmost limits. In any case the very concept of war requires that one party, however bruised and battered, survive with some reserves of strength while the reserves of the other are totally exhausted.

A nuclear conflict does not correspond to this concept of war. The point is never reached in which there is exhaustion of strength and resources of one party, while the other still survives. Even a contestant reeling under the impact of a first strike can unleash destruction upon its opponent with a mere fraction of its available fire power. Indeed, we are now at the stage when machines will take over the fighting from man and go about their preset task of destruction even after human life has been extinguished. As we have seen, an interesting case has already been filed in the U.S. Supreme Court asserting that computers geared for automatic response in the event of nuclear attack

117

are a violation of the U.S. Constitution in that the decision to unleash nuclear weaponry needs to be consciously taken by the human agencies entrusted with that power by the Constitution.

With nuclear weaponry the dialogue thus shifts from war, with all its connotations of victory and defeat, to total destruction. This hypothesis must be more closely examined in the light of three scenarios: theatre nuclear war, nuclear war limited to specific tactical targets, and the new notion of Star Wars. A further factor needing consideration in this context is the launch-on-warning capability (LOWC), which involves the speedy release of nuclear missiles by electronic means in response to the warning of a nuclear attack.

a) Theatre nuclear war.

Possible theatres of tactical nuclear war are the European theatre, the Sino-Soviet theatre, the Middle Eastern theatre, the South African theatre, and the Indo-Pakistan theatre. The question is whether a nuclear exchange could take place in any of these places without escalation to a level at which the superpowers become involved.

It is clear that at least two of these theatres—the European theatre and the Sino-Soviet theatre—will directly involve the superpowers. However, even the theatres which do not directly involve the superpowers have all the potential to draw them in. It is unlikely that the superpowers will choose to remain mere spectators, since a power vacuum will result from the annihilation of one or another of the participants.

In the theatres where the superpowers become directly involved, the scale of devastation alone would render the description of "theatre nuclear war" totally inappropriate. In the European theatre, for example, thousands of short-range tactical nuclear devices available on both sides would be brought into action, resulting in death and destruction on a scale too frightful to contemplate. Moreover, this particular theatre is specially vulnerable because the serried ranks of nuclear missiles confront each other at comparatively close range while the large ground forces of each side face each other. What may begin as a conflict with conventional arms can create a tinder box situation in which either side may suddenly decide to escalate to the nuclear level. In such a situation, a first strike with nuclear weapons would have strategic value; however, this alone would probably be enough to set off a nuclear exchange on a scale sufficient to result in global devastation.

The gravity of the situation is apparent from the fact that neither the U.S. nor the U.S.S.R. is prepared to accept a defeat by conventional weaponry. The U.S.S.R. is reportedly stronger in this theatre in conventional weaponry, and the U.S. has made it plain that it will resort to nuclear weaponry rather than take a defeat based on conventional arms.

In the Sino-Soviet theatre, the conflict will be too important for the other superpower, the U.S., to be a mere spectator. The immense superiority of Soviet firepower over the Chinese creates the necessary backdrop for U.S. intervention.

In regard to the Indo-Pakistan theatre, India announced in May 1985 its grave fears that Pakistan was on the verge of nuclear capability. India has called a halt to this activity, saying that if Pakistan achieves the bomb, India may reconsider its position of not pursuing weapon-manufacturing capability. India has also demanded that the U.S. prevail upon Pakistan to halt this activity. Perhaps this demand is justifiably based, perhaps not—but it does illustrate one way in which superpowers are drawn into what at first appears to be a "local" situation.

In the Middle East, the current Iraq-Iran war illustrates how, in a struggle, all available weaponry is thrown in. If nuclear weapons had been available, they would in all probability have been used too. If they were, there is little doubt that the superpowers would have been drawn in quickly. Maintenance of the oil fields is of vital importance to the superpowers, particularly the U.S. One recalls in this context President Carter's announcement that U.S. interests in the oil fields would be protected even with nuclear weapons.

b) Limited nuclear war.

It is argued by the supporters of limited war theory that nuclear weapons can now be targeted much more accurately. They can reach within a few feet of their intended targets, thereby preventing effective retaliation by enemy nuclear delivery systems. Hence "war-winning" strategy is replacing MAD as a preferred scenario for nuclear war.[8] Supporters of the theory also argue that the confinement of the attack to military targets makes the conflict similar to the actions of conventional warfare and allows the traditional legal principles governing warfare to be invoked.

The defects in such theories are easily seen. In the first place, the range of destruction of even a single nuclear missile is so massive, compared with any conventional weapon, that a great deal of civilian life will be lost whether the missile is accurate or not. It also needs to be remembered that it is not a matter of a single, isolated military target. The series of military targets spreads throughout the length and breadth of a country. Even if one were only attacking military targets, the entire country could easily be destroyed.

In the second place, the doctrine is dangerous because of the inducement it offers for a pre-emptive strike. If the theory works, the power that makes the first attack will be the country to emerge the victor. This places nerves on edge on both sides, for every action needs to be interpreted so as to enable the forecasting of the "enemy's" next move. Such forecasting is never error-proof; sooner or later a misreading of the evidence can precipitate an unwanted war.

It is to be noted, thirdly, that although submarines can also be targeted no less than weapons silos at home, a single submarine such as the Trident can unleash devastation on a nation sufficient to cripple its entire national life. Even with the best information and tracking systems, it is unlikely that all enemy submarines will be instantly destroyed. As for the land-based and air-based forces, only a small percentage of their firepower needs to escape destruction for them to destroy the attacker. In the face of these facts, how can a "war-winning" theory be valid?

Fourthly, the unpredictability of actions of leaders on both sides makes it impossible to guarantee that a "limited" nuclear war will stay limited. For it to work, the "limited war" theory requires that cool and precise calculations be made by the leaders. But even the practice of brinkmanship places a tremendous strain on the ability of leaders to think clearly and rationally. One need only read of the reactions of John Kennedy in the days of the Cuban missile crisis to understand the level of tension involved. Once the nuclear threshold is crossed, the disorientation is likely to be even worse. In the panic, shock, and confusion, there are not likely to be objective, academic discussions about the exact degrees of force to be marshalled.

c) Star Wars: the objections.

The question of whether a "limited" nuclear war can stay limited leads naturally to the question of space-based defence systems and the suggested Star Wars "defence shield" aimed at throwing a blanket of protection over the air space of an entire country.

In a dramatic speech on March 23, 1983, President Reagan expressed the hope that the U.S. would be able to construct for itself a defence shield against incoming nuclear missiles. Such a shield would be based on new advances in such areas as kinetic-energy projectiles, particle beams and lasers. His announcement that research would be done on this project gave a new complexion to the arms debate, for it meant that the superpowers would not necessarily have to base their strategies on the idea of mutual assured destruction.

The concept of mutual assured destruction at least has had the merit of giving reality to deterrence. It has been on the basis of mutual assured destruction, in fact, that negotiations between the superpowers have taken place concerning limitations on the proliferation of missiles.[9] But once the capacity of each side to destroy the other is removed—even in theory—the basis of negotiation is altered. Star Wars therefore assumes a position of key importance in arms negotiations.

There is strong scientific opinion that a complete shield is unattainable. According to Nobel Laureate Hans Bethe, for instance, even being "as optimistic as you can be within the laws of physics and geometry, the system is unworkable."[10] *Time Magazine* commented: "Other experts maintain that even if a Star Wars system could be made operational, it would never be 100% effective."[11] Moreover, the cost, variously estimated at between 500 billion and a trillion dollars,[12] is well beyond the reach of even such an economy as that of the U.S.

Aside from these problems in setting up such a system, there is the problem that work on it would stimulate a Soviet response.

Among the more probable Soviet countermeasures are the following:

1. Releasing a swarm of decoys by the real weapon, thus drawing wasted attacks from the defence system.
2. Causing the missile to spin like a rifle bullet, thus preventing laser or particle beams from concentrating on one spot.

3 . Setting "space mines" in place which can destroy U.S. satellites in orbit.

4 . Multiplying the number of missiles so that more of them get through the "screen."[13]

5 . Another possibility, much discussed recently, is that of devising a "fast-burn" rocket which would do all its burning during the first one minute of flight and hence succeed in avoiding all Star Wars defences based on heat-seeking devices.

There are indeed numerous other possibilities such as super propellants and coatings which reflect laser beams; but we do not need to consider them save to observe that this is an excellent example of escalation breeding escalation. Each advance in methods of attack upon the missiles leads to multipled defences against such attack and the need for further improvements in methods of attack—a never-ending process. Indeed, "a Star Wars capacity might well intensify the arms race, since the Soviets would build more and more ICMs to ensure that at least some of their missiles penetrated U.S. defenses."[14] In the words of a coordinator of research at Livermore, "we are going to be in the counter-counter-measure game forever."[15] As it happens, however, there are financial limits to such games. Escalation cannot go on forever in a situation where the economic resources of the U.S. have been stretched to the limit. As for the Soviet response, each of the measures to evade the defensive "shield" need not involve anything like the same level of expense or sophistication as the "shield" itself.

If it were possible to construct a complete defence, scientific research directed solely towards this objective would indeed be something to be commended. Unfortunately, the moral implications of Star Wars are not quite so easy. For one thing, the projectiles, particle beams or lasers developed for the nominal purpose of defence could be used to perfect offensive weapons. Also, with the development of the Star Wars program the positive contributions of satellites to international security will be threatened.[16]

There is another aspect, too, which should cause concern to scientists and others. In a report released in March 1985 by the Center for Strategic and International Studies at Georgetown University, the Center argued that the shield did not appear to be a realistic possibility and pointed out, among other things, that it would not protect allied populations. Even if Star Wars achieved a 100% capability of protection of the U.S., it would place the U.S. in the position of defending its own population while the lives of its allies were held hostage. Europe, without a nuclear shield, would be an open target for retaliatory attacks. Where is the morality of building a defence shield for oneself alone? Even with the most optimistic hopes, the U.S. will not have its shield in place until the mid-1990s. When will Europe have its shield? The several billions of dollars required for perfection of the American shield would be an even more formidable burden for Europe to bear.

In the words of the Georgetown study, "We must recognize that there is no quick fix, no magic remedy. We cannot expect our nuclear dilemma to be solved, once and for all, by some far-reaching arms control agreement...or by an invisible shield that will protect us from nuclear attack."

It is for informed scientific opinion to advise the lay world whether such a "dream of total safety"[17] is realistic. A more detailed survey of Star Wars appears in Appendix B. The scheme, originally envisaged as a defensive rather than an offensive measure, is not only appearing to be unworkable but is also defeating its objective. It is becoming increasingly clear that instead of making nuclear weapons obsolete, it will inevitably lead to a proliferation of nuclear weapons.

*　　*　　*

It seems, then, that under any of the three scenarios described, nuclear war becomes impossible to contain. Limited war expands once more into mutually assured destruction, and we are back to where we began. Apart from these three scenarios there are some additional reasons why the continued construction (and therefore proliferation) of nuclear weapons is culpable enough to be illegal. They are all aspects that are so obvious or well known as to be within the ordinary knowledge of those engaged in manufacture, who cannot therefore disclaim in law an intention to cause those consequences.

These reasons are dealt with in the next section.

OTHER CONSIDERATIONS

a) The unpredictability of the outbreak of war.

Discussions of nuclear war are often based on the assumption that wars begin because certain rational decisions have been made by rulers. However, this has not been true of a great number of wars. Most serious thinkers on war—Clausewitz, Tolstoy, and Barbara Tuchman among them—have noted the unpredictability of the outbreak of war. Factors totally beyond prediction or analysis can suddenly occur to spark off a major conflagration when the background factors are ready for it. Assassinations (such as the Sarajevo assassination), the acts of a madman, computer error, a mistaken assessment of another's intention, or mere "nerves" can act like a spark in a dry forest. The sparks no one can prevent. But what we are presently doing is loading the forest with the tinder, leaving no doubt that when the spark arrives everything will be destroyed. Those who create this situation cannot disclaim a share of responsibility for the result.

The problem of unpredictable behavior has long intrigued mathematicians, logicians and scientists. Among the manifestations of this phenomenon, sometimes called the chaos factor, are the curling smoke of a burning cigarette, the weather, the stock market, and the economy. Broad patterns can be predicted, but no formula can anticipate the myriad minor factors that determine which of a multitude of alternatives will result. Alvin M. Saperstein, a theoretical nuclear physicist by training and a student of the impact of science on society, has argued in a recent article that war is similarly unpredictable. It is, he says, a "breakdown in predictability: a situation in which small perturbations of initial conditions, such as malfunctions of early warning radar systems or irrational acts of individuals disobeying orders, lead to large unforeseen changes in the solutions to the dynamical equations of the model. There is no way to predict the effect of the actions of any participant—analyst, planner, statesman or general—with any certainty."[18] The chaos factor is so real, argues Saperstein, that security policies based upon any purported ability to predict international events are outmoded. The situation is analogous to that prevailing in the sphere of the economy, which always seems to outwit economists' explanations of it. The fault lies not in bad or incomplete data but in the inherent instability and unpredictability of the system. Mathematical models for the outset of war can be constantly improved, but total predictability will never be achieved.

b) The unpredictability of the course of war.

Once war breaks out, the course it will take is no more predictable than the factors that led up to it. At a Press Conference on January 12, 1945, General Eisenhower observed: "When you once resorted to force...you didn't know where you were going...If you got deeper and deeper, there was just no limit except...the limitations of force itself." An outstanding book on nuclear war by Paul J. Bracken emphasizes this chance element. Bracken writes: "Uncertainties, random phenomena and the general notion of chaos lead to loss of control."[19] Previously orderly events turn chaotic and the scope for the chance factor multiplies, breaking down even the semblance of orderly control possible in peacetime. As this happens, those in positions of command also respond unpredictably as panic, hysteria, and irrationality set in.

c) The uncontrollability of war.

Clausewitz, the philosopher of war, emphasized that the idea of war carried the idea of limitlessless. "War is an act of force," he said, "which theoretically can have no limits."[20] One of the characteristic features of war, according to the Clausewitzean analysis, is that the logic of war is simply a steady thrust towards extremity. As he said, "We can never introduce a modifying principle into the philosophy of war without committing an absurdity." Each party would be taxed to the limits of its strength. The more intense the violence used on one side, the more intense would be the violence used on the other, provided that the means were available to commit violence. There could be no imaginable act of violence, however treacherous or cruel, which would not be used. Each adversary's aim is continually to force the hand of the other.

This is not to say that restraint in the use of force has never occurred. The Vietnam War is a case in point. Although it did have recourse to such means as defoliation, scorched earth, and other practices, the U.S. did not resort to nuclear war when it was facing defeat.

125

But a number of factors distinguish this situation from that of a nuclear war situation. Among these are the following:

1. This was a conflict between a nuclear nation and a non-nuclear nation. Nuclear weapons have never been resorted to in such situations, after their initial use in Japan.
2. The American agencies of control were far removed from the actual theatre of war. Since this High Command was not itself engulfed in war, it could take an objective view of the battlefront.
3. The U.S. homeland was never threatened.
4. There was no serious possibility of the war escalating into conflict with another nuclear power.

In a conflict between nuclear powers there would arise all the uncertainties and lack of restraints discussed above. As Paul J. Bracken observes, "there are strong reasons to believe that any such attacks would initiate an uncontrollable cascading sequence of actions and reactions."[21]

d) Launch on warning capability (LOWC).

It now would take only 30 minutes for a missile launched in the Soviet Union to reach the Midwest region of the United States. A submarine-launched missile can reach there in 15 minutes. West Germany can be hit in less than 10 minutes. The strike times are about the same for a Western attack on the Soviet Union.

If the President of the United States is informed that enemy missiles are on their way, he will scarcely have enough time to collect his thoughts—even if he is awake when the first news comes in. During those few minutes or moments he would have to take one of the most important decisions in human history. Since an evaluation of the pros and cons within this time frame would be beyond human capacity, mechanical aids are employed.

The United States has never officially acknowledged that a "launch on warning" system exists. Nevertheless, a 600 million dollar effort was launched in 1984 to develop supercomputers for the military, anticipating the day when defence systems will need "almost total reliance on automated systems." It is projected that in order for the Pershing 2 missiles installed in West Germany to be launched in time, they will have to be fired within 3 minutes of the beginning of a Russian attack. In the Star Wars scenario the response time may well be as little as 90 seconds. It is thought that only supercomputers will have the speed to allow a response to be made at all.[22]

This increasing reliance on computers has led to fear that the President and the Congress may be abandoning their constitutional decision-making power to a machine. This is the basis of an action instituted in 1985 by Clifford Johnson, a computer specialist, against the U.S. Secretary of State, Mr. Weinberger. Johnson is asking for a declaration that LOWC violates the U.S. Constitution.

Johnson draws attention in his brief to examples of computer error. For example, in 1980 computers at the North American Aerospace Defence Command in Colorado Springs reported the approach of two Soviet missiles. One hundred nuclear bombers readied their engines for take-off, military stations were placed on alert, and the Presidential plane was readied. The cause of all the alarm was a malfunctioning silicon chip. On another occasion, an American defence system in Greenland misinterpreted the rising moon as a Russian missile. Such malfunctioning, which no known system can insure against, could well unleash the havoc of nuclear war. Even if it is caused by a mistake, enemy missiles would respond and the phony war become a real one within a matter of minutes.

Discussing the complexities of nuclear warning systems, Paul Bracken writes: "In the world in which people live, power grids fail, trains derail, bridges and dams fall down, DC-10 engines fall off and nuclear power plants come close to meltdown. These things don't happen often but they do occur."[23] Bracken's point about nuclear power plants has recently been illustrated by the Soviet nuclear disaster at Chernobyl, and to Bracken's list we may now add the sad fact that a space shuttle with humans aboard has exploded soon after take-off. The great power failure in the Northeast in 1965 was traced to a single inexpensive switch that led to a cascading power blackout; experts predicted that such a thing would never happen again; but in 1977 it happened again in New York. With the much more complex systems involved in nuclear responses, anything is possible.

Moreover the signals received are often essentially ambiguous. One would like the machine, if it errs, to err on the side of caution, but caution carried beyond a certain point may be self-defeating. Surprise attack can take many forms. The signals need to be checked and cross-checked within a minute or two. "How can a warning system be designed to prevent this kind of attack? The answer is, it can't."[24]

The ultimate in this regard would be the computer system at the heart of the Strategic Defence Initiative (SDI), which would have to respond unerringly, distinguishing hostile attack from a host of alternative natural and man-made events. Dr. Henry Thompson of the Department of Artificial Intelligence, University of Edinburgh, and 79 other professionals working in computer science, artificial intelligence and related fields, writing to *The Guardian* of July 14, 1985, observed as follows: "...such a system cannot be designed and cannot be built. No design can exhaustively anticipate all relevant detail...These problems are made all the more serious because the extremely short reaction times required of the critical parts of the system preclude effective human supervision...when the cost of a false alarm is an unprovoked attack on the Soviet Union which will then certainly (and probably automatically) respond with a real missile launch, it would literally be suicidal to rely on necessarily unreliable computer systems in this way."

Similar fears have been voiced by computer professionals in America and Canada. The very fact that the Challenger disaster involved an area of lesser complexity should remind us that despite a multiplicity of computer checks and cross-checks and despite the active supervision of teams of technologists, major error can occur in the assessment of a situation. The tragedy of January 28, 1986, occurred not in a split-second decisional situation but against a background of weeks of time for consideration of all possible areas of error. One month later, on Febrary 27, the world was informed of a crippled Soviet satellite weighing 10 tons which was breaking up and likely to hit the Earth's surface in chunks. Fortunately it was not nuclear-powered, as was the Soviet satellite which crashed in 1978.

Robert C. Albridge wrote as follows in 1980: "Three times in seven months the US strategic nuclear forces have been placed on higher alert because of an electronic malfunction. Last November 9 the NORAD indicated an attack by submarine-launched ballistic missiles; on June 3, it indicated a full-scale attack, including sub-launched missiles. Three days later it signalled that missiles had been fired from submarines lurking 1,000 miles off the US Coast—missiles which would reach their targets in 10 minutes or less. The November scare lasted six minutes, and the June alarm lasted three—a considerable portion of the allotted decision time. It is terrifying to think of the consequences had the alert lasted only a few crucial minutes longer."[25]

Against such a record one cannot discount the mounting dangers attendant on a proliferation of weapons.

The role played by supercomputers also has a dramatic impact on the notion of the limited or contained nuclear war. Should the computer systems malfunction, there will be no way to control the extent of a nuclear war; malfunctions could easily lead to the indiscriminate and uncontrolled release of all the missiles. As we have just seen, computer error has occurred with missile systems even under peaceful conditions. Under nuclear war conditions, malfunctioning is far more likely, especially if one takes into account the way electromagnetic pulse wreaks havoc with electronic devices.

e) The electro-magnetic pulse (EMP).

A nuclear blast in space sends out radioactivity in all directions. This has the effect of displacing electrons out of air molecules in the upper atmosphere, and the electrons are deflected by the earth's magnetic field. As they spin down and around the lines of magnetic force, they transmit a sudden and very intensive burst of energy. This burst of energy, or electro-magnetic pulse, knocks out both computers and other electronic devices. It would paralyze all electronic communications, including the vital command and control systems on which the military depends. If those systems go haywire, the attempt to respond defensively will be thrown into chaos.

A sinister aspect of this phenomenon is that it provides an incentive for a first strike. It is useless having vast forces at one's disposal unless one can use them, and one can only use them effectively if the communications network is intact. In situations of heightening tension, the pressure to use them before EMP knocks them out would be quite considerable.[26]

It is to be noted that not only the military control system breaks down from EMP. All civilian communications would be disrupted too, adding immeasurably to the confusion and contributing to the breakdown of the political authority.

f) The absence of a limited war concept in Soviet nuclear strategy.

For it to be practicable, limited war theory depends on mutuality. There is no means of achieving a limited war unless both participants are wedded to the doctrine. Thus even if the U.S. were committed to a limited nuclear exchange, the war would not be a limited one unless on their side the Soviets subscribed to this method of conducting it. When the U.S. talks of limited nuclear war, it is often forgotten that this has never been the Soviet policy position. It has never been part of the strategic thinking of the Warsaw Treaty States. On the contrary, the Soviet Union has expressly stated that if a nuclear conflict begins, the U.S.S.R. will fight a full-scale nuclear war. According to the Soviet Targeting Doctrine, as soon as Russia confirms that a nuclear attack is under way, its bombers and ICBMs will take off even before the U.S. bombs hit the Russian homeland and will retaliate with massive blows against U.S. military, economic, industrial, political and administrative resources.[27] This fact renders quite untenable all discussions of limited nuclear war based upon the resolve of one party only.[28]

g) Incentives towards a first strike strategy.

With the progressive improvement of weaponry, the means of destroying enemy weaponry by first strike keeps increasing in potency. Whether first strike is intended or not, both superpowers are increasing their ability to deliver crippling attacks on their adversaries while the latter's weaponry is still on the ground. Such increased power coupled with the disastrous consequence of being a victim of first strike leads to a temptation to use such first strike capability rather than face the possibility of an immobilization of a large section of one's weaponry before it is used. If indeed Star Wars, as its proponents claim, can confer a substantial defence umbrella on the U.S., such a situation could also be a strong incentive for the Soviets to use their first strike capability before the stage is reached in which the U.S. is relatively invulnerable while still retaining its own first strike capability—a situation the Soviets could not contemplate with equanimity. If the U.S. should in fact achieve such invulnerability, the temptation would be strong to strike before the Soviets could achieve it also.

A disabling first strike could thus become dangerously attractive as a way out of the MAD (Mutual Assured Destruction) stalemate. The development of greater sophistication in weaponry is thus eroding the stability of deterrence and forcing a consideration of other military alternatives—of which first strike is one. In particular, the construction of weapons or weapons systems which are extremely powerful but also relatively vulnerable to others (such as submarines or cruise missiles) gravitates strategy towards first strike. As first strike capability grows on both sides, so will first strike likelihood. Robert C. Aldrige has predicted that this will be very much the case by 1988.[29]

h) Scientific research as an impediment to de-escalation.

One of our fundamental theses has been that the major hope of averting a nuclear conflagration is de-escalation of the weapons race. As long as the race spirals uncontrollably upwards, the prospects for a peaceful resolution diminish accordingly.

New scientific work on nuclear weapons is thus a powerful impediment to peace. The Gorbachev offers in 1985 and 1986 of a moratorium on nuclear testing highlight this aspect. If accepted, they could have been a first step towards that downward turn which is so essential. It is the pressure for new research that has stood in the way. One reason for the continued U.S. testing was to pursue the X-ray laser and other directed energy systems that are part of the Strategic Defence Initiative. The last US test shot of 1985 was part of the X-ray laser system and the first test shot in 1986, carried out on March 22, was, according to Government sources, for an early design of a warhead for the Midgetman mobile intercontinental missile, now in development.

Such new research needs were no doubt among the reasons for the rejection of the Soviet offer, whatever the good or bad faith that may have lain behind the latter. In the U.S. statement issued on March 29, 1986, White House Deputy Press Secretary Peter Roussel rejected the Soviet moratorium offer and reiterated the U.S. position that a nuclear testing moratorium was "not in the security interests of the U.S., our friends and allies."

Naturally, the opportunities for discussion on such matters do not come often. Comparatively rare events such as the succession of a new Soviet head of State may provide such opportunities, but they cannot last for the very reason already mentioned, namely that technological-military pressures are exerted upon all regimes. Mr. Gorbachev would also come under such pressures for resumption of testing from forces within his own country. And so the spiral would continue to soar upwards, powered by the forces pressing for development and manufacture.

Participants in creating the pressures against de-escalation—the military establishment, weapons manufacturers and scientists—keep growing in strength and become more difficult to resist. In the U.S., over 240 firms had by June 1985 submitted bids for 10 or 12 contracts for designing initial strategy, technology and systems for the SDI program. SDI employed 4800 scientists in 1984 and is expected to employ over 18,000 in 1986. The scheme will be several times greater in magnitude than the Manhattan project. When testing components of Star Wars commences in 1988, these forces will be infinitely more powerful. By then the important Anti-Ballistic Missile Treaty will already have been clearly violated by several projected tests. By engaging in similar activities, the Soviets would be guilty of similar violations. Thus as the pressures for escalation grow stronger, the legal obstacles to it would grow weaker, resulting in a two-fold slide towards uncontrollability. In this fashion, continued manufacture and testing would progressively obstruct such pathways as now exist towards global peace.[30]

i) The increase in the likelihood of war.

At several points in this book we have argued that an increase in the number of nuclear weapons and in their locations and support sites means an increase in the risk of nuclear war. Possibilities of accident are increased and so also are the tensions that lead to war.

*Operation Dismantle et al.*v. *The Queen*,[31] a recent Canadian case, raised interesting constitutional issues following from such a contention. The case challenged the decision of the Government of Canada, made pursuant to an agreement with the United States, to permit the testing of the air-launched cruise missile in Canada. The principal allegation was that the testing of the missile in Canada posed a threat to the lives and security of Canadians by increasing the risk of nuclear conflict and thus violated the right to life and security of the person guaranteed by Section 7 of the Canadian Charter of Rights and Freedoms. In the view of the court, the plaintiff failed to prove that there would be an increase in the risk of nuclear war as a result of the test. In the language of Dickson J., "What can be concluded from this analysis of the statement of claim is that all of its allegations, including the ultimate assertion of the increased likelihood of nuclear war, are premised on assumptions and hypotheses about how independent and sovereign nations, operating in an international arena of radical uncertainty, and continually changing circumstances, will react to the Canadian Government's decision to permit the testing of the cruise missile.''[32]

The case is remarkable as taking further than probably any previous case the question of the linkage between missile testing and human rights. In regard to the matter of whether the risk of nuclear war was increased by missile testing, the court's decision did not mean that such increased risk was disproved. On the contrary, the possibility of such increased risk was acknowledged; it was just that the reactions of other powers to the specific decision of the Canadian government could not be predicted with any degree of certainty. The problem we are addressing is a different one: not the particular consequences to a particular State of a particular decision to test a particular weapon, but the overall consequences to mankind of the increase in the global number of nuclear weapons which results from their continued manufacture. It is my contention that the answer to this question is beyond reasonable doubt; if this be so, the Canadian case is important for the linkage it establishes between such a danger and the basic human right to life.

It is not only through the testing of weapons that the right to life is affected of persons who are not citizens of combatant countries. The location of satellite early warning stations also poses hazards. Australia provides cases in point. The Nurrungar Satellite Early Warning Station in remote South Australian desert country doubles from 15 to 30 minutes the warning time the U.S. has of a Soviet attack. The other ground station for American satellite early warning systems is in Colorado, and the Nurrungar facility thus exposes Australia to attack in a U.S.-Soviet confrontation. Mr. Hawke, the Australian Prime Minister, has acknowledged that the presence of U.S. bases at North West Cape, Pine Gap and Nurrungar increases the risk of nuclear attack on Australia.[33] The Prime Minister has contended, however, that the bases help to maintain and enhance the stability of the superpower deterrence relationship. This issue resurfaced in Australian politics with the approach of the biennial Labor Party Conference in July 1986. Though the pro-base view seems certain to prevail, the issue is likely to generate a spirited discussion.

Through the bases and otherwise, Australian research involvement in the U.S. global nuclear defence and offence system is increasing. The Star Wars project is drawing it in even closer.

New Zealand's stance under the Lange government in relation to nuclear vessels is well known. It stems from the same fear of the increase of risk to New Zealand through such linkages, in the event of a nuclear war between the superpowers. Though no question of scientific research or activity is involved in the case of New Zealand, that country's response is indicative of the widespread concern about increased nuclear risk.

THE VIOLATION OF HUMAN RIGHTS

The *Operation Dismantle* case highlights an aspect of the illegality of manufacture which is not often considered. While the *use* of nuclear weapons is clearly a violation of human rights and therefore illegal, as argued in the previous chapter, the *testing* and *manufacture* of weapons can also violate human rights. If this is so, testing and manufacture are also illegal under international law, since basic human rights are now part of the universally accepted body of international law.

The case deals with the violation of the human right to life through the increase in the likelihood of war. In addition, there is a whole series of other basic human rights which are violated by the manufacture of nuclear weapons. Among these are the following:

1. The right to a pure environment. This is violated with every nuclear test and is potentially violated with every manufacture.
2. The right to space as a common heritage of mankind. Every fresh act of militarization of space is a violation of this right and constitutes the use of the property of all mankind as a fresh means of domination. As President Kennedy observed as long ago as 1960, those who control space can control the Earth, "as in past centuries the nation that controlled the seas dominated the continents."
3. The right to health. This is violated with every nuclear test and with nuclear waste.
4. The right to development. The channelling of earth resources into armaments at the rate of over two billion dollars a day represents a diversion of resources from development. The interconnection between the arms race and development is now a well-established tenet of international law.

134

5. The right to self-determination. We have already referred to this in Chapter Two. The gross disparities in power and the compulsive spheres of military influence generated by the escalation of the arms race all but negate the right to self-determination by the numerous smaller members of the family of nations. Though legally and nominally entitled to self-determination, their practical options are being steadily curtailed.

6. The right to a social and international order in which the rights and freedoms set forth in the Universal Declaration can be fully realized. This right, spelled out in Article 28 of the Declaration, is violated inter alia by the consideration in (5) above.

7. The curtailment of human rights (e.g., freedom of expression, freedom of association) in the ranks of employees in the growing nuclear armaments industry.

8. The International Covenant on Economic, Social and Cultural Rights (1966) recognizes the fundamental human right of everyone to freedom from hunger and commits States to take, individually and through international cooperation, the measures which are needed to achieve this. It can be argued that the vast diversion of State resources into nuclear weapons manufacture constitutes a violation of this human right.

9. The link between human rights and peace is spelled out in numerous international documents, commencing with the Preamble and Article 1 of the Charter of the United Nations. Any act that damages the prospects for peace thus affects human rights.

Finally, reference must be made to the U.N. Human Rights Committee's consideration of the question of illegality of nuclear weapons manufacture. At an earlier meeting in 1982, the Committee had observed that the right to life enunciated in Article 6 of the International Covenant on Civil and Political Rights is the supreme right from which no derogation is permitted even in time of public emergency. This right, the Committee observed, is basic to all human rights and is also enshrined in Article 3 of the Universal Declaration. At its 563rd meeting on November 2, 1984, the Committee noted that nuclear weapons not only threaten human life but also absorb resources that could otherwise be used for vital economic and social purposes, particularly for the benefit of developing countries, and thereby for promoting and securing the enjoyment of human rights for all. The designing, testing, manufacture, possession and deployment of nuclear

135

weapons were held to be among the greatest threats to the right to life, and the Committee accordingly made the comment that "The production, testing, possession, deployment and use of nuclear weapons should be prohibited and recognized as *crimes against humanity.*" The General Comments, which appear in Appendix I, reinforce and confirm the conclusions arrived at in this chapter.

*   *   *

In summary, the manufacture of nuclear weapons must always be with the knowledge of their intended use and with such real or reasonably imputable knowledge that, once used, an all-out nuclear war is extremely probable. It must also be with real or reasonably imputable knowledge of those various other considerations, only too well-known today, which render manufacture a source of increased risk and which make manufacture inherently illegal and destructive of human rights. Intention and knowledge of consequences are key factors in determining legal accountability for the consequences of one's action. Concerning nuclear weapons, it is submitted that there can be no justification for placing responsibility for manufacture in a different legal category from responsibility for use. The only difference is the difference between the commission of a crime and preparation to commit a crime.

If a particular article is considered damaging to society, its manufacture is banned as well as its use. This is the case, for instance, with explosives and narcotics. It is an offence to manufacture the first, and it is an offence to grow the plants that yield the latter. Can the most damaging articles in human history—nuclear weapons—attract a different principle?

REFERENCES

1 *New York Times,* November 17, 1982: Text of Administration's Letter to Catholic Bishops on Nuclear Policy.
2 *The Essence of Security: Reflections in Office,* Hodder & Stoughton, 1968.
3 Bellerive Colloquium, Geneva, June 1985.
4 Bellerive Colloquium, Geneva, June 1985.

5　Many of these issues are discussed in W.V. O'Brien, *The Conduct of Just and Limited War*, Praeger, 1981, pp. 127-144. The present author strongly disagrees with O'Brien's conclusion that within strictly defined limits nuclear weapons would be permissible. See on the contrary, Burns H. Weston, "Nuclear Weapons versus International Law: A Contextual Reassessment," 28 *McGill L.J.*, 1983, p. 542, where, after a careful examination of various combinations of the types of warfare (strategic or tactical) and the types of targeting (countervalue/counterforce/theatre/ battlefield) the writer concludes that virtually all potential uses of nuclear weapons are unlawful.

6　Burns H. Weston, *op.cit.*, p. 578.

7　Professor K. Galbraith, "The Politics of Arms Control, the American Context," Groupe de Bellerive Colloquium, June 1985.

8　*SIPRI Yearbook 1979*, p. 449, referred to this seven years ago.

9　Such as was achieved in Strategic Arms Limitation Talks (SALT I) in 1972 and was attempted in SALT II in 1979.

10　*Time Magazine*, Nov. 26, 1984, p. 10. See the article by the same author and others in 251 *Scientific American*, 1984, p. 37.

11　*Ibid.*

12　*Time Magazine*, Jan. 21, 1985, pp. 10-11.

13　*Time Magazine*, March 11, 1985, p. 27.

14　*Time Magazine*, November 26, 1984, p. 10.

15　*Time Magazine*, March 11, 1985, p. 27.

16　For details see Richard L. Garwin et al., 250 *Scientific American*, 1984, p. 27.

17　*Time Magazine*, Jan. 21, 1985, pp. 10-11.

18　"Chaos—A Model for the Outbreak of War," *Nature*, Vol. 309, 24 May 1984, p. 303.

19　Paul J. Bracken, *The Command and Control of Nuclear Forces*, Yale Univ. Press, 1983.

20　Edward M. Collins, *War, Politics and Power*, Chicago, 1962, p. 65.

21　Paul Bracken, *op.cit.*, p. 241.

22　For details regarding LOW strategy, see 250 *Scientific American*, 1984, p. 23.

23　Paul Bracken, *op.cit.*, p. 49.

24　Paul Bracken, *op.cit.*, p. 70.

25　*European Security: Nuclear or Conventional Defence*, IVth International Colloquium, Groupe de Bellerive, Pergamon, 1984, p. 286.

26　A detailed study in German is R. Breuer and H. Lechleitner, *Der Lautlose Schlag [The Silent Strike]*, Meyster-Verlag, Munich, 1982, p. 126. See the review of this work in 7 *Disarmament*, 1984, p. 172.

27　H. Caldicott, *Nuclear Envy*, Bantam Books, 1985, pp. 211-212.

28　See the opening essay by Desmond Ball in J. Schear (ed.), *Nuclear Weapons Proliferation and Nuclear Risk*, St. Martins Press, N.Y., 1984.

29　"First Strike Breakout in 1988," *Ground Zero*, Dec. '83/Jan. '84, p. 1.

30　For these and related items of information, see Helen Caldicott, *Missile Envoy*, Bantam Books, 1986.

31　4 *D.L.R. (4th)*, 481 (1985).

32　At p. 490.

33　Geoffrey Barker, "Thirty Minutes Warning of Armageddon," *The Age*, Melbourne, 18 March 1986.

CHAPTER EIGHT

The Concept of Personal Responsibility in International Law

If then it can be established that illegality attaches to production, the next question for inquiry must center on concepts of responsibility. Responsibility clearly attaches to the statesman who gives the order for manufacture, as it attaches to the general who might order its use.

Responsibility was not always conceived this way in international law. International law traditionally operated at the level of States. States were bound by obligations, were entitled to rights, and could sue and be sued, but personal responsibility was not seen as attaching to heads of State or national leaders. For a long time they were not looked upon as being wilful criminals, whatever the character of the wars they began. They were merely statesmen serving the national interest as best they could and were not therefore to be punished as individuals.[1] The reason underlying this protection was that such an act was an act of State, and those who carried it out were protected by the doctrine of State sovereignty.

The treatment of Napoleon provides a good example of nineteenth-century practice. When he was captured, his former adversaries did not think of bringing him to trial or punishing him, but rather devoted their attention to preventing him from renewing his military activities. The message of the British government to Napoleon, conveyed on board the Bellerophon on July 30, 1815, was in the following terms:

> It would be inconsistent with our duty towards our country and the Allies of His Majesty if General Bonaparte again possessed the means of disturbing the repose of Europe. It is on this account that it becomes absolutely necessary that he should be restrained in his personal liberty, *so far as this may be required by the foregoing important object.* The island of St. Helena has been chosen as his future residence. Its climate is healthy, and its local position will allow of his being treated with more indulgence than could be admitted in any other spot, owing to the indispensable precautions which it would be necessary to employ for the security of his person.[2]

Napoleon felt so affronted by this proposal that he replied in a Protest opening with the words, "I hereby solemnly protest, in the face of Heaven and mankind, against the violence that is done to me and the violation of my most sacred rights in disposing of my person and liberty."[3]

After the defeat of Germany in World War I, the climate of opinion had changed somewhat and there was talk of hanging the Kaiser. There was still enough opposing sentiment to prevent that from taking place. It was the hostilities of World War II, and especially the brutal violations of basic human dignities associated with it, that decisively changed the situation. Had Hitler or Mussolini survived, there is no doubt they would have been brought to trial as war criminals. So strong was the feeling regarding war crimes after World War II that even the direct orders of such heads of State were seen as affording no protection to officials implementing them.

The major manifestation of this feeling after the war was of course the establishment in 1946 of the Nuremberg International Military Tribunal by the governments of France, the United Kingdom, the United States, and the U.S.S.R., "acting in the interests of all the United Nations and by their representatives duly authorized thereto." The Tribunal was to operate in accordance with a Charter annexed to the Agreement under which the Tribunal was constituted.

Article 6 of the Nuremberg Charter provided as follows:

> The following acts, or any of them, are crimes
> coming within the jurisdiction of the Tribunal for
> which there shall be *individual responsibility*:
> (a) Crimes Against Peace: namely, planning,
> preparation, initiation or waging of a war of
> aggression, or a war *in violation of inter-*
> *national treaties, agreements or assurances...*
> (b) War Crimes: namely, violations of the laws
> or customs of war. Such violations shall
> include...wanton destruction of cities, towns
> or villages, or devastation not justified by
> military necessity.
> (c) Crimes Against Humanity: namely...exter-
> mination...and other inhumane acts commit-
> ted against...civilian population, before or
> during the war...

The Convention Relative to the Protection of Civilian Persons
in Time of War (August 12, 1948) authorized similar prosecutions
for offences against civilian populations.

It is important to note in relation to the Nuremberg Charter that
although it was an act of the sovereign countries to which Germany
had unconditionally surrendered, it embodied principles which had
long been deeply embedded in the general principles of international
law. Their authority as such was confirmed not only by the judgment
of the tribunal but by their acceptance by the international community
thereafter, including in particular the countries now engaged in the
nuclear arms race. Those countries are thus bound in a triple sense
to these principles—first, by their being subject to them as members
of the world community; second, by their particular formulation of
these principles in the Charter; and third, by their sponsoring and
endorsement of these principles thereafter at the United Nations.

One of the important submissions of the defendants at the trial
was that international law is concerned with the actions of sovereign
States and provides no punishment for individuals. They submitted
further that where the act in question is an act of State, those who
carry it out are not personally responsible but are protected by the
doctrine of the sovereignty of the State. The Tribunal rejected both
submissions, holding that the imposition of duties and liabilities upon
individuals had long been recognized. The Tribunal drew attention
inter alia to the fact that in a number of cases, individual offenders

had been charged in the American courts with offences against the laws of nations, particularly in regard to the violation of the laws of war.

Under the express provisions of Article 8 of the Charter, the fact that the defendant acted pursuant to an order of his government or a superior does not free him from responsibility, although it may be a factor to be considered in mitigation of punishment. The Tribunal pointed out that this provision was in conformity with the law of all nations and that the fact that a soldier was ordered to kill or torture in violation of the international law of war had never been recognized as a defence to such acts of brutality. According to the Tribunal, the true test, which is found in varying degrees in the criminal law of most nations, is not the existence of the order but whether moral choice is in fact possible. This latter observation is specially pertinent to the case of scientists working under explicit government orders or under government sponsored programs in which freedom of choice is severely curtailed, though not expressly denied.

"Crimes against international law," observed the Tribunal, "are committed by men, not by abstract entities, and only by punishing individuals who counsel such crimes can the provisions of international law be enforced."

Of the 22 individuals indicted, 19 were found guilty on one or more counts and 12 were sentenced to death. In 1946 the General Assembly of the U.N. affirmed "the principles of international law recognized by the Charter of the Nuremberg Tribunal and the judgment of the Tribunal."[4] On the instructions of the General Assembly, the International Law Commission later formulated the Nuremberg Principles in authoritative form (see Appendix I). Similar to the Nuremberg Tribunal was the International Tribunal for the Far East, which tried the Japanese war leaders.

The concept of individual responsibility, thus firmly entrenched, was confirmed by the British Lord Chancellor in 1963 when he stated in Parliament that the United Kingdom looked upon the Nuremberg Principles as generally accepted among States as having the status of customary international law.[5] It received further affirmation from the U.N. with the passing in 1968 of the Convention on the Non-applicability of Statutory Limitations to War Crimes and Crimes Against Humanity.[6]

There was indeed recognition of this principle from the German courts as well during the period between the two World Wars. In the case of the *Llandowery Castle*,[7] it was held by the German Supreme Court that the defence of superior orders would afford no justification, where the act was manifestly and indisputably contrary to international law. Examples were the killing of unarmed enemies or of shipwrecked persons who had taken refuge in lifeboats. It is interesting to note also the concept of individual responsibility contained in the abortive Treaty of Washington, 1922, in relation to submarine warfare. Article 3 of the treaty made a violation punishable as if for acts of piracy, whether or not such a person was under the orders of a governmental superior.

In relation to superior orders, it is of course competent for a court to take into account as a mitigating circumstance the fact that a subordinate acted under fear of immediate and extreme consequences. The force of this defence would vary greatly with different categories of people and would be weak in the case of a civilian not bound by military discipline. A scientist working for a military purpose but not under orders to do so would presumably be in this category. For example, in the *Krupp Trial*,[8] when the accused were charged with using and actively assisting in the use of forced labor of persons deported from enemy territory, it was held that in all likelihood the worst fate that could have overtaken the leading German industrialist Krupp if he disobeyed orders was the loss of his plant. The pressures upon a modern scientist would be, at worst, the loss of a comparatively comfortable position, but would certainly not be of the order of the pressures upon Krupp.

One other fact to be noted in relation to the war crimes tribunals is that apart from the Nuremberg Tribunal, which exercised jurisdiction over accused whose crimes had no specific geographical location, there were numerous other tribunals in a variety of countries which all proceeded to try war crimes on the basis of individual responsibility. Not only the U.S. and Britain, but Belgium, France, Holland, Norway, Czechoslovakia, Poland, Yugoslavia and some other countries conducted such trials and sentenced individuals for war crimes. The notion of individual responsibility for crimes against humanity thus rests upon a broad international basis.

The continuing trend in international law towards holding individuals responsible for criminal acts is also illustrated by the

142

Convention on the Prevention and Punishment of the Crime of Genocide, which was adopted by the General Assembly on December 9, 1948 and entered into force on January 12, 1961. Article I provided that genocide, whether committed in time of peace or in time of war, was a crime under international law which the Parties undertook to prevent and punish. As the crime of genocide has relevance to the devastation caused by nuclear war, Articles II and III deserve to be quoted in toto:

> *Article II.* In the present Convention, genocide means any of the following acts committed *with intent to destroy, in whole or in part, a national, ethnical, racial or religious group, as such:*
> (a) Killing members of the group
> (b) Causing serious bodily or mental harm to members of the group
> (c) *Deliberately inflicting on the group conditions of life calculated to bring about its physical destruction in whole or in part*
> (d) Imposing measures intended to prevent births within the group
> (e) Forcibly transferring children of the group to another group.
> *Article III.* The following acts shall be punishable:
> (a) Genocide
> (b) Conspiracy to commit genocide
> (c) Direct and public incitement to commit genocide
> (d) Attempt to commit genocide
> (e) *Complicity in genocide.*

Those who wage nuclear war cannot disclaim the knowledge of its consequences, and must be taken to have *intended* them.

Article IV provided that persons committing genocide or any of the Acts enumerated in Article III shall be punished, *whether they are constitutionally responsible rulers, public officials or private individuals.* Prosecution is provided for in Article VI which renders prosecution obligatory on the State in the territory of which the act was committed "or by such international penal tribunal as may have jurisdiction with respect to those Contracting Parties which shall have accepted its jurisdiction."

If nuclear warfare exterminates whole populations, then those who engage in it are guilty of genocide and are punishable as such, whatever other offences they may be guilty of. Indeed, as we have seen, the effects of their crime go far beyond mere genocide.

143

While giving jurisdiction to the State in which the act is committed, the Convention looks forward also to competent international criminal tribunals which may be established in the future for the trial of such offences. There can be little doubt that world opinion is moving in that direction.

Even apart from the creation of such a tribunal, this Convention sufficiently conveys the spirit and climate of international law in regard to acts such as these. We do not have to await the creation of a competent tribunal to pronounce on questions of illegality if the illegality already exists under international law. The present illegality of the act, rather than the existence or non-existence of the tribunal, is the criterion by which the individual should guide his conduct.

Humbler officials, well below the level of directors of state policy, are also accountable. Numerous instances can be cited in which individuals have been held accountable and punished for acts contrary to international law. In the case of *ex parte Quirin*[9], the U.S. Supreme Court observed that the Court had from the beginning of its history applied the law of war "as including that part of the law of nations which prescribes for the conduct of war, the status, rights and duties of enemy nations as well as of enemy individuals." The court went on to list cases wherein individuals had been charged with offences against the law of nations, particularly in the context of war. A soldier violating the provisions of the Geneva Conventions on the treatment of prisoners of war can clearly be tried by a belligerent state and punished.

Other illustrations of individual responsibility under international law come from many areas. Piracy has always been regarded as a crime against nations for which individual states could punish offenders. And the Vietnam war produced instances of private accountability for violation of international law norms relating to protection of civilians in time of war.

Although there have been problems in defining the offence of terrorism and making it punishable, hijacking has been made an international offence, and the Tokyo Convention on Offences and Certain Other Acts Committed on Board Aircraft (Sept. 14, 1963) and other Conventions—the Hague Convention for the Suppression of Unlawful Seizure of Aircraft, Dec. 16, 1970; Montreal Convention for Suppression of Unlawful Acts Against the Safety of Civilian Aviators (Sept. 23, 1971)—require any Party either to extradite the offender or bring him to trial.

The Eichmann case showed the possibilities that exist for the trial of an individual for a crime against humanity by the courts of a country considering itself affected—and what country is not affected by genocide or crimes against humanity?

The sentiment of international lawyers is moving towards the punishability of individuals for such offences and the creation of procedures and tribunals for this purpose. It will not be long before they come into existence—certainly within the lifetime of younger scientists.

A well-known modern example of individual accountability for war was the My Lai incident of March 16, 1968 in the Vietnam War. Lt. William F. Calley faced various charges, among which were the killing of a group of 30 or 40 unarmed old men, women and children, and the machine-gunning of 75-100 civilians held in an irrigation ditch.[10] Calley was convicted by U.S. Army court martial of premeditated murder and was sentenced to dismissal from service, forfeiture of all pay, and hard labor for life. Although the conviction was not immediately based on international law, it was under Article 18 of the U.S. Uniform Code of Military Justice, which made the relevant rule of international law part of U.S. domestic law.[11]

An additional factor making for personal responsibility is the growth in authority of the human rights concept. This concept has broken through the barrier once posed by the fact that individuals were not the subjects but only the objects of international law. The growth of human rights doctrine has meant that individuals are vested with an ever-increasing circle of rights. Along with rights must come duties; and if rights can be claimed in the international forum, duties can likewise be enforced. It would be a lopsided international order if the individual were given an increasing circle of enforceable rights and there were left unenforceable the duty not to commit crimes against humanity.

There can thus be little doubt that the liability of the principal actors—the statesmen and the generals—is clear. As the Nuremberg Tribunal observed, "individuals have international duties which transcend the national obligations of obedience imposed by the individual state. He who violates the laws of war cannot obtain immunity while acting in pursuance of the authority of the state if the state in authorizing action moves outside its competence in international law."[12]

145

Finally, reference must be made to the General Assembly Declaration on the Prevention of Nuclear Catastrophe,[13] in which it was resolved that States and statesmen resorting first to the use of nuclear weapons would be committing the gravest crime against humanity. The Declaration categorically affirmed that "There will never be any justification or pardon for statesmen who take the decision to be the first to use nuclear weapons." There has thus been the clearest reference at the highest international level to the concept of personal responsibility in relation to the decision to use nuclear weaponry. It is true that the Declaration confines itself to first use; but for the reasons set out in Chapter 7, it is clear that once culpability is established in regard to the use of nuclear weapons, there is no removal of that culpability on grounds of so-called "self-defence." As it was argued, self-defence in this context is a meaningless and purely vengeful exercise not sanctioned in any way by the law of nations.

Moreover, the use of nuclear weaponry in general terms has been condemned as a violation of the U.N. Charter and a crime against humanity in a number of earlier resolutions. These include: Resolution 1653 (XVI) of November 24, 1961; Resolution 33/71B of December 14, 1978; Resolution 34/83G of December 11, 1979; Resolution 35/152D of December 12, 1980; and Resolution 36/92I of December 9, 1981. The language of the Draft Convention on the Prohibition of the Use of Nuclear Weapons, annexed to Resolution 37/100C of December 13, 1982, is also significant for its second preambular paragraph. It reads: "*Convinced* that *any* use of nuclear weapons constitutes a violation of the Charter of the United Nations and a crime against humanity."

The individual responsibility of statesmen and military leaders for the use of nuclear weaponry must thus be regarded as a well-established proposition in contemporary international law.

The growing recognition of the individual in international law spreads also into areas other than the criminal. In the human rights area, as we have seen, the rights of the individual are the subject of a considerable body of international law. Associated with these rights are specific procedural rights and the recognition of the individual's "procedural capacity." Where formerly an individual would not have standing as such to enforce his rights, a growing body of procedures, e.g. before the Court of Justice of the European Communities, gives him this status. With such rights must come duties.

Another interesting provision recognizing such growing recognition is the 1969 International Convention on Civil Liability for Oil Pollution Damage,[14] by which various items of civil liability are attached to individuals.

Reference must be made, finally, to the ongoing work of the International Law Commission on crimes against the peace and security of mankind. Article 1 of the Draft Code adopted by the Commission at its sixth session in 1954 provided that the *responsible individuals shall be punished* for such crimes. Since then, the General Assembly has encouraged the Commission to proceed with its work, and the Commission at its 37th session in May-July 1985 worked intensively on the responsibility of individuals for such crimes against humanity as apartheid, serious damage to the human environment, and economic aggression. The Commission discussed at length the question of individual criminal responsibility in regard to atomic weapons and expressed its intention to examine the matter in greater depth in the light of the views to be expressed in the General Assembly.[15]

Individual responsibility is thus not only well-recognized, but is a concept of growing importance in international law.

REFERENCES

1 Michael Walzer, *Just and Unjust Wars*, Penguin, 1977, p. 40.
2 Abbott, *Life of Napoleon*, Ward Lock & Co., U.S., 1855, p. 546.
3 *Ibid.*, p. 547.
4 GA Res. 95(1), G.A.O.R. *Resolutions*, First Session Part II, p. 188.
5 Hansard, H.L., Vol. 253, col. 831, 2 Dec. 1963.
6 8 *ILM* 68 (1967).
7 *Annual Digest* 1923-1924, Case No. 235; Cmd. p. 45 (1921).
8 *In re Krupp & Others, War Crimes Report* 10, p. 69 (1949).
9 317 *US* 1 (1942).
10 See *United States v. Calley*, 46 *CMR* 1131 (U.S.C.M.R.) aff'd 22 *CMA* 534, 48 *CMR* 19 (1973); *Calley v. Callaway*, 382 *F. Supp.* 650 (M.D. Ga. 1974) rev'd 519 *F. 2nd* 184 (5th Cir. 1975); cert. den. 425 *U.S.* 911, 96 *S.C.* 1505.
11 For the facts of the Calley case, see the civil habeas corpus proceedings in *Calley v. Callaway*, 519 *F. 2nd* 184, 191-193, 1975, (5th Cir).
12 1 *Trial of the Major War Criminals before the International Military Tribunal* 466 (1948).
13 Resolution 36/100 of December 9, 1981.
14 9 *ILM* 45.
15 Report of the International Law Commission on the work of its 37th Session, 6 May-26 July, 1985, *G.A. Official Records, Fortieth Session Suppl. 10* (A/40/10), pp. 7, 15.

CHAPTER NINE

The Responsibility of the Scientist

What then of the responsibility of the scientist? What of the responsibility of those who *knowingly* participate in the production of the weapon?

The present writer would simply like to point out here that whether the arguments used to justify the development of the first bomb were right or wrong, they cannot be used again *now* to justify current work on nuclear arsenals. The present situation is different in several respects from the previous situation. Among these are:

1. The acute crisis situation of the Hitler war, with all its human rights atrocities and the imminence of an all-out German attack, is no longer present.

2. There is no longer the compulsion of an effort to beat the "enemy" to the punch in obtaining the bomb. The principal possible antagonists now have each obtained the bomb, and attained it several times over.

3. The bombs now stocked in the arsenals of the various world powers exceed, by a million times, the fire-power of the Hiroshima and Nagasaki bombs.

4. The environmental consequences of nuclear war were then largely unknown. They are today the subject of well-known and detailed scientific studies. The nuclear winter findings add a new dimension to the very real possibilities.

5. The demonstrated effect on human populations is now known through the experience of Hiroshima and Nagasaki. Scientists cannot plead ignorance of this horrendous and protracted suffering.

6. The use of nuclear weaponry is no longer confined to one or two target cities, where the damage caused—however extensive—can be isolated from the rest of mankind. The attack, if it takes place, will be on many centers at once and will cause a blanket of destruction.

7. When it was used on Japan, the nuclear bomb could not have drawn a retaliatory nuclear attack; Germany would also not have been able to reply in kind had it been used there. Today nuclear retaliation is certain, making the attacker party to the destruction of his own people as well as those of the adversary.

8. Nuclear exchanges today will not spare neutral countries; they would be destroyed along with the belligerents.

9. Even apart from the special circumstances of the Hitler war, the contrast is inescapable that while the first bombs were made in the context of war, current development is taking place—and has been taking place for 42 years—in the context of peace.

10. The first bombs were made to assist in winning a war. A nuclear war is unwinnable today.

11. If it is right for the scientists of the nuclear powers to develop weapons, it is right also for scientists in up to 25 countries with nuclear potential to do likewise, and we shall in a few years have an unlivable world.

12. The sophistication of today's weapons necessitates an increasing absorption of scientific and other resources urgently needed to alleviate such phenomena as starvation, desertification and pollution which contain the seeds of future wars.

If anything, the responsibility of the contemporary scientist working on nuclear weaponry is many degrees graver than the responsibility of those who worked on the bombs dropped on Hiroshima and Nagasaki. And because his or her work now involves full responsibility to the community of mankind, the principles involved here are those on which international law and the United Nations cannot be without their message to the scientist.

CONSCIOUS INVOLVEMENT

In the discussion that follows, the term "scientist" means not merely one engaged in pure research but also the technologist or technician who lends his expertise to the intricate operations used in modern science. There are many categories of men and women whose expertise is used for the production of nuclear weapons without their knowledge. For example, there may be the case in which a scientist has done some academic research—such as the working out of a new mathematical theorum which is used by the manufacturer of nuclear weapons systems. Or it may be that a scientist is working on an isolated piece of research which is part of an overall nuclear weapons operation; he may not be in a position to find out by intelligent inquiry the purpose for which his research will be used.

As far as this book is concerned, these are peripheral cases. Here we shall concentrate instead on the clearcut case of the scientist who is asked to work on nuclear weapons research or production and accepts the invitation, knowing full well to what end his activity will be used. The general principles of international criminal responsibility certainly apply in this case. For the scientist who *knowingly* engages in such operations, there is no legal principle distinguishing his guilt from that of the more prominent actors. Indeed, such a scientist has a freedom of choice (a "moral choice," as the Nuremberg judgment put it) that is far greater than that of the state official or soldier.

Even if, in a particular nation, the scientist should be *ordered* by public authority to participate in nuclear weapons production, he is not thereby exonerated from liability under the ordinary principles of international law. The Nuremberg principles cover such a situation. The fact that he has been ordered to do it may be considered at best a mitigating factor.

Complicity in a crime against humanity is a crime against humanity. Knowingly being party to the construction of weaponry without which a crime cannot be committed is equivalent to complicity in the crime. For example, a swordsmith who is asked to produce the sharpest possible weapon for a person who desires to use it to kill unlawfully, and who knowingly produces the weapon for that purpose cannot avoid culpability in ordinary criminal law. It does not avail him to plead that he did not know when or against whom the weapon would be used. To use the language of the criminal law, he is a *particeps criminis,* an accessory before the fact. If he recklessly failed to inform himself of the purpose for which the weapon would be used, his conduct would be criminal through his reckless negligence.

Prime Minister Gandhi observed at the 1985 Delhi summit, "Each improvement in accuracy and mobility makes present agreements so much more fragile." Every "advance" the scientist achieves in the sophistication of these weapons is rendering easier the breakdown that will lead to the eventual perpetration of this crime against humanity. Every increase in the arsenals prompts a response from the rival power and propels the spiral that threatens destruction. Every blurring of the distinction between nuclear and conventional weapons, resulting from the increased sophistication of the former, increases the possibility of nuclear war and makes arms control more difficult. Every improvement in accuracy and speed of delivery reduces the time for reflection and judgment before the fatal button is pushed. The scientist is a vital and conscious link in the chain of causation leading to nuclear devastation and can no longer claim the role of innocent bystander.

An important factor in considering scientific responsibility is that new technical weapons ideas do not come from the generals or the politicians but from the weapons laboratories. As Lord Zuckerman, the Chief Scientific Advisor to the British Government from 1966-71, has observed in a recent address to the Groupe de Bellerive in Geneva, multiplying the size or improving the quality of nuclear weapons goes on not for any security reason accepted by rational people, but "because of the inner momentum of the arms race; because in nuclear matters we are governed from below, from the laboratories and their patrons, not from the top."[1] Nowhere is this better illustrated than in the militarization of space, where the ideas of the weapons laboratories have moved upwards from the laboratory. No general or politician could have conceived the ideas which today they have made central to their public stances. Enthusiastic initiative from the laboratories is the cause of this particular escalation of the arms race, as was epitomized in this instance by the influence of Edward Teller upon President Reagan.

Also worth pondering, in relation to the role of scientists, are the words of another famous scientist, Sir Mark Oliphant. "Thus those who seek the abolition of war from earth, beginning by outlawing nuclear weapons, have to overcome the opposition, not only of those whose business is war, but of almost half of all scientists, whose jobs depend upon a continuance of the arms race."[2]

Indeed, in this matter the scientists have brought us to another parting of the roads—another situation where mankind faces two alternative paths of conduct and the choice once made may well be irrevocable. President Nyerere of Tanzania observed at the Delhi Summit of January 1985 that it is too late to stop research on the hydrogen bomb. By contrast, it is not too late to stop the development of nuclear weapons in space. The scientist has more than a routine role to play in this development. As the President observed, emphasizing a viewpoint of the non-nuclear States, "Now we have the threat of a still further escalation of the nuclear arms race, this time into space. Space belongs to all humanity, and thus jointly to Tanzania, and to every other country; it is indivisible. There are already communications satellites, spy satellites and survey satellites in space above Tanzania; we are not consulted and hardly benefit. If we want to share in the communications facility, we can ask permission to buy an opportunity; we were not involved in the decision to place it there. If we want to know what the survey or spy satellites report, we ask for information—and those who put them there can tell us or refuse to do so. Now there is a threat that in future these satellites will be carrying weapons which can be exploded, or in case of accident just explode, above our heads—or which can just fall in our territory. Should we in Tanzania not be concerned?'' Over 2,000 militarily oriented satellites have already been launched by the superpowers. If and when the Star Wars program is in place, the militarization of space will have been completed. The destiny of mankind hangs upon the balance of right decision at this crucial moment, and the role of the scientist in contributing to that decision is critical.

Another aspect of the scientist's role arises from the Nuclear Non-Proliferation Treaty. In the first place, the terms of the treaty are binding on 128 countries and render it illegal for the non-nuclear powers to construct nuclear weapons. Scientists who assist in doing this are clearly committing an illegality. Secondly, in relation to the nuclear powers, scientists who devise further and better nuclear weapons are by their actions assisting such powers in disobeying their treaty obligation to work in good faith towards general and permanent disarmament. No doubt this is arguable, since scientists making and perfecting weapons on either side may see their respective States as being compelled to act the way they do by the intransigence of the opposite party. Yet the overall picture is one of scientists acting as willing agents of their political superiors. If their political superiors are in fact in breach of their treaty obligations and are thereby committing a violation of the Nuclear Non-Proliferation Treaty, the scientists who are in effect aiding them in this process are likewise assisting in the commission of an illegality.

This aspect is only one application of the overall thesis advanced in this book: that the making of nuclear weapons is an illegality in itself, apart from specific violations, and that scientists who know-

152

ingly participate in this activity are party to such illegality and hence culpable.

THE PRINCIPLE OF CAUSATION

The foreseeable intervention of third parties is no excuse for a wrongful act. For example, leaving a car unlocked and unattended on a slope when there are children around would suffice to attach liability to the owner if children are injured as a consequence; it is foreseeable that the children might enter the car and release the brake. Another illustration would be that of an explosive left unattended, without warning, in a public place. Responsibility and accountability in such instances would be both moral and legal, for there is always a duty of reasonable care to avoid foreseeable injury to others.

One of our great contemporary jurists, Julius Stone, explained the application of this principle to the question of nuclear weapons. He observed, "Unless, then, we indulge a belief in such a miraculous transformation of the known world, we must attribute moral responsibility to those who, after they realized that their work would lead 'almost inevitably' to nuclear weapons, nevertheless continued on this path."[3] This statement must be read subject to the qualification that scientists who knowingly worked on the first nuclear weapon may well have had compelling mitigating circumstances or indeed a compelling argument for exoneration. This would not be true, however, of workers on later weapons.

When scientists reach a point in their research where they can anticipate its use for dangerous and destructive purposes, it is naive for them to plead that they exercised their freedom of research in the expectation that this knowledge would be left unused despite its great commercial or military value. They bear the same responsibilities that would normally attach to any person who foresees the reasonable probability of damage from his action but who nevertheless chooses to act in the manner productive of such probable harm.

A difficult problem arises when a particular line of research is foreseen as having both beneficial and potentially destructive uses, e.g. nuclear irradiation which can be useful for both peaceful purposes and armaments. There is here a problem beyond the competence of the individual scientist, and it should be possible for him or her to seek advice under a set of ethical guidelines from an advisory body.

153

Such a set of guidelines is urgently required for all scientists, not just weapons specialists. An advisory body to formulate such guidelines should comprise not only scientists but laymen as well, very much in the fashion of interdisciplinary ethical committees in hospitals, to which sensitive issues are referred. It is beyond the scope of this book to examine this difficult question in detail. It will require the combined wisdom of lawyers, scientists, and others.

THE PRINCIPLE OF FORESEEABILITY

Under ordinary principles of law, foreseeability is one of the well-recognized tests of actionability. The current trend in the law is to include an ever-widening circle of persons among those foreseeably affected by an act; the growing reach of modern technology is one of the reasons for this extension. The case of *Donoghue v. Stevenson*[4] provides an illustration of this principle. It extended the common law in regard to liability for manufactured products to the entire circle of those who could be foreseeably injured by negligence in manufacture. It thus broke through the earlier limitations which confined actionability to direct purchases from the manufacturer. Similarly, the case of *Rylands v. Fletcher*[5] recognized the principle of absolute liability to all who might be foreseeably injured by the accumulation of a deleterious substance on one's premises.

These same principles would certainly suffice according to ordinary principles of municipal law to fix responsibility upon a scientist for the consequences of his actions. Suppose, for instance, a dangerous virus were negligently released from a laboratory which was pursuing research in recombinant DNA experimentation. The scientist and the laboratory would be liable in damages for this foreseeable harm, despite the fact that the work was done in the pursuit of knowledge.

The proposition is not without its difficulties. Situations can arise where possible dangerous consequences are not foreseen. For example, Lord Rutherford's pioneering work on the atom was continued in the belief that "whoever talks of extracting power from the atom talks moonshine."

Although such problem cases exist, however, they do not detract from the general principle that a scientist who knowingly lends his skill to the active production of a nuclear weapon cannot avoid moral or legal blameworthiness for the consequences of its use.

CHANGES IN PUBLIC ATTITUDE

It is true that there is today no public condemnation of the work of nuclear weapons scientists. But public attitudes on such matters can change, and a major accident involving nuclear weaponry could turn public opinion around very quickly. The Three Mile Island incident had a dramatic effect on opinion concerning nuclear power plants, and the incident at Chernobyl will no doubt produce even more far-reaching effects. Already it has shocked public opinion into the realization that safety precautions thought to be more than adequate were far from being so. Even without an accident or war, it is inevitable that sooner or later there will be a change of heart in regard to nuclear weapons. Worldwide, a reaction will set in which will condemn and attempt to destroy the nuclear weapons already made. In that changed climate of opinion, those who have actively contributed to their manufacture may well attract opprobrium as knowing parties to the manufacture of weapons calculated to destroy mankind. While their activities are today permitted to proceed uncondemned, they may well at that stage attract censure for their past actions, if not be actively branded as guilty of a crime against humanity.

Such changes of heart are not rare or unknown. A striking example from the last war is the postwar attitude towards Bomber Command's fire-bombing of German cities. During the war this was permitted and even applauded; the story was different when peace arrived. While comparable commanders were decorated for their actions, Air Marshall Harris received a marked lack of recognition and retired with few of the honors he might otherwise have received.[6]

That change of attitude was within the ranks of a victorious power. Still greater will be the change of attitude if we move towards a peace where there are neither victors nor vanquished, and where world opinion rather than national opinion is dominant. Certainly international law at that date will be readjusting its principles and attitudes in regard to those actively associated with the manufacture of nuclear weapons.

LEVELS OF SCIENTIFIC INVOLVEMENT

In the production of nuclear weapons there are levels of scientific work besides pure or applied front line research. One can distinguish five different levels:

(a)   Front line research, pure or applied.

(b)   High-level application of existing scientific knowledge to the processes of manufacture. At certain levels this can be done only by the highly-trained scientist or technician.

(c)   High-level maintenance in service order of the weapons systems that scientists and technicians have devised.

(d)   Manufacture of weapons systems. This area, currently requiring middle-level expertise, will be progressively taken over by less-trained technicians as the procedures become more stereotyped.

(e)   Low-level technology, intricate but mainly mechanical.

In the opinion of the present writer, liability should be applicable to at least levels "a" through "c". Whether it should apply further down the line is a matter for later discussion and determination.

Some would claim that the liability should extend well into the range of the comparative amateur. Enough information is available in published literature that a gifted college-level physics student could discover the theory behind the manufacture of a crude nuclear device. From this circumstance an argument could be made that any legal restrictions would be an attempt to close the stable door after the horse has bolted. Such an argument overlooks the fact, however, that nuclear weapons manufacture as practised by states calls for a much higher level of scientific expertise. Weapons now manufactured are very sophisticated indeed, especially those at the cutting edge of technology. Therefore, the legal inhibitions remain meaningful and productive of worthwhile results.

SCIENTIFIC INVOLVEMENT THROUGH INFORMATION TECHNOLOGY

It is not merely through the manufacture of nuclear weaponry that the scientist is involved in the arms race. He also contributes through information technology.

In a study released in July 1983, World Watch Institute reported that the new technologies of communication increase the temptation for a country to launch a nuclear attack rather than help to control weapons of mass destruction.[7] They expand the amount of information available to the point that it overwhelms those in command.

The public, preoccupied with the destructive power of nuclear weapons, has overlooked the increasingly central role of communication and information technology such as satellites and computers in the arms race. Lightning-quick communication and information retrieval systems have shifted the focus of the arms race away from the power and speed of weapons to the ability to detect and target the enemy's forces. Some say that the harnessing of information technology for military tasks already has become the principal driving force in weapons design and in shaping the arms race.

Information technologies are highly vulnerable to enemy attack. The World Watch Institute report comments: "Sensors themselves are easily smashed or blinded and the links of processing centers and users are easily severed...Infrared optical and radar systems will be unable to detect objects amid the maelstrom of fire, dust and electrical turbulence."[8] Since the technologies will be of greatest use to the side that has them intact, the result is greater pressure to strike first in crisis situations.

ALLEGED JUSTIFICATIONS FOR SCIENTIFIC INVOLVEMENT

Defence 1. The principle of freedom of scientific research.

There was a time when it was assumed that among human rights was the right to uninhibited scientific inquiry. Scientific knowledge was thought to be solely beneficial; man had not yet reached the stage where the concept of "forbidden knowledge" had any relationship to reality. The voluntary moratorium in the 1970s by scientists in the field of recombinant DNA research provided the first important practical recognition of the concept that there could be situations where knowledge may need to be constrained in the public interest.

Knowledge now enables man to destroy his planet, alter his species, and create new forms of life. Earlier assumptions on the role of knowledge all need to be re-evaluated in light of this development. A scientist who is himself altruistic may be opening up the opportunity for others to use the knowledge for very questionable purposes. There is never a dearth of such persons acting for purposes of political or personal power.

It might be argued that it is not the discovery of knowledge that is at fault here but its uncontrolled use. However, this is not an adequate answer to the present situation, where the use manifestly cannot be controlled. The scientist discovering the new knowledge knows this as well as anyone.

157

Like all the other freedoms, academic freedom is not an absolute right. The right of freedom of speech gives way to the right of others to preserve their reputations; the law against defamation prevails. The right to freedom of trade gives way to the right of the citizen not to be the victim of artificially manipulated prices; the law against monopoly prevails. The freedom of the individual, therefore, always has limits. In Kantian terms, one must act according to a rule of conduct which can be adopted as a governing rule of conduct by everyone else. In Christian terms, there is the golden rule that one must do as one would be done by.

There are various cases that fall into a borderline area, a sort of no-man's-land lying between where A's freedom ends and B's begins. In other cases, A's freedom clearly trespasses upon the territory belonging to B, or vice-versa. It seems to me that work on nuclear weapons is an example, *par excellence,* of the latter. To work knowingly in an activity that can contribute to the destruction of humanity, and of life as we know it, is clearly an unwarranted extension of one's individual freedom and a deep intrusion upon the freedom of every other human being on this planet.

Defence 2. Patriotic duty.

Patriotic duty is sometimes cited as justification for placing one's talent at the disposal of one's country in situations of peril. The purpose of such devotion is no doubt to save one's country from peril, but even patriotism does not afford a justification for violating the rules of war. Patriotism is not a viable defence to a charge of genocide, for example, nor ought it to be a defence to the charge of "eco-cide." Thus a defence based on patriotic duty could not have saved the defendants at the Nuremberg trials; if that were a viable defence, the laws of war would have no meaning.

Defence 3. Defence of political beliefs or economic interests.

Since neither political nor economic systems can survive the horrors of nuclear war, this deprives such an argument of validity.

It is true the powerful countries have made statements to the effect that they are prepared to resort to nuclear war to defend their vital interests, as in the Gulf Region. However, such actions would be just

158

as much a crime against humanity as if the nation were to resort to genocide in the name of protecting its strategic interests. No matter how vital its objectives may be, they are no excuse for the commission of a crime against humanity.

Defence 4. The slippery slope argument.

It might be claimed that if scientific research into nuclear weaponry is curbed, it will establish a precedent for further curtailments of academic and scientific freedom. Since freedom of scientific research and inquiry is a principle of far-reaching importance, it might therefore be better not to start down the slippery slope of beginning to ban things.

The answer to this is that prohibitions—whether in the moral, the legal, or the merely administrative areas—always involve questions of degree. In some cases a rule clearly and unequivocally applies; in other cases the rule may or may not be applicable. In the same way, one may ask the old scholastic question of how many hairs make a beard or how many books make a library. When the hairs or books are few, it may be very debatable; however, it is not debatable that there are beards and libraries.

There are many areas of scientific research in which it may be very debatable whether a danger is posed to humanity. It is submitted, however, that in the case of nuclear weaponry the case is so manifest as to admit little debate.

Defence 5. Belief in self-defence, deterrence, or the concept of a contained nuclear war.

If scientists actively working on nuclear weapons projects could be polled, this justification for their actions would probably be the one most frequently cited by them. This does not necessarily mean that the matter has been thought about deeply by them; but there is little excuse for not doing so. At a time when the attention of all thinking persons has been directed at the problems of nuclear war, the scientist involved in the production of these very weapons must be expected to give his very special attention to all their implications.

It is true many legal issues are involved, and the scientist is not trained as a professional lawyer. However, both moral and theological discussions of the issues do verge very closely on the legal. Such concepts as deterrence and just war, for example, have been well within the area of non-legal discussion. To illustrate this point, I would like to cite two extracts—one from the Anglican viewpoint and one from the Catholic.

In his speech during the British Council of Churches debate on nuclear weapons (November 1980), the Archbishop of Canterbury said: "It is impossible when talking of nuclear warfare to talk about the just war—the war prosecuted in a just cause in which gains can be judged to outweigh the inevitable injuries inflicted on individuals and societies. After the Second World War, even the defeated nations, Germany and Japan, were able to recover fairly rapidly. This would not be true after a Third World War."[9]

In 1976 the National Conference of Roman Catholic Bishops of the U.S. resolved that: "With respect to nuclear weapons, at least those with massive destructive capability, the first imperative is to prevent their use. As possessors of a vast nuclear arsenal, we must also be aware that not only is it wrong to attack civilian populations, but it is also wrong to threaten to attack them as part of a strategy of deterrence."[8]

Since these are considerations well within the range of concern of the average layman, the scientist cannot plausibly excuse his own lack of concern with them. Even ignorance of the legal issues cannot be fully excused, in the respect that works dealing with those issues, such as this book, are available to him if he wishes to consult them.

Perhaps there are some scientists who sincerely believe that they should act in accordance with the concept of national self-defence, despite the arguments offered to the contrary both in this book and elsewhere. To them I would merely like to point out that their position will be no different from that of the persons who mistakenly believed that the fire-bombing of Dresden or the nuclear bombing of Hiroshima were justified by the exigencies of national defence. The arguments considered under the head of "necessities of war" cover this situation as well. If ever the matter of their guilt under international law should come up for consideration, their bona fide but mistaken belief in the justifications for such action would not excuse them.

Defence 6. Belief that nuclear weapons control 'small wars' and prevent big ones.

One hears this argument often advanced, along with the claim that the nuclear bomb has held back the onset of World War III for a longer period than the interval of peace between World War I and World War II. In this scenario the nuclear powers play the role of policemen, keeping the non-nuclear nations under control.

The scenario is not in accord with facts, as one can see from the "small war" between Iraq and Iran. The conflict has not shown any amenability to control by the nuclear powers; nor, for that matter, have many of the other disputes ranging from international wars to internal liberation struggles.

When the nuclear nations fall out, there is no superior force to control them. They must play the game of brinkmanship, each attempting to stretch the other's restraint as far as they think it can be stretched. It is by a series of happy accidents and a run of good luck that a nuclear war between the big powers has been delayed. A realistic forecast of probabilities is that a nuclear war will occur within the next ten years. The Stockholm Institute of Peace Research has made even more pessimistic forecasts.

Defence 7. The futility of individual protest.

There is a widely-shared view that nuclear arms issues are decided at the summit level and that there is no scope for individual protest. The present author believes that in fact individual protest can have a considerable impact on nuclear weapons policy, although it does not fall within the compass of this book to detail the ways in which individual opinion affects those in control of a nation's affairs. Let us rather consider here what scientists can do. They are an indispensable link in the chain leading to the construction and improvement of nuclear weaponry; they are willing participants in the enterprise, not conscripted labor; and they form an elite group within their respective nations. They have an ethos and a conscience of their own. It was through their assistance in the first place that nuclear arms originally emerged. It would be idle to contend that a body of persons in this key position can make no impact. If they choose to avoid the moral and legal issues involved in their work, they will of course make no impact. But if they do face these issues fairly and squarely, the consequences will be felt all the way up the chain of command.

Defence 8. Culpability and responsibility lie with the decision makers.

This has already been dealt with in chapter 8 under the topic of individual responsibility.

Defence 9. Superior orders.

The Nuremberg trials dealt specifically, as we have seen, with the defence based on superior orders. In military and international law, it has never been sufficient to plead this excuse; even if a scientist is ordered by a government to engage in illegal work, this does not exonerate him. When the Nuremberg Tribunal was set up in August 1945, there was, in addition to the Charter, a framework of principles issued by the Allied Commanders in Berlin relating to the prosecution of individuals charged with crimes under international law. This document—Control Council No. 10 of December 20, 1945—provided in Article II(4)(b) that an individual was not freed from culpability if he acted "pursuant to the orders of his government or of a superior." Such a plea could be used in mitigation of the sentence but not for exoneration.

Control Council No. 10 also identified several categories of people who could be brought to trial. They included those who were "accessory to the commission of the crime," those who "took a consenting part therein," and those who "were connected with plans or enterprises involving its commission."[11] The phraseology of these provisions clearly takes in the case of the consenting scientist.

The present situation of most scientists involves even greater difficulty than that of those accused at Nuremberg, for the choice of employment is voluntary. If the scientist opts to work in the nuclear weapons field and remains in it even after knowing its objective, he cannot rely on the defence that he was forced into it.

Defence 10. Lack of official position.

The Nuremberg trials expressly rejected the contention that individuals who do not hold public office and do not represent the state are not criminally responsible under international law. It is not essential that one be a policy maker or a state leader. *The Ministries Case*[12] showed that liability extended even to the level of humbler officials who aided

162

in the implementation of those policies *with knowledge* of their nature.

Indeed, the trials went even further than this, reaching those who held no official position whatsoever. Two striking illustrations are the *Flick Case* and the *Zyklon B Case*.[13]

In the *Flick Case,* German industrial leaders, who formed no part of the official structure of state administration, asserted in their defence that international law was a matter wholly outside the work, interest and knowledge of private individuals. The Tribunal rejected this contention, observing that "International law as such binds every citizen just as does ordinary municipal law. Acts adjudged criminal when done by an officer of the government are criminal when done by a private individual. The guilt differs only in magnitude, not in quality."[14]

The *Zyklon B Case* is even more in point in regard to the responsibility of scientists. The defendants in this case were civilians who supplied prussic acid for use in concentration camps. While prussic acid itself is capable of being used in beneficial ways, here it was used to give lethal doses to the inmates of the camps. The defendants pleaded lack of specific knowledge that it was to be used for a criminal purpose; they also pointed out that they were not government officials. The Tribunal rejected these pleas, holding that in these circumstances the defendants could not plead ignorance of the purpose. They also held that a civilian who is an accessory to a violation of the laws and customs of war is himself also liable as a war criminal.[15]

Defence 11. Economic necessity.

Like most others, scientists need to earn their living, and they may not always have a choice of positions. Once employed by a government or an arms producer, the shift to alternate skilled employment may be very difficult or next to impossible. Nuclear weapons production may be the only employment in which the scientist can put his special skills to use.

It must be admitted that such a situation is a difficult one indeed. However, the crisis of conscience he must experience is not peculiar to the nuclear weapons scientist. There are other walks of life in which economic necessity is not a strong enough answer. A similar problem might be faced by a skilled employee who works for a company which does business with South Africa and thereby helps to bolster its apparatus of apartheid. A debt collector may be faced with this choice when he discovers that his employer is pursuing totally unprincipled business methods. While it may not be to their economic advantage, such employees may have to leave their jobs for reasons of conscience. A scientist in the nuclear industry is also forced to face an uncomfortable decision; but if he is convinced that his job is dangerous to the future of humanity, the choice should be clear. And as the climate of scientific opinion opposing involvement with nuclear weapons grows, the choice should become clearer still.

SOME IDEOLOGICAL OBJECTIONS

Apart from these defences, a number of ideological objections which are commonly advanced in justification of uninhibited scientific research need to be briefly noted. These have been well set out by John Ziman in a paper contributed to the UNESCO/Pugash Symposium on Scientists, the Arms Race and Disarmament.[16] Singly or cumulatively, these ideological objections may be capable of being built into a legally acceptable defence, and they must hence be examined.

a) *The neutrality of science.*

There is great debate in this area ranging from the views of scientists such as J.D. Bernal, who see science as involved in the social and political currents of the time, to those of Michael Polyani, who see science as a neutral and unfettered activity. In 1942, R.K. Merton formulated disinterest as one of the qualities which win prestige for science.[17] However, this norm has become heavily obscured, especially in the post-war years, by the trend to seek funds, recognition, and advancement from such sources as political and commercial ones, whose criteria for evaluation are other than academic.

It is no longer true of workers in many areas of science that they can function without regard to the social, political or commercial interests on which they are dependent for employment, research funds and awards. The idea that scientific activity, by reason of its detachment from external interests, is or ought to be immune from concepts of moral, social or legal responsibility is thus no longer valid. Science can be and often is as politically and socially involved as any other activity.

b) The worthiness of the scientific endeavor.

According to this belief, scientists engaged in scientific research are imbued with certain intellectual and moral virtues—detachment, independence, open-mindedness, being logical—which society should respect and protect. Moreover, the scientist is a leader in his field and hence his expert views should be respected.

Although respect for truth and integrity in research are cardinal scientific tenets, it does not follow that these alone can keep science true to its social function of service to society. The scientist adhering to those values alone can do work which is socially harmful. Nor does he have the expertise in other disciplines—sociology, ethics, psychology—which are essential for a proper determination of values and goals.

It is said further that the quest for knowledge is the most worthy of all human activities and should be pursued for its own sake. Such a contention can result in a total concentration of effort and will to the task in hand regardless of the social consequences. Science cannot be thus disconnected from other human activities or concerns.

As a matter of fact, scientists can be so carried away by their research as to lose their sense of perspective. An example is the fact that when news reached Los Alamos that the atom bomb had been successfully exploded at Hiroshima, scientists rushed to telephones to arrange dinner parties at nearby restaurants.[18]

Another aspect of the argument of "worthiness" is that "all science is good science."

No such general principle exists. Each case must be weighed on its own merits. Science may have been beneficial to humanity as a whole, but the concentration camps and vivisection and mind manipulation techniques show the need for evaluation of each project. Such evaluation is a moral obligation that cannot be avoided.

c) The truthfulness and rationality of science.

It is argued that science never lies, and that a strict rationality always underlies the entire scientific endeavor. Hence the pursuit of truth through scientific research is the duty of the scientist, just as much as it is the duty of society to permit such pursuit without interference. The doctrine that scientific "truth" is absolute is now thoroughly discredited with the greater realization of the relativity and fallibility

165

of scientific knowledge. Science and its application touch the social sciences at many points, and in the interface areas scientific truth is not the criterion of validity. It does not exclude discussion and debate.

The history of science has shown, moreover, how subjective have been some of the major scientific theories of the past. Science is not an ivory tower activity conducted with machine-like detachment from the human researcher. A claim to deference and protection based upon this supposed quality is untenable.

d) The openness of science.

The argument is that freedom to acquire knowledge and to disseminate it is an aspect of academic freedom and therefore inviolate. Such an argument, couched in terms of absolutes, again overlooks the social interest. In national society no one would advocate the propagation of knowledge as to how a nuclear weapon is made. In international society we impose no limitations upon the pursuit of such knowledge purely because the seekers after such knowledge are sovereign states that place no restraints upon themselves. Yet if the danger in the one case is obvious, so is the danger in the other, for sovereign states are no more moral than individuals. Looked at therefore from a global standpoint—the only one available where human rights and the security of mankind are involved—the international activity is no less offensive than the national.

e) The unpredictibility of scientific consequences.

No one blames a scientist for the unpredictable consequences of his research, just as in ordinary life no one is blamed for the unpredictable consequences of his actions. When the results of an action are foreseeable and predictable, however, we must face the problem of the culpability of the actor.

This concept was forcefully formulated by Professor Julius Stone, one of the outstanding jurists of our time. He wrote: "Unless then we indulge a belief in such miraculous transformation of the known world, we must attribute moral responsibility to those who, after they realized that their work would lead 'almost inevitably' to nuclear weapons, nevertheless continued on that path."[19]

With the moral culpability will come an increasing consideration of the legal. Scientists often reach a point in their research where

166

they can anticipate that the knowledge they will unravel will be capable of use for irreversible or destructive purposes. It is naive to expect that knowledge of great commercial or military value will be left unused. However, where there is no foreseeability, there can be no liability, whether moral or legal.

f) The misapplication of science by others.

Scientists often know who the customers are for the product they evolve. They often know why it is needed and to what use it will be put. It is insufficient for the scientist who has this knowledge to claim that he has had no hand in the end product evolved by the technologist, the politician, or the arms manufacturer. The duty to give concerned thought and attention to this problem can no longer be disclaimed.

SOME INTERNATIONAL DECLARATIONS
ON SCIENTIFIC RESPONSIBILITY

In the postwar years there has been a growing recognition of the social responsibilities of scientists, and former notions of the neutrality of science and of the scientist's lack of moral responsibility for the consequences of his work have been discarded. This recognition was indeed slow in evolving in the postwar years, despite the scientific horrors of the concentration camps and despite the nuclear bomb. The old belief that science, technology and the human freedoms marched hand-in-hand died hard. But by 1968, the Proclamation of Teheran (Final Act of the International Conference on Human Rights, May 13, 1968) registered a definite international recognition that scientific and technological advance could endanger rights and freedoms, and hence required close and continuing attention. The Teheran Conference recommended in Resolution XI that "the organizations of the U.N. family should undertake a study of the problems with respect to human rights arising from developments in science and technology."

At that stage attention was focused on such matters as advances in biology, medicine, biochemistry, and electronics; nonetheless, a significant milestone had been reached in recognizing the possible dangers of science and technology. (Needless to say, the Conference also was not unmindful of the enormous benefits that science and technology could confer upon society.)

167

This new attitude became entrenched in the numerous other documents that ensued. For example, Resolution 10(XXVII) of March 18, 1971 was passed by the Commission on Human Rights. It recognized the need during the Second U.N. Development Decade to concentrate attention on the most important and basic problems of protecting human rights and fundamental freedoms in the context of scientific and technological progress. One of the particular matters stressed was "the prevention of the use of scientific and technological achievements to restrict fundamental democratic rights and freedoms." Similarly, a series of major reports was prepared between 1971 and 1976 by the Secretary-General of the U.N. and the various specialized agencies; they were considered by the Commission on Human Rights and the General Assembly. Among them was a report on the deterioration of the human environment and the hazards arising from the increasingly destructive power of modern weapons and from atomic radiation.[20]

The 1972 Stockholm Declaration of the U.N. Conference on the Environment[21] stressed in Principle 18 that science and technology must be applied to the avoidance and control of environmental risks and for the common good of mankind. This is a principle which perhaps no scientist engaged in the manufacture of armaments would venture to controvert in words, though many continue to act in a manner which inevitably violates it in practice.

The theme of the use of scientific and technological progress in the interests of peace was taken up by the General Assembly in 1975 in its Declaration on the Use of Scientific and Technological Progress in the Interests of Peace and for the Benefit of Mankind.[22] The Declaration has an added significance in that, for the first time, all States were placed under a duty to promote international cooperation "to ensure that the results of scientific and technological developments are used *in the interests of strengthening international peace and security, freedom and independence, and also for the purpose of the economic and social development of peoples and the realization of human rights and freedoms in accordance with the Charter of the U.N.*" In addition to this duty stated in Principle I, the fourth principle of this Declaration required all States "to refrain from any acts involving the use of scientific and technological achievements for the purpose of violating the sovereignty and territorial integrity of other States, interfering in their internal affairs, waging aggressive wars, suppressing national liberation movements..." It went on to stress that "such acts are not only a flagrant violation of the Charter of the United Nations and principles of international law, but *constitute an inadmissible distortion of the purposes that should guide scientific and technological developments for the benefit of mankind.*" The Declaration thus elevated this principle to the level of a State duty, and this principle will assuredly build itself into the norms of international law. Associations of scientists cannot afford to ignore these principles and in particular that relating to the devotion of science and technology to projects which are for the benefit of mankind.

Numerous resolutions and declarations have followed this Declaration. Among these are the 1976 Resolution of the General Assembly on the Implementation of the Declaration on the Use of Scientific and Technological Progress in the Interests of Peace and for the Benefit of Mankind.[23] The General Assembly requested all States and specialized agencies concerned to take the provisions of the Declaration fully into account in their programs and activities, and requested the Commission on Human Rights to give special attention to the implementation of the provisions of the Declaration. More specifically, a 1982 General Assembly Resolution again called upon all States, specialized agencies, intergovernmental and non-governmental organizations to take necessary measures to ensure that the results of scientific and technological progress *are used exclusively in the interests of international peace, for the benefit of mankind* and for promoting and encouraging respect for human rights.[24]

Both associations of scientists and the individual scientists themselves must look at these international documents, which provide the guiding principles in the body of internationally accepted principles and point to the scientists' obligations as currently understood. To ignore the use of science and technology for peace, and to use their undoubted gifts for purposes of war and destruction of human rights, is to act contrary to the currently accepted scientific ethic as reflected in these leading documents.

Similar norms have been stated even more forcefully in declarations of unofficial bodies of scientists and other concerned individuals. There is space here only to refer to some of them.

One of the earliest groups of scientists to concern themselves with these problems was the Pugwash Group, a group of 22 distinguished scientists who assembled in Pugwash, Nova Scotia in 1957 to seek

169

ways of ending the nuclear war. They called for an end to the arms race at that time and have kept up their activities ever since. Pugwash scientists have stressed the duty of scientists to inform and educate governments and peoples about the dangers of the nuclear arms race. They fully support the General Assembly's declaration of 1978 at the First Special Session on Disarmament, which emphasized that mankind must halt the arms race or face annihilation. It is a pity that so few in the scientific community have decided to follow their lead.[25]

The regular annual Conferences of Pugwash and their numerous symposia and workshops have been immensely influential in bringing better understanding between East and West in matters relating to nuclear war, especially in educating decision makers about the folly of expecting a victory in a nuclear war. Josef Rotblat has said of them, "Surely, at a time when a very high proportion of the scientific manpower is engaged in military research and development, when it is alleged that scientists are the instigators, and dictate the pace of the nuclear arms race, it is of the utmost importance to realize that a group of scientists voluntarily give their time, talent and thought in the reverse direction, to stop the nuclear madness."[26]

The Dai Dong Independent Conference on the Environment, held in Sweden in 1972,[27] formulated seven guiding principles on the Earth-Space Environment. The seventh principle declared that war constituted an accelerating threat to human survival. They pinpointed military technology as a major cause of global pollution and resource depletion, pointing out that nuclear proliferation had vastly increased the danger to the environment.

In 1972 the Oi Committee International sponsored a conference of 41 nations on Problems of the Third World and the Human Environment.[28] The Oi Committee was an International Committee of Young Scientists and Scholars; its name comes from the Swahili proverb "Ote Iwapo!" which means "All that is, must be considered." The Committee was emphatic about the need to humanize technology and to create social responsibility in science. It declared: "The new technology must be based on a new concept of science intended only for the social well-being of all peoples...Scientists and other workers alike have the responsibility to participate in the economic and social development of all people...We reject the concept of 'neutrality of science'..."

The "Poona Indictment"[29] of 1978 was couched in even stronger terms. Entitled "The Perversion of Science and Technology: An Indictment," the document drew particular attention to the perversion of science and technology inherent in advanced military technology. It said, "When one superpower develops a more destructive weapons system...the other superpower redoubles its R & D effort to overcome the disadvantage...The result is both increasing appropriation of world resources by the arms race between the superpowers and growing militarization of Third World countries." The report went on to say that alternative modes are required for science and technology, which must henceforth be directed especially towards the needs, skills and knowledge of the underprivileged peoples of the world. It noted that all resources pumped into the arms race are resources diverted from the needs of development. This interrelationship between the human right to development and the arms race emphasizes another aspect of the immorality of engaging in the manufacture of weapons. Apart from actively producing the weapons of death, it also has the effect of denigrating basic human rights, which suffer from the diversion of resources.

The Bucharest Symposium of September 1981, attended by 68 scientists from 38 countries and held under the patronage of President Ceausescu of Rumania, drew attention to the arms race which, it said, seriously increased "the danger of conflagrations that can destroy the whole planet, the very civilization created over the millennia." It called for the setting up of an international committee—"Scientists and Peace"—which would ensure that opinions of scientists would be heard in all forums which debate questions of disarmament, peace, security and international cooperation.

The world's agenda is now crowded with international events dealing with the role of science and technology in economic, social and political change. Among these have been UNCTAD V, the 1979 U.N. Conference on Science and Technology for Development, UNIDO III and the General Assembly's Special Session on the Third Development Decade in 1980. Scientists have been repeatedly urged to build up the pressure for facing squarely the issues. Yet there has been little inclination among the scientific elites in the First, Second or Third Worlds to really discuss the critical underlying issues. It is a responsibility which scientists cannot afford to avoid much longer.

171

UNILATERAL SCIENTIFIC ABSTENTION

At some forums at which the author has set out some of the propositions in this book, the point has been made that there are countries where scientists are free to change their sphere of work and others where such freedom does not exist. Consequently, if scientists in the former group desist from nuclear weapons activity, the countries where scientists are not so free would forge ahead.

I accept that the degrees of freedom to choose one's occupation would vary from country to country, but I argue also that the difference is not at present as great as it would seem to be, for the following reasons:

a) Scientists in the countries where movement is theoretically "free" are not in fact practically free owing to the heavy economic and group pressures operating upon them. They have been trained for such work to the exclusion of other skills, it brings them rich rewards, their security and careers depend upon it, and the pressures of their peer group, their employers, and of the competitive spirit keep them at the task. Moreover, the folklore of the nuclear age induces the belief that their work is essential for freedom, thus blunting their conscience. There are of course the rare exceptions who opt out, but this requires great intellectual and moral fortitude. The nuclear scientific establishment moves on, confined to the rails of conformity and compliance by pressures they can scarcely avoid.

b) For every scientist who voluntarily opts out, there will be a dozen prepared to take his place. The attitude of the establishment toward those who drop out may well be that such exodus is so minuscule under the current regime of scientific ethics that it can be ignored. The dogs may bark but the caravan marches on.

On the other hand, I would argue also that the opposition by scientists to nuclear weaponry on the other side of the Iron Curtain is not as mute or non-existent as is often supposed. The free participation of Soviet scientists in inquiries into the nuclear winter on committees such as SCOPE/ENUWAR and the Appeal to World Scientists by the Presidents of the Academies of Science in the socialist countries when they met in Bulgaria in October 1981 are examples of this. The latter document was signed by the representatives of the scientific academies of Bulgaria, Hungary, Vietnam, the German Democratic Republic, Cuba, Mongolia, Poland, Rumania, the USSR, and

Czechoslovakia. It was addressed to the scientists of the world and called upon them all to come forward against the arms race. It also supported the idea of setting up an international committee of scientists and welcomed the initiatives of scientific forums and individual scientists for rallying the efforts of scientists in the defence of peace.[30]

In the West likewise the voices of scientists against armaments are gathering momentum. The Federation of American Scientists (FAS), which includes about half of all living American Nobel Prize Laureates among its more than 5000 members, the Union of Concerned Scientists and the Bulletin of Atomic Scientists, are important manifestations of this. International organizations such as the World Federation of Scientific Workers and the Pugwash movement add to the momentum. There is thus in existence a not inconsiderable nucleus of scientific opinion ranged against nuclear weaponry. If all these forces can be joined in a common voice of protest against nuclear weaponry, the global result could be significant.

One of the purposes of this book is to revive the debate and give it an additional dimension by raising the issue of legality which has not thus far received the attention it deserves. With the highlighting of the moral and legal issues and their adoption by national and international bodies of scientists on both sides of the power confrontation, governments themselves can become more sensitive, especially in the context of a global groundswell of popular opinion against nuclear weapons.

There is, it must be noted, a growing sense of unity among the scientists of the world. Through international gatherings of one sort or another and through the realization that most scientific issues are global rather than parochial or national, an esprit de corps is growing up among scientists. This is comparable to the collegiate spirit that has grown up among international lawyers, who are agreed upon certain basic principles of international law, even though those principles might operate against the political interests of their respective countries. This body of international scientific opinion has considerable collective power and moral authority which must not be discounted.

However, as long as the present tendency of the bulk of scientists to sweep the problem under the carpet continues, the position on nuclear weaponry will continue very much as before.

CURRENT ETHICAL CONCERNS AMONG SCIENTISTS

The enormity of the current U.S. military buildup is causing an increasing number of scientists and technologists engaged in the armaments industry to give thought to their situation. According to the Institute of Electrical and Electronic Engineers, 25 per cent of its more than 10,000 members considered it important to be assigned to non-Department of Defence work when changing a career.[31] Only one-eighth had a positive attitude toward assignment to Department of Defence work. Since there are 330,000 engineers now working on defence research and development projects in the U.S., these figures indicate there must be tens of thousands of engineers in the U.S. seriously concerned about the military implications of their work.

There are several different attitudes which scientists have taken towards the situation. Basically they fall into the following categories:

a) Deny that there is a problem, and identify with one's work. "We are under a duty to guard our society and one's work is a noble contribution to this end."

b) Shut one's mind to the problem and abstain from inquiries that may raise questions of conflict. "One is doing a job like anyone else in society. Give good value to one's employer for the pay one receives. What happens thereafter is society's business—the business of politicians, trained administrators, expert soldiers, and others." "The issues after all are too complex for the average layman, and if there were something seriously amiss no doubt the courts and/or the churches and/or the political opposition and/or the media would step in. In our society these are among the numerous built-in checks and balances which ensure that democracy is alive and well and its enemies kept at bay."

c) Accept that there is a problem but seek moral justification for one's involvement. "Society has trained me for the job and therefore society is to blame." "I am not an expert in the business of government or military strategy." "I do not know all the facts and therefore am not competent to decide." Alternately, one could rely on one or another of the various ideological justifications set out in the text.

d) Accept that there is a problem in general with armaments work, but rationalize that one's own particular work is not socially harmful. "My work in computers will be a stabilizing factor in evaluating a military crisis."

174

e) Accept the contradiction that one's conscience militates against one's work and resign oneself to being torn by pangs of conscience, but accept the lack of any practical alternative. Suffer in silence.

f) Accept the contradiction and opt out. This means sacrifice and requires fortitude.

As a growing proportion of national populations are drawn directly or indirectly into the military juggernaut, the issue is becoming one of the great questions of conscience of our time. It is my purpose to assist in the resolution of this problem by pointing out that the issues are far clearer than most scientists suppose and that, morality aside, legality demands a certain course of conduct. People in each one of the groups mentioned will need to give some thought to this aspect.

Increased awareness of the problem is causing some high technologists to band together to help each other towards alternative employment in peaceful work. High Technologists for Social Responsibility is one such organization.[32] High Technology Professionals for Peace, with national headquarters at Cambridge, Massachusetts, has 325 members. Computer Professionals for Social Responsibility, based in California, has 1,100. There are also church-inspired organizations such as Exodus in Providence, Rhode Island, and Peace Alternatives in Louisville, Kentucky, which offer emotional support to workers who contemplate leaving the weapons industry.

In a feature article on "Conscience and the Defense Worker," the *Boston Globe* on March 11, 1986, discussed several cases of the real anguish felt by workers who found themselves caught in the dilemma. "I spent a lot of sleepless nights," said one worker, "just being wracked with the pain of this conflict." The worker was an engineer who sold oxygen systems for nuclear submarines including Trident submarines at General Dynamics' Electric Boat Division in Groton, Connecticut. "The choice was, should I choose to live according to my conscience and risk financial disaster and the well-being of my family." He came to the view that passively looking on and contributing to a nuclear weapons build-up was analogous to the conduct of those Germans who did not intervene to stop the Nazis. The worker eventually left his job and took a job at a salary of one-third his former pay. "I live a heck of a lot more peaceful life now," he is quoted as saying.

THE NEED FOR AN ETHICAL CODE
FOR NUCLEAR SCIENTISTS

Even in the initial stages of nuclear research, various efforts were made by concerned scientists to register their moral concerns about the nature of their work. As we have seen in the first chapter, some were prepared to penetrate to the heart of the political power structure to express their views. However, their attempts to assert themselves soon ran out of steam. Like the lawyers, the scientists became acclimatized to the nuclear weapons situation. They became victims to the folklore of nuclear weaponry, and in the process became minor cogs in the wheels of power, more or less content to do as they were asked.

In 1955 scientists attempted to strike another blow in assertion of their moral values. The Russell-Einstein manifesto appealed to men to remember their humanity above all, warning that if mankind could not think in this fashion, it must face the risk of universal death. The manifesto was of course a landmark and alerted scientists to their duty to warn the general public of the dangers of nuclear war. Unfortunately it did not go further and warn scientists of their ethical duty as scientists to refrain from being contributory parties to a nuclear holocaust. To date scientific bodies have thus far been slow to make authoritative pronouncements concerning it, and individual scientists have often overlooked it.

In 1957 Dr. Linus Pauling, one of the signatories to the Russell-Einstein manifesto, organized a petition urging a test ban. It was signed by 2,875 scientists. It was significant that only a dozen scientists working at Atomic Energy Commission facilities, including the Los Alamos weapons laboratory, placed their signatures on the petition.

Pauling also obtained the signatures of 13,000 scientists around the world, including a large number of Nobel laureates. This was a notable instance of unilateral action by a concerned scientist. Pauling took his petition to Dr. Dag Hammarskjold at the United Nations, and his actions helped to persuade the public that nuclear testing should stop. He played a real role in achieving the first partial test ban treaty.

But scientists cannot stop at persuading others. They must act themselves on the basis of these convictions. So long as they lend their expertise to the making of arms, the arms race goes on. What is needed is an authoritative commitment by their profession to the ethic of non-participation in such activities.

It is noteworthy that Dr. Pauling's petition was the result of individual action. A few concerned individuals worked on their own to achieve it. It did not have the backing of the scientific establishment as such; no organizations of scientists endorsed the petition or helped it on its way. Indeed, the professional organizations preferred to steer clear of such activities. Like all other citizens, the scientists seem to be caught in the nuclear trap; the difference is that they are among the few who are in a position to enable mankind to escape before the trap door finally closes.

If anything, the freedom of action by scientists seems to be decreasing. An increasing segment of scientists depends, either directly or indirectly, upon the military-industrial complex for a living. An important form of indirect dependence occurs through some of the military-related work undertaken even by universities.

Considerable pressures are applied to scientists who deviate from the orthodoxies of the weapons culture. Even a two-time Nobel laureate such as Dr. Pauling was pilloried on the basis that he was aiding the Communist cause. The power of the military establishment is so great that it requires considerable courage for the individual scientist to openly assert his convictions.

The *Washington Post* has recently reported that some 80% of research and development money spent by government is for military projects. It also points out that "The longest sustained military build-up in U.S. peacetime history is sending money cascading through the U.S. economy. In 1984 the Defence Department signed $146 billion in prime contracts, compared with $32 billion ten years earlier...Every major aero-space industry except Boeing now depends primarily on government sales...The Pentagon will spend $140 billion on defence electronics this year [1985], $10 billion more than consumers will spend on electronics products."[33]

On the Soviet side, there can be little doubt that the proportion of military spending to civilian is likewise rising owing to the arms race, and that there is a similar emphasis on weapons research. It appears, then, that the peace-oriented alternatives for the scientist's work are being steadily reduced on both sides of the Iron Curtain.

One must of course appreciate that scientists will be of varied views. There will be the doves and the hawks, the concerned and the apathetic, the orthodox and the radical. Granting all this, the common core of scientific fact about the known effects of nuclear weapons should be enough to cause deep concern to all nuclear weapons scientists, regardless of their political stripe. From the time of Szilard and Bohr, through Einstein and Russell, Pauling and the Union of Concerned Scientists, scientific evidence has been gathered which makes at least a prima facie case regarding the possible extinction of humanity through nuclear war. Even if the extinction of humanity is not an absolute certainty, the fact that it is a very strong possibility means the scientific conscience cannot be at ease in assisting in this enterprise.

Against this background, it is clear that there is an imperative need for an ethical code for nuclear scientists. Individual scientists need to be strengthened by a collective ethic of their profession, just as individual workers need to be strengthened in the assertion of their rightful claims by the collective strength of their union. For example, an individual worker once could not agitate for greater safety conditions in the workplace, but through the collective strength of a union the safety conditions were brought about. In the same way, an individual scientist with moral scruples regarding his work on modern weapons cannot now indicate his views, but the collective ethic of the profession as a whole may enable him to do so.

If the profession as a whole cannot agree on the ethical stance, it can at least agree on the principle that scientists who have moral scruples regarding weapons research ought to have a right to express their views without fear of repercussions. As matters stand, scientists are made to feel that if they voice their objections to such research, adverse consequences will follow concerning their livelihood and employability. This is becoming more and more the case as the military establishment tightens its grip over the industry, making the need for a professional ethic even more urgent.

Scientists engaged in any occupation capable of causing danger to society cannot avoid considering the consequences of their actions. The Bhopal tragedy shows what lack of foresight, and perhaps lack of scruples for the public welfare, can do. Scientists working on nuclear reactors or on recombinant DNA experimentation cannot shut their eyes to the possible consequences of their work. They cannot plead, for example, that their employers required them to relax safety standards; and they cannot ignore the impact of their work on society. Can the scientist manufacturing nuclear arms argue otherwise?

In its current membership application form, the American Society of Civil Engineers sets out a Code of Ethics consisting of Four Fundamental Principles and Seven Fundamental Canons. If elected to the Society, members pledge themselves to conform to these norms. The first of the Four Fundamental Principles states that engineers are to advance the integrity, honor and dignity of the profession by "using their knowledge and skill for the enhancement of human welfare." The first of the Canons says, "Engineers shall hold paramount the safety, health and welfare of the public in the performance of their professional duties." Moreover, there is an Engineer's Creed which appears on the reverse side of the annual certificate of good standing of the National Society of Professional Engineers in the U.S. It begins: "As a Professional Engineer, I dedicate my professional knowledge and skill to the advancement and betterment of human welfare."

This engineering ethic can serve as a model for all those involved in scientific work. Many of those at work in making and improving nuclear weapons are professional engineers and are already bound—at least in theory—to that ethic. Certainly the fact that they are working in the nuclear weapons field does not discharge them from that ethic; but it is an ethic which needs to be implemented, both by those who are engineers and by those scientists who work alongside them. All must refuse to wear blinkers regarding the effects of their work. Least of all can an attitude of non-inquiry be adopted by those whose basic discipline trains them to pursue the habit of independent inquiry.

*   *   *

As a postscript to this chapter, I should add that I have drafted a proposed United Nations Declaration on the responsibility of scientists engaged in the manufacture of nuclear weaponry. It has been circulated to all member states of the United Nations and to scientific societies in various countries. It has drawn responses ranging from strong opposition through lukewarm support to enthusiastic endorsement. Some smaller countries not directly engaged in the nuclear race are prepared to support it but not to raise it themselves, presumably for fear of adverse consequences from more powerful countries if they are seen to take a leadership role in such an enterprise. The late Olof Palme, Prime Minister of Sweden, expressed the view[34] that while the proposed Declaration contained many elements of value for further discussions on the elimination of the nuclear threat, it was up to the scientific community rather than the General Assembly to consider the drafting of an ethical code concerning the involvement of scientists in research and development of nuclear weapons.

There would be the need for a member state to sponsor such a Declaration, but once such a proposal is brought before the United Nations by a member State, the author believes it will be possible for it to gather a fair measure of support—especially if the scientific associations of member countries become more active in furthering such a proposal. If the ethical code in question should achieve the status of being incorporated in a United Nations document, we will have gone a long way towards the global acceptance of such a scientific ethic.

REFERENCES

1 "Nuclear Reality, Military Illusion, Political Responsibility," in M. de Perrot (ed.), *European Security: Nuclear or Conventional Defence*, 4th International Colloquium, Groupe de Bellerive, Pergamon Press, N.Y., 1984, 15 at 21.
2 Mark Oliphant, "Comment on the Social Responsibilities of Scientists," in J. Ritvkat (ed.), *Scientists, The Arms Race and Disarmament:* A UNESCO/Pugwash Symposium, Taylor & Francis, London, 1982, p. 193.

3 "Knowledge, Survival and the Duties of Science," 23 *American Univ. Law Review*, 1973, p. 259.

4 [1932] A.C. 562.

5 L.R. 3 H.L. 330 (1868).

6 J. Keegan & A. Wheatcroft, *Who's Who in Military History*, Weidenfeld & Nicholson, London, 1976, p. 155: "despite his long tenure of command [he] received only a baronetcy in the victory honours."

7 See *The New York Times*, July 31, 1983.

8 *Ibid.*

9 Geoffrey Goodwin (ed.), *Ethics and Nuclear Deterrence*, Croom Helm, London, 1983, p. 191.

10 *Ibid.*, p. 190.

11 Control Council No. 10, Art. II(2).

12 22-23 *Trials of War Criminals before Nurnberg Military Tribunals under Control Council Law No. 10 (1952)*.

13 For these cases, see Friedmann, *The Law of War: A Documentary History*, vol. II, pp. 1284 and 1487. See also the discussion of them in Falk, et al., 20 *Indian Journal of International Law*, 1980, pp. 587-8.

14 See Friedmann, *op.cit.*, p. 1284.

15 Friedmann, *op.cit.*, p. 1498.

16 John Ziman, "Basic Principles," in J. Rotblat (ed.), *Scientists, The Arms Race and Disarmament:* A UNESCO/Pugwash Symposium, Taylor & Francis Ltd., London, 1982, pp. 161-178.

17 See R.K. Merton, "Science and Technology in a Democratic Order," in *Journal of Legal and Political Science*, Vol. 1, 1942, pp. 115-126.

18 R.W. Reid, *Tongues of Conscience*, Constable, 1969, pp. 103, 104.

19 Julius Stone, "Knowledge, Survival, and the Duty of Science," in 23 *American Universities Law Review*, 1973, p. 259.

20 A/10146.

21 Stockholm, June 10, 1972, 11 *Int. Legal Materials*, 1972, p. 1416.

22 Resolution 3384(XXX) of November 10, 1975.

23 31/128 of December 16, 1976.

24 37/189A of December 18, 1982.

25 See generally on the Pugwash record of achievement J. Rotblat (ed.), *Scientists, The Arms Race and Disarmament:* A UNESCO/Pugwash Symposium, Taylor & Francis Ltd., London, 1982, pp. 133-144.

26 *Ibid.*, p. 143.

27 See 1 *Alternatives—A Journal of World Policy*, 1975, p. 406.

28 Weston, Falk, and D'Amato, *Basic Documents in International Law and World Order*, West, 1980, p. 427.

29 Adopted by participants in the 14th Meeting of the World Order Models Project held in Poona, India, July 2-10, 1978; reprinted in 4 *Alternatives—A Journal of World Policy*, 1979, p. 413; Weston, Falk, D'Amato, *op.cit.*, p. 421.

30 For the text of this document, see J. Rotblat (ed.), *Scientists, The Arms Race and Disarmament:* A UNESCO/Pugwash Symposium, Taylor & Francis, London, 1982, pp. 111-112.

31 *Boston Globe*, March 11, 1986.

32 H. Caldicott, *Missile Envy*, Bantam Books, 1985, p. 362.

33 The Washington Post, April 1, 1985, p. A7.

34 In a letter to the author dated December 6, 1985.

181

CHAPTER TEN

Consequences of the Thesis Advanced in this Book

CONCLUSION: PRACTICAL ADVANTAGES OF UNDERLINING SCIENTIFIC RESPONSIBILITY

1. Clarification of the issues for scientists.

It is hoped that the information in this book will assist scientists to debate and clarify the principal issues concerning their role in nuclear arms production. Systematic discussions of these tend to be confined to the legal literature, which may not be easily accessible to scientists. Clarification of the legal issues should help to make much clearer the choices that lie before scientists. Perhaps a large number of scientists already hold the view that work on nuclear weapons systems is immoral. This book has attempted to show that it is also illegal, criminal, and tortious.

2. Sharpening of the scientific conscience.

With the exception of medicine, the scientific enterprise has been largely shielded from having to grapple with matters of conscience. The pursuit of knowledge, irrespective of where it may lead, has been considered a legitimate goal. At the same time, there has been a rather complacent confidence that any questions of conscience would be adequately handled by each individual scientist in his or her capacity as a person of conscience and integrity.

As we have shown, however, recent developments in many branches of science have shaken this confidence in the adequacy of individual judgment. Over the past decade, in particular, there has been a marked increase in the scientist's concern with issues of conscience. The area of nuclear arms provides the sharpest possible confrontation between freedom of research and these issues of conscience.

3. Creation of a climate of scientific opinion.

In charting his course of action, the individual scientist will be helped greatly by the growth of a climate of scientific opinion. It is hoped that the discussions in this book will help to promote a stronger general feeling regarding scientific responsibility and thereby make it easier for the individual scientist to refuse to participate in the nuclear enterprise. At the least it should provide further testimony for the fact that the scientist cannot exonerate himself by trying to pass on the responsibility to others.

4. Evolution of codes of ethical conduct for nuclear scientists.

Doctors have the Hippocratic oath as an ethical code for their profession, but there are many branches of scientific activity which function without any explicit ethical codes whatsoever. This is the case, for example, with physicists, chemists, botanists, and zoologists. Computer scientists, engineers and some other scientists are beginning to evolve codes for themselves. It is time an ethical code emerged for nuclear scientists, and it is hoped that the previous discussion will help such a code to emerge.

5. International declarations.

Declarations in regard to the duties of scientists engaged in nuclear weapons manufacture are long overdue. This book has based itself upon propositions of international law; and if those propositions are correct, the code of conduct consequent on them is a matter for the world community and for international law.

This code needs to be worked out by international bodies at all levels. Councils of scientists must deliberate on these issues and formulate a code, possibly one which has the approval of a body like a World Council of Scientists or the International Council of Scientific Unions. Appropriate organs of the U.N. and the U.N. itself could also adopt such declarations in the light of international law. Once adopted, such declarations could reinforce the current set of norms applicable to this matter under customary international law.

183

6. Greater public awareness.

Every means of increasing public awareness regarding the nuclear peril is useful. To date there has been no general awareness that a well-developed body of international law exists on this matter; instead, there is a general sense of powerlessness and futility concerning feasible forms of action. More than 25 years ago the Pugwash movement stressed the need for scientists to inform the general public and governments about the dangers of the nuclear arms race.[1] All disciplines, and not science alone, share this duty. Hopefully this book is a means by the which the discipline of the law can play its part in spreading such awareness.

7. Reinforcing of anti-nuclear moral sentiment.

To date most anti-nuclear sentiment has been based on moral grounds. This book should have made it clear that the sentiment should be grounded on both moral and legal considerations rather than on morality alone. While this book has been written expressly in regard to the obligations of scientists, its general thesis has been the illegality of the use and manufacture of nuclear weapons. Obviously this concerns all persons, not scientists alone.

8. Strengthening the wall of resistance to the use of nuclear weaponry.

There is a certain degree of inhibition that naturally attaches to the act of pressing the nuclear button. The survival of humanity may depend on how much that natural inhibition can be strengthened. At the time of Hiroshima, there was a chance for a wrong decision to be corrected. There was the need to transport the bomb to its destination by conventional aircraft and there was a time cushion of 5 to 8 hours before the device was actually dropped. Whoever gave the command could reconsider it and cancel the command if necessary. Today a Pershing II or an SS20 takes about one minute to cover the distance between Bonn and Prague. A Pershing takes seven minutes to go from Europe to Moscow. That means that if the nuclear button is ever pressed, we are irrevocably committed to a nuclear war. It is a matter of overriding importance, therefore, that this button never be pressed. The knowledge that using nuclear weaponry is inherently illegal should increase the inhibition and hestitation about pressing the button. Perhaps that alone will buy us a portion of extra time. However small that time may be, it is likely to be valuable.

9. Clarifying the distinction between destruction and war.

A war is fought with certain objectives. It is a form of settling disputes; it is a prelude to the peace that is to follow; it assumes the continued possibility of co-existence of victors and vanquished. Within that framework international law has worked out a series of precepts and principles.

As this book has pointed out, the matter of nuclear weaponry cannot be conceived within this traditional framework. A nuclear "war" is not war but sheer destruction; it has not even the shred of rationality and meaning that wars have. It is destruction which proceeds to the ultimate conceivable limits. If scientists can realize this, it is less likely that they will consent to participate in this totally senseless enterprise.

10. Reliance on existing principles rather than future treaties.

It may be that in another 10 or 15 years the superpowers will decide to end the arms race and instruct their negotiators to enter into disarmament treaties. Such negotiation would take up still more time. There are thousands of pages of international documentation on disarmament,[2] and if one were to study these, it would be the study of a lifetime. The problem is that we just do not have the kind of time required by these procedures. Nuclear war threatens every moment. If regulation by treaty is not available, we need to fall back on the other limb of international law, namely regulation in consequence of principles already deeply embedded in international law. We do not need to wait until disarmament is formalized by treaty; there is already a sufficiently well-established body of international law in existence concerning the issue. International law already outlaws weaponry of this nature. All that is needed is for these principles to be fully recognized by nations and individuals, and for them to be implemented.

185

11. More affirmative use of the legal system.

If the thesis advanced in this book be correct, there is room in all countries for a series of legal actions challenging the validity of numerous enterprises and activities which amount in fact to a violation of international law. International law receives recognition in one form or another in all countries. Human rights law has worked its way into the statute books of most countries, and the various international human rights treaties are binding upon the States that are parties to them. Indeed, various affirmative obligations to implement their provisions have been imposed upon the signatory States. Scientists and scientific associations could in one forum or another test out these principles. The *Operation Dismantle* case is one example of how attention can be focussed on the issue.

Legal action can take so many forms that it is beyond the scope of the present work to attempt to enumerate them. Some examples, however, may be cited. In *Weinberger v. Catholic Action of Hawaii/Peace Education Project*,[3] an injunction was sought against the building of structures for the storage of nuclear weapons, until an environmental impact statement had been filed by the Navy under the National Environmental Policy Act. In *Hellman v. United States*,[4] an action was brought by executors and the daughter of a deceased serviceman for wrongful death caused by his participation in numerous atomic tests. From the time of the Vietnam war there have been challenges to taxation on the basis of the taxpayer's belief in the immorality or illegality of the relevant operation.[5] In 1969 an action was brought by a college professor seeking to declare the Vietnam conflict unconstitutional as it "contributed to a serious inflation, diminished funds available for social welfare, and led to the death or wounding of innumerable Americans including the wounding of one of the plaintiff's own relatives."[6] These actions failed for one reason or another, some of them technical. The need to keep these matters constantly under scrutiny is, however, vital. The legal system is not being used as effectively as it ought to be in the cause of peace. It is to be remembered also that two powerful circumstances keep constantly improving the chance of success. They are the growing body of human rights doctrine and the increasing scientific consciousness, both collectively and individually, of their role in the arms race.

In this context it is to be noted that there is room for more linkages between international law and U.S. constitutional law. The Procedural Aspects of International Law Institute (PAIL) Conference of September 1983 noted the significant gap that exists between international and constitutional legal scholars,[7] despite the Supreme Court's celebrated injunction that "international law is part of our law."[8]

12. Channelling science towards peace.

One of the prime needs of our time is the devising of methods to channel to peaceful uses all the enormous scientific and technological talent that is now channelled into the needs of war. Scientists and technologists have not thus far given sufficient active consideration to this important practical means of reducing escalation. It is hoped that with a clearer knowledge of the issues involved, they will give more consideration to this aspect, which cannot be effectively handled without their active co-operation and concern. This is especially important as the extreme sophistication of current military hardware and technology makes it much more difficult than ever before to turn swords into ploughshares.

The concentration upon military-related aspects has caused an imbalance in the overall advancement of science and technology. Peace-related areas are suffering through a channelling of the major share of funds into military R&D. Shortage of funds is causing the U.S. to slip from its lead even in the exploration and commercial development of space, according to a report released on April 3, 1986, by Notre Dame University's Business-Higher Education Forum, whose 28 member committee is made up largely of university presidents and chairmen of major industrial corporations.

With scientists becoming more aware of the illegality of their work, it is hoped that they will give more attention to redressing this imbalance, and at the same time help the economy to free itself from dependence on military spending. There are great opportunities here for the scientist to contribute not merely to the advancement of scientific knowledge, but also to the service of humanity. An example of the type of project which might evolve is the Japanese Human Frontier Project, also called the Human and Earth Sciences Program (HESP). Initial plans for the project called for an expenditure of between 7.8 billion and 15.6 billion dollars. At the time of writing,

187

Mr. Nakasone, the Japanese Prime Minister, was expected to unveil this plan as the Japanese equivalent in terms of outlay to the SDI and the European Community's Eureka Science Project. It would develop such peaceful advances as intelligent robots and robots which incorporate aspects of organic locomotion. It would study in much greater depth than ever before the functions of the human body and brain, and aim at energy conservation and protection of the environment.

*　　*　　*

In the midst of superpower politics and summit diplomacy, one must not underestimate the strength and resolve of ordinary human beings at every level. Once their conscience awakens, once they realize how much is at stake and what they can do about it, their activities can impinge upon state policy and international relations. The ordinary citizen has done this in the past. The scientist can do no less. The most powerful in the world are but his clients; he must be more conscious of the power he wields. He must also be more conscious of the responsibility that goes with that power.

REFERENCES

1 For the Pugwash contribution on the arms race and disarmament, see Joseph Rotblat (ed.), *Scientists, The Arms Race and Disarmament:* A UNESCO/Pugwash Symposium, Taylor & Francis, London, 1982.
2 See generally J. Dahlitz, *Nuclear Arms Control with Effective International Agreements,* McPhee Gribble, 1983.
3 454 *US* 139 (1981); 102 *S.Ct.* 197.
4 731 *F. 2nd* 1104 (1984).
5 E.g., *United States v. Malinowski,* 472 *F. 2nd* 850 (1973).
6 *Velvel v. Nixon,* 415 F. 2nd. 236 (1969).
7 79 *AJIL* 158-163 (1985).
8 *The Paquete Habana,* 175 *US* 677, 700 (1900).

Appendix A

THE NUCLEAR WINTER ACCORDING
TO LORD BYRON, 1816

In 1815 the Indonesian volcano Tambora erupted, producing the greatest atmospheric effects on record. Though the eruption was in the Southern Hemisphere, the injection of dust and smoke into the atmosphere was so great that the summer of 1816 in Europe was and is the coolest on record for that period. Worldwide crop failures and darkness caused 1816 to be described as the year without a summer.

Lord Byron wrote the poem "Darkness," reproduced below (and reproduced also in *Scientific American,* March 1984, p. 58). At a hearing on the effects of nuclear war in the Senate Caucus Room of the U.S. Senate in December 1983, the Russian physicist Sergei Kapitza called attention to the poem. Kapitza said the poem was well known to many Russians because it had been translated by the novelist Ivan Turgenev.

Here is the poem in full.

Darkness

I had a dream, which was not all a dream.
The bright sun was extinguished, and the stars
Did wander darkling in the eternal space,
Rayless, and pathless, and the icy earth
Swung blind and blackening in the moonless air;
Morn came and went—and came, and brought no day,
And men forgot their passions in the dread
Of this their desolation; and all hearts
Were chill'd into a selfish prayer for light.
And they did live by watch fires—and the thrones,
The palaces of crowned kings—the huts,
The habitations of all things which dwell,
Were burnt for beacons; cities were consumed,
And men were gather'd round their blazing homes
To look once more into each other's face.
Happy were those who dwelt within the eye
Of the volcanos, and their mountain-torch:

A fearful hope was all the world contain'd;
Forests were set on fire—but hour by hour
They fell and faded—and the crackling trunks
Extinguish'd with a crash—and all was black.
The brows of men by the despairing light
Wore an unearthly aspect, as by fits
The flashes fell upon them; some lay down
And hid their eyes and wept; and some did rest
Their chins upon their clenched hands, and smiled;
And others hurried to and fro, and fed
Their funeral piles with fuel, and look'd up
With mad disquietude on the dull sky,
The pall of a past world; and then again
With curses cast them down upon the dust,
And gnash'd their teeth and howl'd. The wild birds shriek'd
And, terrified, did flutter on the ground,
And flap their useless wings; the wildest brutes
Came tame and tremulous; and vipers crawl'd
And twined themselves among the multitude,
Hissing, but stingless—they were slain for food.
And War, which for a moment was no more,
Did glut himself again;—a meal was bought
With blood, and each sat suddenly apart
Gorging himself in gloom. No love was left;
All earth was but one thought—and that was death,
Immediate and inglorious; and the pang
Of famine fed upon all entrails—men
Died, and their bones were tombless as their flesh;
The meagre by the meagre were devour'd,
Even dogs assail'd their masters, all save one,
And he was faithful to a corse, and kept
The birds and beasts and famish'd men at bay,
Till hunger clung them, or the dropping dead
Lured their lank jaws. Himself sought out no food,
But with a piteous and perpetual moan,
And a quick desolate cry, licking the hand
Which answer'd not with a caress—he died.
The crowd was famish'd by degrees; but two

Of an enormous city did survive,
And they were enemies. They met beside
The dying embers of an altar-place,
Where had been heap'd a mass of holy things
For an unholy usage; they raked up,
And shivering scraped with their cold skeleton hands
The feeble ashes, and their feeble breath
Blew for a little life, and made a flame
Which was a mockery. Then they lifted up
Their eyes as it grew lighter, and beheld
Each other's aspects—saw, and shriek'd and died—
Even of their mutual hideousness they died,
Unknowing who he was upon whose brow
Famine had written Fiend. The world was void,
The populous and the powerful was a lump,
Seasonless, herbless, treeless, manless, lifeless—
A lump of death—a chaos of hard clay.
The rivers, lakes, and ocean all stood still,
And nothing stirr'd within their silent depths;
Ships sailorless lay rotting on the sea,
And their masts fell down piecemeal; as they dropp'd
They slept on the abyss without a surge—
The waves were dead; the tides were in their grave,
The Moon, their mistress, had expired before;
The winds were wither'd in the stagnant air,
And the clouds perish'd; Darkness had no need
Of aid from them—She was the Universe.

Appendix B

THE FALLACY OF STAR WARS

The concept of "Star Wars" is of particular importance to the central thesis of this book, for if the Star Wars concepts should be aimed, as is claimed, at producing a defence shield, it could afford a complete refutation of the contention that the activity of the weapons scientist is blameworthy. Even those scientists worried morally by their work on nuclear weapons can seek to justify their work on the basis of the supposed defensive nature of Star Wars. Indeed, many do already.

It will be submitted, however, that far from producing this effect, the Star Wars concept and the work accompanying it only escalate potential nuclear war, increase the risks of its outbreak, and multiply the need on either side to produce weapons of attack. Moreover, the concept militarizes space, an important domain that has been kept free of nuclear weaponry and must be preserved so in the interests of the survival of mankind. Battles can now begin in outer space and spread to earth, thus opening up another possible theatre of conflict.

The reasons for concluding that Star Wars research will lead to graver dangers than we now face are as follows:

1. It is technologically impossible to produce an effective defence shield.
2. It will be viewed by the Soviets as an offensive rather than a defensive program, and will provoke an appropriate offensive response.
3. It represents a dangerous escalation of the arms race.
4. It militarizes space.
5. It unsettles existing treaties on arms limitation.
6. It endangers the Anti-Ballistic Missile Treaty.
7. From Star Wars on, the arms race will career completely out of control.

The technical impossibility of a defence shield.

To understand the technical difficulties involved, it is necessary to know something of the phases of ballistic flight. From the moment the silo cover slides back to enable the missile to commence its journey of destruction, the following phases can be identified: the boost phase, the post-boost phase, the mid-course phase, and the re-entry phase. When the boost phase ends and the thrusting engines fall away, what is left is a "bus" carrying several warheads, which are independently released to strike different targets. The bus contains small thrusters to help them on their way. Most modern ICBMs carry such multiple independently targetable re-entry vehicles (MIRVs). The various phases of the flight of an ICBM are indicated in the subjoined diagram.

CHART: Phases of ICBM flight

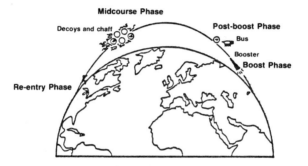

Source: Union of Concerned Scientists, J. Tirman (ed.), *The Fallacy of Star Wars*, Vintage Books, N.Y., 1984, p. 55.
Note: An ICBM attack launched from 1,000 silos would include more than 100,000 decoys.

Confronted with a Star Wars shield, an attacking ICBM would release a multitude of decoys (100 or more) and clouds of confusing debris in addition to its 10 or more warheads. Although the decoys would be much lighter than the true weapons, they would travel through the vacuum of space in much the same way, and the Star Wars defence would not be able to distinguish between the true weapons and the decoys. Some 100 or more counter-missiles would hence be needed to neutralize each attacking ICBM at this stage.

It must be realized that although the U.S. has often spoken of limited war, the Soviets have never spoken in terms of a limited nuclear war. If they should decide to launch a nuclear attack, they will attack with everything they have. With over 1,000 ICBMs at their disposal, the Star Wars program would have to put out hundreds of thousands of missiles to meet this invading armada.

There is of course the possibility of attacking the missile in the boost phase, before the multiple warheads have been released. That has the great advantage that one hit destroys its entire cargo of warheads. Also, it is a larger target and therefore easier to hit, and its booster flame makes it instantly detectable. If the missiles can be destroyed in the boost phase, there can be a substantial defence shield (assuming, that is, that at least 90 per cent of the attacking missiles can be thus destroyed).

But attack during boost phase presents insurmountable problems. In the first place, boost phase is very short—around 180 seconds in the case of an MX and this can be curtailed even to 40 seconds. Moreover, the boost phase attack must take place virtually within enemy territory, and the shield defending the U.S. must therefore be, rather, a shield over the Soviet Union, preventing their attacking weapons from getting out.

The final possibility is to attack the incoming missiles at the re-entry phase. The heavy warheads now survive atmospheric re-entry while the decoys and the chaff vaporize. "Terminal defence," as this operation is called, can preserve such "hard" targets as weapon silos, which need to be struck precisely or at a very low altitude. But it cannot protect larger targets such as cities, because very large urban areas can be destroyed by explosions which occur at one kilometer above them; the "small" Hiroshima bomb, it must be remembered, was itself detonated at a height of two thousand feet above Hiroshima. The incoming missiles are likely to be "salvage-fused," i.e., set to detonate the moment they sense interception.

It is also theoretically possible to use laser weapons to attack missiles in the boost phase. The lasers would reach their targets with the speed of light, but here, too, there are difficulties.

a) There are a number of delivery systems which can be devised to evade an otherwise perfect ballistic missile defence by using low trajectories. Such missiles as the ground-hugging cruise missiles cannot be reached by a space-based defence system,[1] and launched from submarines they would punch a hole in a Star Wars defence.

b) It is not difficult to coat the attacking missile with a kind of surface which would reflect back the laser beam. The cost of doing so would be negligible compared with the cost of a laser-based defence.

c) All boost-phase interceptions must be carried out at long distance since the target would be in Soviet airspace or very close to it. For such attacks one needs either a low orbit battle station or a geostationary battle platform; the latter is more than ten times further away from its target. In the former case the cost of lifting fuel to power the laser beams would run to billions of dollars in addition to the cost of lifting the station.[2] In the latter case enormously greater accuracy is needed, for the distance involved is 40,000 kilometers. To attain such accuracy, a telescope several times larger than that at Mt. Palomar would be required.[3] Moreover, commercial grids cannot provide the enormous power needed for short, sharp bursts—a power requirement estimated at 20-60 per cent of the entire present power output of the U.S. A reasonable cost figure for constructing new plants to generate such power is 40-110 billion dollars.[4]

d) Since it is not feasible to generate such power in space, it would have to be generated on the ground. This means that the laser beams would have to be directed from the ground and reflected off geostationary mirrors in space. Such mirrors would have to be enormously large and have a plane surface superior to that of any mirror now in existence.

e) The Soviets could always work on reducing the boost phase from the current average of 100 seconds to shorter periods, thus multiplying the difficulties of targeting them. The Fletcher Commission has thought that even a 50-second boost phase is feasible.

f) Systems placed in space clearly increase the cost of defence, as they themselves must be defended from attack. Indeed, any such systems would be obvious early targets in a nuclear war.

One could go on with a practically endless catalog, but sufficient has been said to indicate the immense expense involved in any Star Wars defence. Each step improving the apparatus would be met by a countermeasure, and the scale of expense involved in meeting it would rise exponentially. Under current projections, the scheme seems likely to sap all available financial resources of the U.S. The Stockholm Peace Research Institute has predicted that a runaway arms race could destroy the economy of its participants, and this is likely to happen to the U.S. if Star Wars needs should ever multiply. We are already reaching the saturation point in military expenditure. If that saturation point is reached, there would be pressure to use what armaments we possess before they become financially impossible to maintain or improve.

Morever, such a defence system is clearly incompatible with the 1972 Anti-Ballistic Missile Treaty and will endanger it.[5] In his President's Fiscal Year 1984 Arms Control Impact Statement, President Reagan himself acknowledged that the Treaty "bans the development, testing and deployment of all ABM systems and components that are sea-based, air-based, space-based, or mobile land-based." He also noted that the ban on space systems applied to energy-directed technologies. Both the U.S. and the U.S.S.R. are limited by the Treaty and its 1974 Protocol to a maximum of 100 interceptor missiles and to a single deployment area.

Like the Non-Proliferation Treaty, the ABM Treaty has great symbolic value in addition to the practical limitations it imposes on the superpowers. A full-blown Star Wars defence commitment would be open to the interpretation that it constitutes a unilateral repudiation of the Treaty. This would have repercussions which would be felt in all areas of the disarmament process. It would strengthen the case of non-nuclear powers who argue that the superpowers are not keeping their part of the compact embodied in the Non-Proliferation Treaty, thus leading to a scramble for nuclear weapons by the non-nuclear states.

This is not to say that it is only the Star Wars program which constitutes a threat to the ABM Treaty. Before the Star Wars program was seriously proposed, there was conduct on both sides which threatened the Treaty. There was the development of anti-satellite and advanced air defence systems with some ballistic missile defence capability. This led to charges and countercharges of Treaty violations.[6]

Nevertheless, the abrogation of the Treaty would have disastrous consequences for the entire process and concept of arms control. It would also have serious consequences for the NATO powers, who would be gravely affected if the Soviets were released from the constraints imposed by the Treaty.

Far from repudiation of the existing Treaty, the need is for the creation of a new Treaty restricting the further development of space weapons. In May 1983, three members of the Union of Concerned Scientists presented a model treaty on this topic to the Senate Foreign Relations Committee. In 1981 the Soviet Union had placed a draft before the U.N. of "A Treaty on the Prohibition of the Stationing of Weapons of Any Kind in Outer Space,'' followed in 1983 by another draft called ''A Treaty on the Prohibition of the Use of Force in Outer Space or from Space Against the Earth.'' It is submitted that there is sufficient desire for such treaties, and that the path to peace lies in the relaxation of tensions and not in the exacerbation of them which would follow from a Star Wars program.

Addressing the Groupe de Bellerive in 1983, Lord Zuckerman said: ''We hear now about ambitious R&D projects to devise a space defence against ballistic missiles using laser and charged-particle beams. This is space fiction—whether or not President Reagan's recently declared 'agreement in principle' to go ahead with an R&D program that would cost tens of billions of dollars were ever to become agreement in fact.''[7] He also observed: ''There is no technical expert in armaments and certainly no military chief who could give a guarantee to his political masters that he knew a certain way of destroy-ing, say, at best, three out of four incoming missiles. The quarter that would get through would be enough to lay waste where they struck.''

On May 18, 1983, three members of the Union of Concerned Scientists gave testimony before the Senate Foreign Relations Committee. They said: ''Even though there is no scientific justifica-tion for holding out hope for a leak-proof space-based defense against nuclear weapons, the quest for such a defense will, even if futile, have destabilizing consequences. In particular, the prospect of a space-based BMD (Ballistic Missile Defence) system is certain to spawn the development of space mines by the adversary, which will hound the BMD platforms to assure penetration of ICBMs. Space mines will be developed even if, as is most probable, no BMD capability is ever achieved, and these mines will then threaten all objects in space, whether they carry weapons or not. This could lead to a war in space as a prelude to war on Earth.''[8]

In summary, Star Wars research suffers from the following legal and strategic objections:

1. It is incompatible with treaty obligations under the ABM Treaty. There could be more than a dozen violations of its several provi-sions. For example, it would violate Article II(1), by which each Party undertakes not to place in orbit around the Earth weapons for destroying, damaging, rendering inoperable or changing the flight trajectory of space objects. It would also violate Article II(3), by which each party undertakes not to test such weapons in space

or against space objects. Star Wars also undermines the entire rationale of the Treaty.

2. It undermines an evolving rule of customary international law under which Earth orbit is considered part of outer space, thus making it subject to international space law.[9]

3. Techniques of attack upon incoming missiles may be defensive but are capable of being put to offensive use. Communications and warning satellites would be extremely vulnerable to attack, and there may be a temptation to use them against such comparatively softer objects, thereby crippling the opponent's command and control system.

4. As discussed previously in the text of the book, work on Star Wars creates a strong temptation for a first strike by the Russians before the system becomes operative.

5. Directed energy space vehicles (as opposed to directed energy weapons) are permissible under the ABM Treaty. They employ the same technology as directed energy weapons, and this legal loophole could be exploited by both parties.[10]

6. It will undermine the SALT II Treaty, since the Soviets would not be able to contemplate the Treaty limitations on their missile force if the U.S. were acquiring a defence shield.

7. With the undermining of the ABM and SALT II Treaties, two of the major treaty roadblocks on the path to nuclear war would be removed.

8. Numerous new scenarios of possible conflict situations will be created which will greatly enhance the risk of nuclear war. There will be special sensitivity, for instance, to any interference with communications and warning satellites, and such an event in space could well trigger a nuclear conflict.

9. Tactically there is no doubt that it will set off a massive Soviet arms buildup to counter any weapons destruction by the defence shield. This would be rather inexpensive for the Soviets compared to the cost of Star Wars.

10. There will also be numerous counter-measures which will escalate the cost of the counter-counter-measures required to meet them. The arms race could spiral uncontrollably.

11. Economically the effect on both antagonists could be devastating. Moreover, the diversion of increasing proportions of Earth

resources on such a sterile objective could be politically disastrous and damaging to global peace.

12. It will increase, on both sides, the grip of the military-industrial complex over all aspects of national life, particularly the development of scientific research.

Star Wars and the Reykjavik Summit Meeting

The meeting between Mr. Reagan and Mr. Gorbachev at Reykjavik, Iceland in October 1986 came close to producing dramatic breakthroughs in the banning of intermediate range nuclear missiles from Europe and a ceiling on the number of warheads on each side. As the world now knows, however, the meeting ended in failure and no agreement was reached. Reportedly, Star Wars was the issue that undid the whole package.

In this book we have argued that Star Wars is essentially unworkable as a defensive system. It might be asked why, if that is true, the Russians seem to take the program so seriously that an historic agreement was destroyed because of it. If the system were as poor as we have suggested, it would seem to be in the Russian interest to let the US go ahead and bankrupt itself in constructing an unworkable system; certainly they should not have let it stand in the way of an agreement. Is it a superstitious fear of the possible prowess of Western technology? Or is it that they already know something about Star Wars which has not been disclosed in the literature that has appeared in the West? Neither of these, I think, is the case. Rather, the answer lies in an entirely different direction.

When the SDI program has been presented to people in the West, emphasis has always on the defensive nature of the weapon. In the very month of the Reykjavik Summit, for instance, President Reagan compared SDI to the development of radar and declared at a campaign rally that "SDI is a purely defensive, purely peaceful, technology." By way of contrast, Soviet presentations of the program to its people have highlighted its potential capacity as the means for a first strike by the West. This concern led to special Soviet studies of the system's offensive capability.

The results of such studies appeared in a major Soviet report released in October 1986, and they must have weighed heavily at the Summit. They indicated that a Star Wars-type program had immense potential as the medium for a first strike. Four recent Western studies have independently corroborated these results.[11] In a way, they are not so surprising. The language of armaments tends to disguise the truth that modern weapons are not like the shields of medieval warfare, which were incapable of being used for offence. There is scarcely a technology of modern defence which is not also one of potential offence.

In the case of Star Wars, the defensive power to strike down a missile *in* space and *from* space inevitably entails the deployment, *in* space and *from* space, of weapons of greater accuracy than anything known thus far. Moreover, SDI develops not only their accuracy but also their power. Several studies have shown the frightening ability of Star Wars laser stations to attack targets on the ground. They would have the capacity to destroy aircraft, to burn ships, and even to incinerate entire cities.

The intensity of concentration of radiant energy necessary to burn through the metal skin of a missile in flight—about 10,000 joules per square centimeter—is said to be several times that required to ignite fires in urban surroundings. According to a study by Caroline Herzenberg of the Argonne laboratory in Illinois, the amount of laser energy necessary to cause a missile to fail, according to the minimum set by the SDI's own program, is more than 100 times greater than the amount necessary to ignite urban fires.[12] Consequently Star Wars would have the capability to trigger off firestorms like those which devastated Dresden and Tokyo, and it could do so with a hundred cities at the same time. If this is not bad enough, the Argonne studies and those conducted at the University of Marburg in West Germany suggest that use of lasers alone could be sufficient to trigger off the ultimate catastrophe of a nuclear winter.

Even if the Soviets were to accept at their face value the bona fides of Western advocates of SDI, there is no guarantee that later American officials would restrain themselves from using the offensive potential of the system against the Russian people. For the Russians this means that in the short run they dare not accept a disarmament proposal which would cut back their nuclear stockpile. In the longer run, it forces them to develop their own form of SDI in order to achieve equilibrium. Research on such a system is reportedly already underway, but of course the full implementation of such a system would be an incredible strain on the Russian economy. Even the US, with its far greater resources, would be forced into serious cutbacks in welfare services and other vital fields; for the Russians, it would mean sacrificing virtually all economic benefits on the domestic side.

Even if the two sides cannot see that with every escalation and every response one gets further from a solution and closer to catastrophe, it may be hoped that the hard facts of economics will bring them to their senses and drag them back to the conference table. If there is another hopeful feature in all this, it is that the momentum for Star Wars has depended so largely upon the passionate personal commitment of President Reagan. He has laid so much store by the program that a retreat from it would be politically damaging for him. Under his successors the political and personal stakes may not be so high. Negotiations may revive; and if the illegality of the role of scientists is more strongly perceived by the scientific community, this could be an additional circumstance lending weight to the forces in favor of de-escalation.

REFERENCES

1 For further details relating to the matters set out in this section, see Union of Concerned Scientists, *The Fallacy of Star Wars*, J. Tirman (ed.), Vintage Books, N.Y., 1984, ch. 4, "The Elements of a Strategic Attack."

2 *Ibid.*, p. 101.

3 *Ibid.*, p. 105.

4 *Ibid.*, p. 109. Former Secretary of Defence James Schlesinger estimated the total cost at one trillion dollars, observing that even with such expenditure "there is no serious likelihood of removing the nuclear threat from our cities in our lifetime or in the lifetime of our children." *Science*, 4 November 1984, p. 673.

5 On this incompatibility see (1984) 78 *American Journal of International Law*, pp. 418-423.

6 See generally chap. 8 of Tirman (ed.), *op.cit.*

7 7 *Disarmament*, 3 at 4.

8 Tirman (ed.), *op.cit.*, p. 286. See also the articles by members of the Union of Concerned Scientists in 251 *Scientific American*, 1984, p. 37 and 250 *Scientific American*, 1984, p. 27.

9 On the dangers of militarization of space, see *Common Security: A Programme for Disarmament*, The Report of the Independent Commission on Disarmament and Security Issues under the Chairmanship of Olof Palme, Pan Books, 1982, pp. 123-4, 154-5.

10 See Vlasic, "Disarmament Decade, Outer Space and International Law," (1981), 26 *McGill Law Journal* pp. 135, 176-77.

11 *The Boston Globe*, November 10, 1986, p. 61.

12 *Ibid.*, p. 61.

Appendix C

Albert Einstein
Old Grove Rd.
Nassau Point
Peconic, Long Island
August 2, 1939

F.D. Roosevelt
President of the United States
White House
Washington, D.C.

Sir:

Some recent work by E. Fermi and L. Szilard, which has been communicated to me in manuscript, leads me to expect that the element uranium may be turned into a new and important source of energy in the immediate future. Certain aspects of the situation which has arisen seem to call for watchfulness and, if necessary, quick action on the part of the Administration. I believe therefore that it is my duty to bring to your attention the following facts and recommendations:

In the course of the last four months it has been made probable—through the work of Joliot in France as well as Fermi and Szilard in America—that it may become possible to set up a nuclear chain reaction in a large mass of uranium, by which vast amounts of power and large quantities of new radium-like elements would be generated. Now it appears almost certain that this could be achieved in the immediate future.

This new phenomenon would also lead to the construction of bombs, and it is conceivable—though much less certain—that extremely powerful bombs of a new type may thus be constructed. A single bomb of this type, carried by boat and exploded in a port, might very well destroy the whole port together with some of the surrounding territory. However, such bombs might very well prove to be too heavy for transportation by air.

The United States has only very poor ores of uranium in moderate quantities. There is some good ore in Canada and the former Czechoslovakia, while the most important source of uranium is the Belgian Congo.

In view of this situation you may think it desirable to have some permanent contact maintained between the Administration and the group of physicists working on chain reactions in America. One possible way of achieving this might be for you to entrust with this task a person who has your confidence and who could perhaps serve in an inofficial capacity. His task might comprise the following:

a) to approach Government Departments, keep them informed of the further development, and put forward recommendations for Government action, giving particular attention to the problem of securing a supply of uranium ore for the United States;

b) to speed up the experimental work, which is at present being carried on within the limits of the budgets of University laboratories, by providing funds, if such funds be required, through his contacts with private persons who are willing to make contributions for this cause, and perhaps also by obtaining the cooperation of industrial laboratories which have the necessary equipment.

I understand that Germany has actually stopped the sale of uranium from the Czechoslovakian mines which she has taken over. That she should have taken such early action might perhaps be understood on the ground that the son of the German Under-Secretary of State, von Weizacker, is attached to the Kaiser-Wilhelm-Institut in Berlin where some of the American work on uranium is now being repeated.

Yours very truly,

Albert Einstein

Appendix D

NIELS BOHR'S MEMORANDUM TO
PRESIDENT ROOSEVELT, JULY 1944

It certainly surpasses the imagination of anyone to survey the consequences of the project in years to come, where, in the long run, the enormous energy sources which will be available may be expected to revolutionize industry and transport. The fact of immediate preponderance is, however, that a weapon of an unparalleled power is being created which will completely change all future conditions of warfare.

Quite apart from the question of how soon the weapon will be ready for use and what role it may play in the present war, this situation raises a number of problems which call for most urgent attention. Unless, indeed, some agreement about the control of the use of the new active materials can be obtained in due time, any temporary advantage, however great, may be outweighed by a perpetual menace to human security.

Ever since the possibilities of releasing atomic energy on a vast scale came in sight, much thought has naturally been given to the question of control, but the further the exploration of the scientific problems concerned is proceeding, the clearer it becomes that no kind of customary measures will suffice for this purpose, and that the terrifying prospect of a future competition between nations about a weapon of such formidable character can only avoided through a universal agreement in true confidence.

In this connexion it is particularly significant that the enterprise, immense as it is, has still proved far smaller than might have been anticipated, and that the progress of the work has continually revealed new possibilities for facilitating the production of the active materials and of intensifying their efforts.

The prevention of a competition prepared in secrecy will therefore demand such concessions regarding exchange of information and openness about industrial efforts, including military preparations, as would hardly be conceivable unless all partners were assured of a compensating guarantee of common security against dangers of unprecedented acuteness.

The establishment of effective control measures will of course involve intricate technical and administrative problems, but the main point of the argument is that the accomplishment of the project would not only seem to necessitate but should also, due to the urgency of mutual confidence, facilitate a new approach to the problems of international relationship.

The present moment where almost all nations are entangled in a deadly struggle for freedom and humanity might, at first sight, seem most unsuited for any committing arrangement concerning the project. Not only have the aggressive powers still great military strength, although their original plans of world domination have been frustrated and it seems certain that they must ultimately surrender, but even when this happens, the nations united against aggression may face grave causes of disagreement due to conflicting attitudes toward social and economic problems.

A closer consideration, however, would indicate that the potentialities of the project as a means of inspiring confidence under these very circumstances acquire real importance. Moreover, the present situation affords unique possibilities which might be forfeited by a postponement awaiting the further development of the war situation and the final completion of the new weapon...

In view of these eventualities the present situation appears to offer a most favourable opportunity for an early initiative from the side which by good fortune has achieved a lead in the efforts of mastering mighty forces of Nature hitherto beyond human reach.

Without impeding the immediate military objectives, an initiative, aiming at forestalling a fateful competition, should serve to uproot any cause of distrust between the powers on whose harmonious collaboration the fate of coming generations will depend.

Indeed, it would appear that only when the question is raised among the united nations as to what concessions the various powers are prepared to make as their contribution to an adequate control arrangement, will it be possible for any one of the partners to assure himself of the sincerity of the intentions of the others.

Of course, the responsible statesmen alone can have insight as to the actual political possibilities. It would, however, seem most fortunate that the expectations for a future harmonious international cooperation, which have found unanimous expressions from all sides within the united nations, so remarkably correspond to the unique opportunities which, unknown to the public, have been created by the advancement of science.

Many reasons, indeed, would seem to justify the conviction that an approach with the object of establishing common security from ominous menaces, without excluding any nation from participating in the promising industrial development which the accomplishment of the project entails, will be welcomed and be met with loyal cooperation in the enforcement of the necessary far-reaching control measures.

It is in such respects that helpful support may perhaps be afforded by the world-wide scientific collaboration which for years has embodied such bright promises for common human striving. Personal connexions between scientists of different nations might even offer means of establishing preliminary and unofficial contact.

It need hardly be added that any such remark or suggestion implies no underrating of the difficulty and delicacy of the steps to be taken by the statesmen in order to obtain an arrangement satisfactory to all concerned, but aims only at pointing to some aspects of the situation which might facilitate endeavours to turn the project to the lasting benefit of the common cause.

Appendix E

A REPORT BY SEVEN SCIENTISTS TO
THE SECRETARY OF WAR, JUNE 1945

Summary

The development of nuclear power not only constitutes an important addition to the technological and military power of the United States, but also creates grave political and economic problems for the future of this country.

Nuclear bombs cannot possibly remain a 'secret weapon' at the exclusive disposal of this country for more than a few years. The scientific facts on which construction is based are well known to scientists of other countries. Unless an effective international control of nuclear explosives is instituted, a race for nuclear armaments is certain to ensue following the first revelation of our possession of nuclear weapons to the world. Within ten years other countries may have nuclear bombs, each of which, weighing less than a ton, could destroy an urban area of more than ten square miles. In the war to which such an armaments race is likely to lead, the United States, with its agglomeration of population and industry in comparatively few metropolitan districts, will be at a disadvantage compared to nations whose populations and industry are scattered over large areas.

We believe that these considerations make the use of nuclear bombs for an early unannounced attack against Japan inadvisable. If the United States were to be the first to release this new means of indiscriminate destruction upon mankind, she would sacrifice public support throughout the world, precipitate the race for armaments and prejudice the possibility of reaching an international agreement on the future control of such weapons.

Much more favorable conditions for the eventual achievement of such an agreement could be created if nuclear bombs were first revealed to the world by a demonstration in an appropriately selected uninhabited area.

In case chances for the establishment of an effective international control of nuclear weapons should have to be considered slight at the present time, then not only the use of these weapons against Japan, but even their early demonstration, may be contrary to the interests of this country. A postponement of such a demonstration will have in this case the advantage of delaying the beginning of the nuclear armaments race as long as possible.

If the government should decide in favor of an early demonstration of nuclear weapons, it will then have the possibility of taking into account the public opinion of this country and of the other nations before deciding whether these weapons should be used against Japan. In this way, other nations may assume a share of responsibility for such a fateful decision.

Composed and signed by

J. FRANCK

D. HUGHES

L. SZILARD

T. HOGNESS

E. RABINOWITCH

G. SEABORG

C.J. NICKSON

Appendix F

THE RUSSELL-EINSTEIN MANIFESTO
issued in London, July 9th 1955

In the tragic situation which confronts humanity, we feel that scientists should assemble in conference to appraise the perils that have arisen as a result of the development of weapons of mass destruction, and to discuss a resolution in the spirit of the appended draft.

We are speaking, on this occasion, not as members of this or that nation, continent, or creed, but as human beings, members of the species Man, whose continued existence is in doubt. The world is full of conflicts; and, overshadowing all minor conflicts, the titanic struggle between Communism and anti-Communism.

Almost everybody who is politically conscious has strong feelings about one or more of these issues; but we want you, if you can, to set aside such feelings and consider yourselves only as members of a biological species which has had a remarkable history, and whose disappearance none of us can desire.

We shall try to say no single word which should appeal to one group rather than to another. All, equally, are in peril, and, if the peril is understood, there is hope that they may collectively avert it.

We have to learn to think in a new way. We have to learn to ask ourselves, not what steps can be taken to give military victory to whatever group we prefer, for there no longer are such steps; the question we have to ask ourselves is: what steps can be taken to prevent a military contest of which the issue must be disastrous to all parties?

The general public, and even many men in positions of authority, have not realized what would be involved in a war with nuclear bombs. The general public still thinks in terms of the obliteration of cities. It is understood that the new bombs are more powerful than the old, and that, while one A-bomb could obliterate Hiroshima, one H-bomb could obliterate the largest cities, such as London, New York, and Moscow.

No doubt in an H-bomb war great cities would be obliterated. But this is one of the minor disasters that would have to be faced. If everybody in London, New York and Moscow were exterminated, the world might, in the course of a few centuries, recover from the blow. But we now know, especially since the Bikini test, that nuclear bombs can gradually spread destruction over a very much wider area than had been supposed.

It is stated on very good authority that a bomb can now be manufactured which will be 2,500 times as powerful as that which destroyed Hiroshima. Such a bomb, if exploded near the ground or under water, sends radioactive particles into the upper air. They sink gradually and reach the surface of the earth in the form of a deadly dust or rain. It was this dust which infected the Japanese fishermen and their catch of fish.

No one knows how widely such lethal radioactive particles might be diffused, but the best authorities are unanimous in saying that a war with H-bombs might possibly put an end to the human race. It is feared that if many H-bombs are used there will be universal death—sudden only for a minority, but for the majority a slow torture of disease and disintegration.

Many warnings have been uttered by eminent men of science and by authorities in military strategy. None of them will say that the worst results are certain. What they do say is that these results are possible, and no one can be sure that they will not be realized. We have not yet found that the views of experts on this question depend in any degree upon their politics or prejudices. They depend only, so far as our researches have revealed, upon the extent of the particular expert's knowledge. We have found that the men who know most are the most gloomy.

Here, then, is the problem which we present to you, stark and dreadful and inescapable: Shall we put an end to the human race; or shall mankind renounce war? People will not face this alternative because it is so difficult to abolish war.

The abolition of war will demand distasteful limitations of national sovereignty. But what perhaps impedes understanding of the situation more than anything else is that the term "mankind" feels vague and abstract. People scarcely realize in imagination that the danger is to themselves and their children and their grandchildren, and not only to a dimly apprehended humanity. They can scarcely bring themselves to grasp that they, individually, and those whom they love, are in imminent danger of perishing agonizingly. And so they hope that perhaps war may be allowed to continue provided modern weapons are prohibited.

This hope is illusory. Whatever agreements not to use H-bombs had been reached in time of peace, they would no longer be considered binding in time of war, and both sides would set to work to manufacture H-bombs as soon as war broke out, for, if one side manufactured the bombs and other did not, the side that manufactured them would inevitably be victorious.

Although an agreement to renounce nuclear weapons as part of a general reduction of armaments would not afford an ultimate solution, it would serve certain important purposes. First: any agreement between East and West is to the good in so far as it tends to diminish tension. Second: the abolition of thermo-nuclear weapons, if each side believed that the other had carried it out sincerely, would lessen the fear of a sudden attack in the style of Pearl Harbor, which at present keeps both sides in a state of nervous apprehension. We should, therefore, welcome such an agreement, though only as a first step.

Most of us are not neutral in feeling, but, as human beings, we have to remember that, if the issues between East and West are to be decided in any manner that can give any possible satisfaction to anybody, whether Communist or anti-Communist, whether Asian or European or American, whether White or Black, then these issues must not be decided by war. We should wish this to be understood, both in the East and in the West.

There lies before us, if we choose, continual progress in happiness, knowledge, and wisdom. Shall we, instead, choose death, because we cannot forget our quarrels? We appeal, as human beings, to human beings: Remember your humanity, and forget the rest. If you can do so, the way lies open to a new Paradise; if you cannot, there lies berfore you the risk of universal death.

Resolution

We invite this Congress, and through it the scientists of the world and the general public, to subscribe to the following resolution:

In view of the fact that in any future world war nuclear weapons will certainly be employed, and that such weapons threaten the continued existence of mankind, we urge the Governments of the world to realize, and to acknowledge publicly, that their purpose cannot be furthered by a world war, and we urge them, consequently, to find peaceful means for the settlement of all matters of dispute between them.

Max Born
Percy W. Bridgman
Albert Einstein
Leopold Infeld
Frederic Joliot-Curie
Herman J. Muller

Linus Pauling
Cecil F. Powell
Joseph Rotblat
Bertrand Russell
Hideki Yukawa

Appendix G

DECLARATION BY THE
CANADIAN PUGWASH GROUP

*on the 25th Anniversary of the holding of
the First Pugwash Conference at Pugwash, Canada,
in July 1957*

A quarter of a century ago, a small group of 22 distinguished scientists from 10 East-West countries assembled in Pugwash, Nova Scotia, on the invitation of Mr. Cyrus Eaton, to seek ways of ending the Cold War, preventing a hot war and avoiding a nuclear holocaust. They were inspired by the Russell-Einstein Manifesto pointing to the dangers of a nuclear war that could put an end to the human race.

That meeting gave its name to the Pugwash Movement which has spread around the world and now encompasses some 2000 scientists from 75 countries.

Today, on the invitation of Canadian Pugwash, another small group of scientists, including signers of the Russell-Einstein Manifesto and participants in the first Pugwash Conference, have gathered in Pugwash to commemorate the 25th Anniversary of that first meeting. There follows the statement adopted by the Canadian Pugwash Group.

The nuclear peril facing the nations and the peoples of the world is now much greater than it was 25 years ago. Nine multilateral treaties and thirteen bilateral American-Soviet treaties and agreements on arms limitation have failed to halt the arms race which continues to escalate. The arms race, and in particular the nuclear arms race, is proceeding in a more dangerous way than ever before. The threat it poses to human survival knows no parallel in all history.

Increasing numbers of scientists and the public realize that peace and security cannot be found in the vast and continuing accumulation of weapons of destruction or in the current concepts of deterrence. Unfortunately, however, others, including some in positions of authority, speak of fighting, surviving and even winning a limited nuclear war, a protracted nuclear war or an all-out nuclear war. We believe that these illusions verge on insanity and can only lead to a mad race to oblivion.

We agree with and fully support the declaration of 1978 of the United Nations General Assembly's First Special Session on Disarmament:

> Removing the threat of world war—a nuclear war—is the most acute and urgent task of the present day. Mankind is confronted with a choice: we must halt the arms race and proceed to disarmament or face annihilation.

There now exist some 50,000 nuclear weapons whose destructive power is more than one million times greater than the bomb that destroyed Hiroshima. Not only is the number of weapons increasing but, what is worse, the nuclear arms race is now mainly a qualitative race rather than a quantitative one. The rapid pace of technological innovation and the development of new, more accurate and more devastating weapon systems so far exceeds the slow pace of arms control and disarmament negotiations as to make a mockery of the efforts to halt and reverse the arms race. The threat of nuclear annihilation, either by design or as a result of accident, desperation, miscalculation, or panic, grows greater year by year.

In these circumstances, the only sure way of halting the nuclear arms race is by freezing the testing, production and deployment of all nuclear weapons and their delivery vehicles by the two superpowers. Such a freeze is a necessary first step to major reductions in the stockpiles of these weapons and toward the goal of their eventual elimination. Indeed, a reduction in the number of nuclear weapons and their delivery systems, without a freeze, could be meaningless. The modernization of older weapon systems and the development of even more horrible and threatening new ones could completely negate the effect of any reduction in numbers. A technological freeze is as necessary as numerical reductions, and even more urgent. Moreover, if small nuclear delivery vehicles, such as cruise missiles, are produced and deployed in large numbers, it will be extremely difficult, if not impossible, to verify their limitation and reduction. Thus, time is indeed running out on efforts to halt and reverse the nuclear arms race.

Recently there have been several hopeful developments as people all over the world have become alerted to the dangers of the nuclear arms race. Millions have rallied to demand a stop to the arms race, and a great human cry for a nuclear freeze is surging around the world.

Another hopeful development is the growing demand that additional Governments pledge not to be the first to use nuclear weapons. [Note: Such pledges were made by China in 1965 and by the U.S.S.R. during the Second U.N. Special Session on Disarmament in 1982.] Declarations of no-first-use by all the nuclear weapon powers would be tantamount to declarations never to use these weapons. We believe that any imbalance in conventional forces is not of such dimensions as to prevent the making of no-first-use pledges; the making of such pledges, however, could be more readily agreed to if there were agreement on mutual balanced conventional forces in Europe.

It is also encouraging that several scientific inventors of some of the most sophisticated nuclear weapons systems ever conceived by the mind of man now oppose their use and urge their abolition.

In the light of these developments, we believe that the scientists of the world—and particularly those who are members of the Pugwash Movement—have a duty to help inform and educate the governments and peoples of the world about the dangers of the nuclear arms race and to explore ways of improving international security in order to avoid a nuclear war.

The members of the Canadian Pugwash Movement and the distinguished guests invited to join them at this 25th Anniversary Commemorative Meeting at Pugwash, Canada, call on the Pugwash Movement and the scientists of the world to intensify their efforts and to rededicate their energies and activities to the abolition of the threat of nuclear war and to the establishment of a just and secure world order.

Appendix H

*A Statement in Support of the
Five Continent Peace Initiative*

Human technology is now able to destroy our global civilization and perhaps our species as well. The lives of all those who inhabit the Earth today, and of all generations yet to come, are in jeopardy. Nations and peoples, even those far removed from the probable nuclear war target zone, now face unprecedented devastation. The danger of nuclear war cuts across religious, economic, social, and ideological boundaries. Whatever our aspirations, prospects and ambitions for the future, whatever our hopes for our children and their children, all are now imperiled by the prospect of nuclear war. The United States, the Soviet Union, Britain, France and China would be among the nations most completely disintegrated by the nuclear war, but both the danger and the responsibility for a nuclear war must now be parceled out among all the nations of the planet.

The world yearns for a dramatic change from the reckless accumulation of still more nuclear weapons and still more delivery systems. People all over the planet long for a safe, multilateral, verifiable, and massive decline in the global arsenal of nuclear weapons and their delivery systems. If we are not so foolish as to destroy ourselves, future generations will look back on this time as a critical crossroads in human history, when we had the wisdom to break with the burdens of the past, to adopt a new way of thinking, to choose life and not death.

We welcome the Five Continent Peace Initiative by world leaders, and support their call for an urgent reordering of planetary priorities. There is a pressing need for such a group to play an effective third party role in ending the long deadlock in nuclear negotiations. We call upon the nuclear weapons states to seize this new opportunity to protect and preserve our global civilization.

H-1

We share a small planet, and an intricate and delicate life-support system. In the name of our common humanity, and on behalf of all the human beings who have been, who are, and who are yet to be, we urge the peoples and the nations of the Earth to support this new Initiative and to build bonds among adversary nations, to reverse the nuclear arms race, and to speak for our species and our planet.

Partial List of Signatories

Carl Sagan
Cornell University
USA

Hannes Alfven
Nobel Prize for Physics, 1970
Sweden

Philip W. Anderson
Nobel Prize for Physics, 1977
USA

Christian B. Anfinsen
Nobel Prize for Chemistry, 1972
USA

Werner Arber
Nobel Prize for Physiology or Medicine,
Switzerland   1978

Kenneth J. Arrow
Nobel Prize for Economics, 1972
USA

Julius Axelrod
Nobel Prize for Physiology or Medicine,
USA   1970

Nikolai G. Basov
Nobel Prize for Physics, 1964
USSR

George W. Beadle
Nobel Prize for Physiology or Medicine,
USA   1980

Samuel Beckett
Nobel Prize for Literature, 1969
Ireland

Baruj Benacerraf
Nobel Prize for Physiology or Medicine,
USA   1980

Paul Berg
Nobel Prize for Chemistry, 1980
USA

Hans A. Bethe
Nobel Prize for Physics, 1967
USA

Nicolass Bloembergen
Nobel Prize for Physics, 1981
USA

Baruch Blumberg
Nobel Prize for Physiology or Medicine,
USA   1976

Heinrich Theodor Boll
Nobel Prize for Literature, 1972
West Germany

Norman E. Borlaug
Nobel Peace Prize, 1970
USA

Willy Brandt
Nobel Peace Prize, 1971
West Germany

Herbert C. Brown
Nobel Prize for Chemistry, 1979
USA

F. MacFarlane Burnet
Nobel Prize for Physiology or Medicine,
Australia   1960

Carlos Chagas
President, Pontifical Academy of Sciences,
Brazil   the Vatican

Subrahmanyan Chandrasekhar
Nobel Prize for Physics, 1983
USA

John Cornforth
Nobel Prize for Chemistry, 1975
Australia/Britain

Francis Harry Compton Crick
Nobel Prize for Physiology or Medicine,
Britain   1962

Jean Dausett
Nobel Prize for Physiology or Medicine,
France   1980

Gerard Debreu
Nobel Prize for Economics, 1983
USA

Christian Rene de Duve
Nobel Prize for Physiology or Medicine,
Belgium   1974

Leo Esaki
Nobel Prize for Physics, 1973
Japan

Adolfo Perez Esquivel
Nobel Peace Prize, 1980
Argentina

William A. Fowler
Nobel Prize for Physics, 1983
USA

Kenichi Fukui
Nobel Prize for Chemistry, 1981
Japan

Daniel Carleton Gajdusek
Nobel Prize for Physiology or Medicine,
USA   1976

Alfonso Garcia-Robles
Nobel Peace Prize, 1982
Mexico

Donald A. Glaser
Nobel Prize for Physics, 1960
USA

Sheldon L. Glashow
Nobel Prize for Physics, 1979
USA

William Golding
Nobel Prize for Literature, 1983
Britain

Stephen Jay Gould
Harvard University
USA

Ragnar Granit
Nobel Prize for Physiology or Medicine,
Sweden   1967

Gerhard Herzberg
Nobel Prize for Chemistry, 1971
Canada

Dorothy Crowfoot Hodgkin
Nobel Prize for Chemistry, 1964
Britain

Roald Hoffmann
Nobel Prize for Chemistry, 1981
USA

Robert Hofstadter
Nobel Prize for Physics, 1961
USA

Robert W. Holley
Nobel Prize for Physiology or Medicine,
USA   1968

David H. Hubel
Nobel Prize for Physiology or Medicine,
USA   1981

Brian D. Josephson
Nobel Prize for Physics, 1973
Britain

H. Gobind Khorana
Nobel Prize for Physiology or Medicine,
USA   1968

Polykarp Kusch
Nobel Prize for Physics, 1955
USA

Luis F. Leloir
Nobel Prize for Chemistry, 1970
Argentina

Fritz A. Lipmann
Nobel Prize for Physiology or Medicine,
USA   1953

William N. Lipscomb
Nobel Prize for Chemistry, 1976
USA

Andre Lwoff
Nobel Prize for Physiology or Medicine.
France   1965

Edwin M. McMillan
Nobel Prize for Chemistry, 1951
USA

James E. Meade
Nobel Prize for Economics, 1977
Britain

Peter B. Medawar
Nobel Prize for Physiology or Medicine,
Britain   1960

Bruce Merrifield
  Nobel Prize for Chemistry, 1984
  USA

Robert S. Mulliken
  Nobel Prize for Chemistry, 1966
  USA

Alva Myrdal
  Nobel Peace Prize, 1982
  Sweden

Gunnar Myrdal
  Nobel Prize for Economics, 1974
  Sweden

Daniel Nathans
  Nobel Prize for Physiology or Medicine, 1978
  USA

John H. Northrop
  Nobel Prize for Chemistry, 1946
  USA

Severo Ochoa
  Nobel Prize for Physiology or Medicine, 1959
  USA

Linus C. Pauling
  Nobel Prize for Chemistry, 1954
  Nobel Peace Prize, 1962
  USA

Arno Penzias
  Nobel Prize for Physics, 1978
  USA

Max F. Pertuz
  Nobel Prize for Chemistry, 1962
  Britain

George Porter
  Nobel Prize for Chemistry, 1967
  Britain

James Rainwater
  Nobel Prize for Physics, 1976
  USA

Burton Richter
  Nobel Prize for Physics, 1976
  USA

Joseph Rotblat
  University of London
  Signatory, Einstein/Russell Memorandum, July
  Britain   1955

Carlo Rubbia
  Nobel Prize for Physics, 1984
  Italy

Abdus Salam
  Nobel Prize for Physics, 1979
  Pakistan

Jonas Edward Salk
  Co-developer, first poliomyelitis vaccine
  USA

Frederick Sanger
  Nobel Prize for Chemistry, 1980
  Britain

Glenn T. Seaborg
  Nobel Prize for Chemistry, 1951
  USA

Kai M. Siegbahn
  Nobel Prize for Physics, 1981
  Sweden

Roger W. Sperry
  Nobel Prize for Physiology or Medicine,
  USA   1981

Richard L.M. Synge
  Nobel Prize for Chemistry, 1952
  Britain

Henry Taube
  Nobel Prize for Chemistry, 1983
  USA

Lewis Thomas
  Chancellor, Memorial Sloan-Kettering
  USA   Cancer Center

Jan Tinbergen
  Nobel Prize for Economics, 1969
  Holland

Nikolaas Tinnbergen
  Nobel Prize for Physiology or Medicine,
  Britain   1973

Alexander R. Todd
  Nobel Prize for Chemistry, 1957
  Britain

Desmond M. Tutu
  Nobel Peace Prize, 1984
  South Africa

Simon van der Meer
  Nobel Prize for Physics, 1984
  Switzerland

George Wald
  Nobel Prize for Physiology or Medicine,
  USA   1967

Steven Weinberg
Nobel Prize for Physics, 1979
USA

Victor F. Weisskopf
Massachusetts Institute of Technology
USA

Patrick White
Nobel Prize for Literature
Australia

Torsten N. Wiesel
Nobel Prize for Physiology or Medicine, 1981
USA

Maurice Hugh Frederick Wilkins
Nobel Prize for Physiology or Medicine, 1962
Britain

Robert W. Wilson
Nobel Prize for Physics, 1978
USA

Appendix I

HUMAN RIGHTS COMMITTEE

GENERAL COMMENTS UNDER ARTICLE 40,
PARAGRAPH 4, OF THE COVENANT

*Adopted by the Committee at its 563rd meeting
(23rd session) held on November 2, 1984*

General comment 14(23)c/(article 6)

1. In its general comment 6(16) adopted at its 378th meeting on 27 July 1982, the Human Rights Committee observed that the right to life enunciated in the first paragraph of article 6 of the International Covenant on Civil and Political Rights is the supreme right from which no derogation is permitted even in time of public emergency. The same right to life is enshrined in Article 3 of the Universal Declaration of Human Rights adopted by the General Assembly of the United Nations on 10 December 1948. It is basic to all human rights.

2. In its previous general comment, the Committee also observed that it is the supreme duty of States to prevent wars. War and other acts of mass violence continue to be a scourge to humanity and take the lives of thousands of innocent human beings every year.

3. While remaining deeply concerned by the toll of human life taken by conventional weapons in armed conflicts, the Committee has noted that, during successive sessions of the General Assembly, representatives from all geographical regions have expressed their growing concern at the development and proliferation of increasingly awesome weapons of mass destruction, which not only threaten human life but also absorb resources that could otherwise be used for vital economic and social purposes, particularly for the benefit of developing countries, and thereby for promoting and securing the enjoyment of human rights for all.

4. The Committee associates itself with this concern. It is evident that the designing, testing, manufacture, possession and deployment of nuclear weapons are among the greatest threats to the right to life which confront mankind today. This threat is compounded by the danger that the actual use of such weapons may be brought about, not only in the event of war, but even through human or mechanical error or failure.

5. Furthermore, the very existence and gravity of this threat generates a climate of suspicion and fear between States, which is in itself antagonistic to the promotion of universal respect for and observance of human rights and fundamental freedoms in accordance with the Charter of the United Nations and the International Covenants on Human Rights.

6. The production, testing, possession, deployment and use of nuclear weapons should be prohibited and recognized as crimes against humanity.

7. The Committee accordingly, in the interest of mankind, calls upon all States, whether Parties to the Covenant or not, to take urgent steps, unilaterally and by agreement, to rid the world of this menace.

Appendix J

At the very first session of the U.N. General Assembly in 1946, the Nuremberg Principles were unanimously adopted. These Principles were later reformulated, in 1950, by the International Law Commission. The ensuing document is the authoritative ILC text. The ILC is a United Nations body of expert international lawyers functioning away from political and ideological conflicts and devoted to the technical task of formulating and developing the body of international law.

Principle I
Any person who commits an act which constitutes a crime under international law is responsible therefor and liable to punishment.

Principle II
The fact that internal law does not impose a penalty for an act which constitutes a crime under international law does not relieve the person who committed the act from responsibility under international law.

Principle III
The fact that a person who committed an act which constitutes a crime under international law acted as Head of State or responsible government official does not relieve him from responsibility under international law.

Principle IV
The fact that a person acted pursuant to order of his Government or of a superior does not relieve him from responsibility under international law, provided a moral choice was in fact possible to him.

Principle V
Any person charged with a crime under international law has the right to a fair trial on the facts and law.

Principle VI

The crimes hereinafter set out are punishable as crimes under international law:

    a. Crimes against peace:

        (i) Planning, preparation, initiation or waging of war of aggression or a war in violation of international treaties, agreements or assurances;

        (ii) Participation in a common plan or conspiracy for the accomplishment of any of the acts mentioned under (i).

    b. War crimes:

        Violations of the laws or customs of war which include, but are not limited to, murder, ill-treatment or deportation to slave-labour or for any other purpose of civilian population of or in occupied territory, murder or ill-treatment of prisoners of war or persons on the seas, killing of hostages, plunder of public or private property, wanton destruction of cities, towns, or villages, or devastation not justified by military necessity.

    c. Crimes against humanity:

        Murder, extermination, enslavement, deportation and other inhuman acts done against any civilian population, or persecutions on political, racial or religious grounds, when such acts are done or such persecutions are carried on in execution of or in connexion with any crime against peace or any war crime.

Principle VII

Complicity in the commission of a crime against peace, a war crime, or a crime against humanity as set forth in Principle VI is a crime under international law.

Appendix K

PROPOSED U.N. DECLARATION
OF SCIENTIFIC RESPONSIBILITY
IN RELATION TO NUCLEAR WEAPONRY

Preamble

THE GENERAL ASSEMBLY

Recognizing that in an age dominated by science and technology, it is essential that science and technology should be devoted to the service of humanity

Gravely concerned that the development and production of nuclear weapons and the nuclear arms race are endangering the future of humanity and indeed of life on this plant

Conscious that the most recent and meticulous scientific inquiries have established the probability of a nuclear winter with disastrous consequences to humanity and our planet in the event of a nuclear confrontation

Realizing that the nuclear arms race would be impossible to sustain without the active cooperation of scientists and technologists

Taking account of the fact that the general principles of international law as contained in

    a. International custom

    b. The general principles of law recognized by civilized nations

    c. Judicial decisions and the teachings of jurists

    d. International Covenants

place beyond doubt the illegality of the use of nuclear weaponry, having regard inter alia to its violation of the principles of proportionality, discrimination, aggravation of pain and suffering, nullification of a return to peace and inviolability of neutral states

Aware that the use of nuclear weaponry would undoubtedly result in ecocide, genocide and, if there are any survivors, in massive intergenerational damage

Convinced that the concept of a limited nuclear war is unrealistic and a nuclear war once started is totally unlikely to be contained

Persuaded that the concepts of self-defence and deterrence have become meaningless in the context of nuclear weaponry and thus afford no justification for their production, possession, testing or deployment

Mindful that the use, production, testing, possession and deployment of nuclear weapons thus constitute a violation of international law and a crime against humanity

Recalling that this Assembly by Resolution 3384(XXX) of 10 November 1975 proclaimed the Declaration on the Use of Scientific and Technological Progress in the Interests of Peace and for the Benefit of Mankind and has since taken numerous steps towards the implementation of this resolution, including the passing of Resolution 37/189A of 18 December 1982 calling upon all States, specialized agencies, intergovernmental and non-governmental organizations to take the necessary measures to ensure that the results of scientific and technological progress are used exclusively in the interests of international peace, for the benefit of humanity and for promoting and encouraging respect for human rights and fundamental freedoms

Noting that the Human Rights Committee of the United Nations at its 563rd meeting (23rd session) held on 2 November 1984 in its general comment 14(23)c/(article 6) declared that the production, testing, possession, deployment and use of nuclear weapons should be prohibited and recognized as a crime against humanity

Noting also that the said Committee in the said general comment called upon all States, whether Parties to the Covenant or not, to take urgent steps unilaterally and by agreement to rid the world of this menace

Persuaded that the legal and moral responsibility borne by scientists participating in such activities is today infinitely greater than at the time of the creation of the first nuclear weapons by reason inter alia of the greater knowledge now available of the disastrous atmospheric, agricultural, medical and social impacts of the use of nuclear weaponry, the possibility of nuclear retaliation, the enormously enhanced destructive power of current nuclear weaponry and the vast nuclear arsenals now available in the event of nuclear war

Deeply moved by the consideration that the power of science is such, in the words of the Russell-Einstein Manifesto, as to open the way to a new paradise or lead to the risk of universal death

Believing that the participation of scientists and technologists is crucial to the determination of the choice between these alternatives

Convinced that the principle of individual responsibility for crimes against humanity is well established in international law

Convinced also that superior orders do not constitute a defence in international law in regard to crimes against humanity

and *Determined* that in the light of the above circumstances a consideration of the responsibility of scientists and technologists engaged in the nuclear weapons enterprise should no longer be further delayed by the international community,

This Assembly hereby *reaffirms* the principles that

(a) the use, production, possession, testing and deployment of nuclear weapons are contrary to international law and constitute a crime against humanity

(b) the participation in scientific or technological research in this area is contrary to international law and is a crime against humanity

(c) those who consciously participate in the manufacture of nuclear weapons and nuclear weapons research are personally guilty of a violation of international law and of a crime against humanity and/or of complicity in such acts

(d) such activity is incompatible with the dominant principle underlying all scientific activity, namely service to humanity, and is therefore unethical and contrary to the express Declarations of this Assembly

and *calls upon* all scientists and technologists throughout the world to abide by the legal and ethical obligations outlined in this document and to desist from any activity involving the development, production, testing, possession, deployment or use of nuclear weapons.

INDEX

abrogation, of international law 98
accidental nuclear war 15, 127-129, 132
African customary law 95
Aga Khan, Sadruddin 23
aggression, definition of 73
agricultural effects 37-39
aircraft, offences concerning 144
Al-Shaybani 71
Aldridge, Robert C. 128, 131
Alfonsin, President 109
Alamagordo trial 10
American Society of Civil Engineers 179
Anglican Church 160
Anti-Ballistic Missile Treaty, see Treaties
Antarctic 20
Apartheid 147
Appeal to World Scientists 172
Aquinas, Thomas 74, 77, 78
Aristotle 74, 77, 91
arsenals 50-62
asphyxiating gases 87, 95-6
atmospheric effects, see TTAPS,
    SCOPE-ENUWAR
Atomic Energy Commission 19, 176
Augustine, St. 71, 74, 77, 78, 91
Austin, John 66
Australian bases 133
automatic response, to nuclear attack
    56, 117-118, 126-127

Baruch Plan 19
Bellerive, Groupe de 23, 46, 151, B9
Berlin crisis 15
Bernal, J.D. 164
Bhopal tragedy 178
biological weapons 29
Birks, J.W. 29
Bohr, Niels 4, 5, 8, 9, 178, D14-16
bombers 56
Bracken, Paul J. 125, 126, 127
Bucharest symposium 171
Bulletin of Atomic Scientists 173
Byron, Lord A1-3

C3 stability 15
Canadian Pugwash Group G23
Canadian Royal Society, study by 45
Canadian Charter, of Rights and
    Freedoms 132
Carter, President 48, 119
Catholic bishops, of US 111, 160
Challenger disaster 128
Chadwick, James 6
chaos factor 124
Chernobyl disaster 127, 155
Cherwell, Lord 9, 99
chemical warfare 83
China 61
Chinese law 84, 95
Christian morality 158
Churchill, Winston 1, 9, 114-115
Civil and Political Rights, International
    Covenant 80
civilians, protection of 140
Clausewitz 76, 91, 92, 117, 124, 125
climatic effects, see TTAPS,
    SCOPE-ENUWAR
Cockroft, J.D. 6
Cold War 18
Computer Professionals for Social
    Responsibility 175
Compton, A.H. 10
computer error 127-129
Conventions, see Treaties
contained nuclear war 116-123,
    159-160
concentration camps 167
Crutzen, P.J. 29
Cuban missile crisis 15, 120

Dai Dong declaration 170
Declarations
    Delhi, on Disarmament 70
    Hague, re Asphyxiating Gases 87, 95
    of scientific responsibility 167-171,
        179,-180, 183
    on nuclear weapons 69, 70

on Prevention of Nuclear Catastrophe
146
on the Use of Scientific and
Technological Progress 168
St. Petersburg 87, 89, 100
Stockholm, on Environment 70, 81,
168
Universal, on Human Rights, *see*
Universal Declaration
Definition of Aggression Resolution 73
Delhi Declaration, on Disarmament 70
Delhi Summit, on Nuclear Disarmament
109, 150, 151
delictual liability 97
De Martens clause 90
deterrence 24, 111-116, 119, 121, 159-60
development, right to 134
de Vitoria, *see Vitoria*
Disarmament
Commission 20, 22
Conference on 22
Delhi Declaration on 70
Research, Institute of 22
DNA experimentation 178
Dresden bombings 98, 99-100, 160
Dunant, Henry 89

economic aggression 147
economic necessity, as defence 163-4
economic rights 80
eco-system, destruction of 87, 92-93,
158
Eichmann case 145
Einstein 2, 4, 5, 8, 13, 47, 176, 178,
C12, F19
Eisenhower, President 20, 80-81, 125
electro-magnetic pulse 129
Engineer's Creed 179
environmental consequences 149
environmental rights 134
environment, protection of 92-93, 147
ethical codes, for scientists 176-179, 183
ethical concerns, of scientists 174-5
Exodus 175

Falk, Richard 87
Federation of American Scientists 173
Fermi, Enrico 5, 6, 10, C12
fire bombing 155, 160, *see also*
Dresden
first strike strategy 130-131
fission, nuclear 2, 3, 12
Five Continent Peace Initiative H26
Flerov, G.N. 11
"folklore" of nuclear war 16-20
foreseeability, principle of 154-155
Franck, Joseph 10
freedom of research 153, 157-158
Frisch, Otto 5
fusion 12

Gandhi, Rajiv 23, 24, 150
Gas Protocol, Geneva 88, 89, 95, 96
General Assembly resolution, on nuclear
winter 46
genetic damage 95
Geneva Conventions, *see under Treaties*
Geneva Gas Protocol 88, 89, 95, 96
genocide 80, 86-87, 94, 143, 144, 158
Georgetown Center, for Strategic Studies
122-123
Gorbachev, Mikhail 131
Gratian 71, 77
Grotius 71, 78, 79, 108
Groves, Leslie 6, 7

Hague Convention, on land warfare 90
Hague Declaration on Asphyxiating
Gases 87, 95
Hammarskjold, Dag 176
health, right to 134
Heisenberg, Werner 3
High Technologists for Social
Responsibility 175
Hindu law 71, 84
Hippocratic oath 183
Hiroshima 1, 2, 10, 11, 12, 18, 22,
30, 41, 47, 88, 98, 100, 148, 149,
160, 165, 184, B6

Hitler, Adolf 3, 6, 7, 99, 139, 148
Hobbes, Thomas 79, 107
Houtermans, Fritz 3
humanity, crimes against 140, 150
  see also Nuremberg
human rights 134
Human Rights Commission 168
Human Rights Committee, comment on
  nuclear weapons 131
hydrogen bomb 12, 13, 19

ICBMs 55
illegality, of nuclear weapons 111-137
India 26
individual protest 161
Indo-Pakistan theatre 118, 119
information technology 156
intergenerational damage 95
International Court of Justice, Charter
  of 83
international law
  of war 71-80
  sources of 66-67
  status of 64
  swings towards 70-71
International Law Commission 147, J33
international lawyers, inactivity of
  18, 19
Iran-Iraq War 119, 161
Islamic law 71, 79, 84, 90

Japan 4, 5, 7, 8, 10, 126. *See also*
  Hiroshima, Nagasaki
Judaic law 71, 84
Jungk, Robert 12
jurists, opinions of 86
jus ad bellum 71-77, 116
jus in bello 71, 77-81, 116
"just war" concept 102

Kaiser William II 139
Kant, Immanuel 91, 158
Kapitza, Piotr 11, 13, 21
Kautilya 107
Kellogg-Briand Pact 72

Kennedy, President 25, 120, 134
Kennedy, Senator Edward 114-115
Korean War 15, 18, 19, 20
Kurchatov, Igor 11

Lateran Council, Second 77, 87
Latin America, prohibition of nuclear
  weapons in 69
launch-on-warning systems 56, 118,
  126-127
Lawrence, Ernest 10
leukemia 88
life, right to 109, 132
limited nuclear war 116-123
Locke, John 79-80
Los Alamos 1, 6, 7, 165, 176

Machiavelli 107
Mahabharata 90
Malinowski, B. 66
Manhattan project 6-7, 9
manufacture of weapons, illegality of
  111-136
McCarthyism 18
McCloy-Zorin principles 21
McDougal, M. 67
McNamara, Robert 113
medical effects 40-42
Melanesian customary law 95
Merton, R.K. 164
Middle East theatre 118-119
military industrial complex 21
military law 84
military manuals 84, 88
monopoly, U.S., of bomb 16, 19
Mussolini, Benito 139
mutually assured destruction 119, 121,
  130. *See also Deterrence*
My Lai 145

Nagasaki 10, 11, 12, 98, 100, 148, 149
Nanking, Japanese bombing of 85
Napoleon 138
"necessities of war" 160
neutral states, damage to 96

neutrality of science 164-165
New Zealand 26, 134
Nishina, Yoshio 4, 5
Nobel laureates, against nuclear war
176, 177
non-combatants, protection of 84
Non-Use of Nuclear Weapons,
Resolutions on 69
NORAD 128
Nuclear Non-Proliferation Treaty, see
Treaties
nuclear winter 29-48
Nuremberg Charter and trials 68, 85,
93, 94, 98, 99, 116, 139, 140, 141,
145, 150, 158, 162, J33
Nyerere, President 151

Oi Committee 170
Oliphant, Mark 5, 6, 27, 151
Oppenheimer, Robert 1, 5, 6, 10, 13

Palme, Olof 24, 113, 179
Partial Test Ban Treaty 21
Pastoral Letter, of U.S. bishops 76
Paul VI, Pope 77
Pauling, Linus 176, 177, 178
Peace Alternatives 175
Pentagon, spending power of 177
permissive action links (PALS) 62
personal responsibility, in international
law 138-147
Physicians for Prevention of Nuclear
War 42
plutonium bomb 10
Polanyi, Michael 164
"Poona Indictment" 171
positivism, in international law 108
Procedural Aspects of International
Law Institute 187
proliferation 61-63
proportionality, principle of 90-91, 115
Pugwash 164, 169-170, 173, 184, G23

Quemoy-Matsu crisis 15

Ramayana 84
Reagan, President 103, 121, 151, B9
Red Cross 89, 100
Reisman, M. 67
Resolutions
General Assembly, on environment 93
General Assembly, on nuclear
weapons 102, 146
on Definition of Aggression 73
on implementing Declaration on Use
of Scientific Progress 169
on limiting belligerents' rights 85
on Non-Use of Nuclear Weapons 69
Roosevelt, President 8, 9
Rotblat, Josef 5, 6
Russell-Einstein manifesto 176, 178,
F19
Rutherford, J. 5
Rutherford, Lord 154

Sagan, Carl 45-46, 59
Sakharov, Andrei 13
Saperstein, Alvin 124
satellites 153, 157 see also Star Wars
Schell, Jonathan 107
Schwarzenberger, G. 18, 71
science
misapplication of 167
neutrality of 164-165
openness of 166
perversion of 171
rationality of 165-166
truthfulness of 165-166
unpredictability of 166-167
worthiness of 165
scientific conscience, sharpening of 182
scientific opinion, climate of 183
scientific research, as impediment to
de-escalation 131-132
scientific responsibility, declarations of
167-171
scientist, responsibility of 148-180
SCOPE-ENUWAR 32-39, 44, 172
SDI. see Star Wars
seabed 20, 21

self-determination, right to 135
self-defence 102-105, 159-160
Seven Scientists' Report E17-18
Shimoda case 68, 85
Singh, Nagendra 18
Sino-Soviet theatre 118-119
SLBMs 55
Snow, C.P. 5
social effects 42
South African theatre 118-119
Soviet bomb, first 12, 19
Soviet nuclear strategy 129-130
space
    militarization of 151, 152, see also
        Star Wars
    right 134
Speer, Albert 3
Stalin 1, 11, 20
Star Wars 52, 104, 121-123, 128, 130,
    131, 132, 152, Appendix B
Stimson, Secretary 8
Stockholm Delcaration, on environment
    70, 81, 168
Stone, Julius 153, 166
submarines 55, 63, 120
Summit, Six Nations' 23, 24
superior orders, defence of 142, 162,
    see also Nuremberg
Swedish nuclear debate 49n
Szilard, Leo 5, 7, 8, 21, 178, C12

Tambora eruption 30, A1
Teheran, Proclamation of 85, 167
Teller, Edward 5, 12, 13, 151
theatre nuclear war 118-119
Thirty Years War 108
Thompson, J.J. 5
Three Mile Island 155
Tolstoy 124
Treaties
    Anti-Ballistic Missile 69, 132, B8, B9
    Convention on Protection of Civilians
        140
    Convention on Use of Conventional
        Weapons 88

Geneva Conventions 68, 69, 80,
    85-86, 89, 90, 92, 102, 144
Geneva Gas Protocol 88, 89, 95, 96
Genocide Convention 80, 143, 144
Hague Convention for Suppression of
    Seizure of Aircraft 144
Hague Convention on Land
    Warfare 90
International Covenant on Civil and
    Political Rights 80, 135
Kellogg-Briand Pact 72
Limitation of Underground Weapons
    Tests 21
Montreal Convention on Unlawful
    Acts Against Civilian Aviators 144
Non-Proliferation of Nuclear Weapons
    21, 22, 23, 69, 70, 116, 152, B8
    B9, B10
Oil Pollution Damage, Convention on
    147
Partial Test Ban 21
Prohibition of Emplacement of
    Nuclear Weapons on Seabed 21
SALT ABM Treaty 21
Tlatelolco 69
Tokyo Convention on Offences
    on Board Aircraft 144
Washington, on submarine warfare
    142
Truman, President 1, 94
TTAPS study 30, 31, 47
Tuchman, Barbara 124

UNCTAD v 171
UNIDO III 171
unilateral scientific abstention 172!3
unintentional nuclear war 15
Union of Concerned Scientists 173,
    178, B9
U.N. Charter 23, 65, 72, 73, 74, 135,
    146
U.N. Human Rights Committee
    135-136
Universal Declaration of Human Rights
    80, 135

unpredictability of nuclear war 124
uranium bomb 10
U.S. National Academy of Sciences,
  study by 45
U.S. Office of Science and Technology
  Policy 45
Ussuri clashes 15

Vernoek 4
Vietnam war 18, 20, 125-6, 144
Vitoria, Francisco 71, 77

World Federation of Scientific Workers
  173
World Order Models Project 108
World Watch Institute 156, 157

Yalta conference 8
Yasuda, Takeo 4

Zorin, Valerian 21
Zuckerman, Lord 50, 62, 151, B9